Piety
In The
Public School

Piety
In The
Public School

TRENDS AND ISSUES IN THE RELATIONSHIP
BETWEEN RELIGION AND THE PUBLIC SCHOOL
IN THE UNITED STATES

Robert Michaelsen

Professor of Religious Studies and
Chairman of the Department of Religious Studies
The University of California at Santa Barbara

THE MACMILLAN COMPANY
COLLIER-MACMILLAN LTD., LONDON

Library of Congress Catalog Card Number: 72–87896

First Printing

The Macmillan Company
866 Third Avenue, New York, N.Y. 10022
Collier-Macmillan Canada Ltd., Toronto, Ontario
PRINTED IN THE UNITED STATES OF AMERICA

FOR *Florence*

Contents

Preface   ix

I   **Religion and Piety in America**   1

II **The Public School as "Established Church"?**   45

III **Common School, Common Religion?** Issues and   67
    Trends in the Nineteenth Century

IV **Church Religion or No Religion?** The Religious   109
    Context of the Common School at the End of
    the Century

V **Common School, Common Faith?** Issues and   134
    Trends in the Early Twentieth Century

VI **Faiths and the Common Faith;** Church Religion   160
    and the Public School to Mid-Century

VII **A "Wall of Separation";** Religion, the Supreme   192
    Court, and the Public School

VIII **The Churches, the Public, and the "Wall," 1947-**   219

IX **Piety and Learning, Unity in Diversity;** A Con-   254
    cluding Positional Postscript

Index   269

Preface

This book has a double focus—on trends and issues. On the one hand, high points in the history of the relationship between religion and the public school are examined. On the other hand, since this relationship has always involved important issues of public policy, many of which continue to be debated and decided upon in our own time, the book also focuses on issues.

I have depended primarily upon three types of sources: selected materials related to American religious history; the work and thought of some major educational leaders such as Horace Mann and John Dewey; and significant court cases. Court cases are useful both historically and philosophically. They often deal with controversies which throw light on local practices and bring into focus major questions having to do with the relationships between religion and public life.

The subject of religion in the public school is likely initially to suggest to many Americans such practices as prayer and Bible reading. While they are relevant, this book is concerned with considerably more than these practices in and of themselves. These and similar practices are as important as symbols as they are for themselves. For example, they can help us to understand what public functions Americans expect from their religion. There are also larger issues of relevance to our subject for which prayer and Bible reading might not be of great significance— for example, the roles which Americans generally assign to their public school. Furthermore, even in attempting to understand the possible *religious* role of the public school it might be as important to consider the pledge of allegiance to the flag and the required use of certain textbooks as it is to look at prayer and Bible reading.

Reference to a possible *religious* role of the public school immediately opens the question of terminology. Words should be convenient and meaningful devices for expressing and describing realities of human experience. The richness and subtleties of that experience, however, often put vocabulary to the test. For example, when scholars such as Robert N. Bellah and Sidney E. Mead speak of "civil religion" or the "religion of the Republic"[1] in the United States they use the word "religion" in an uncommon manner. Americans tend to associate "religion" primarily with churches or such practices as prayer and Bible reading. Nevertheless, Bellah and Mead do describe a significant aspect of our national experience which does manifest characteristics which might be called religious.

By choosing to use "piety" instead of "religion" in the title of this book I intend to indicate that the book deals with both civil and churchly realities. "Piety" seems more fluid than "religion" and hence better suited to suggest this inclusiveness. I understand "piety" to mean both more and less than "religion." Generally it is understood in terms of acts and attitudes having to do with one's relationship to God (or the gods) or to one's family, superiors, community, people, or nation. It is an active virtue which is manifested in carrying out one's faith or obligations. In this sense, it is a function of one's religion or status. I use "piety" primarily, however, according to the third definition offered in Webster's unabridged Third International Dictionary: "the moral or spiritual resources of an individual or a group." For example, "public piety," as I use it, refers to "the moral or spiritual resources" of the American community, especially as they relate to the nation, and to attempts to articulate these resources in word, ceremony, and act. Obviously these "moral or spiritual resources" are closely related to what is commonly called "religion." This matter of terminology is discussed in greater detail in Chapter I.

A word about perspective: Obviously no one—scholar or otherwise—can jump out of his skin. Hence, for those concerned about such things (and those who may wish to have this

[1]Robert N. Bellah, "Civil Religion in America," *Daedalus*, XCVI (Winter 1967), 1-21; Sidney E. Mead, "The 'Nation with the Soul of a Church,'" *Church History*, XXXVI (September 1967), 262–83, especially 275. Also by Mead, *The Lively Experiment* (New York: Harper & Row, 1963), Chapters IV, V, and VIII; and "The Post-Protestant Concept and America's Two Religions," *Religion in Life*, XXXIII (Spring 1964), 191–204.

author's skin), and with apologies to others for the personal note, I point out that my father is a second generation Danish-American who did not entirely escape the influence of Danish Lutheranism and my mother was an "old American" of predominantly English stock who led both my father and me to Methodism. After thirteen years in the public schools I went to a Methodist college and then to a nondenominational but predominantly Protestant seminary. For more than fifteen years I worked in a state university school of religion which was by deliberate structure interreligious in nature. I am pleased to count among my friends Jews, Catholics, Protestants of many varieties, Hindus, Buddhists, Muslims, and not a few non-believers.

Of more relevance than these personal details is the perspective I have on the relationship between religion and the public school, a perspective which seems to me to be more the result of my own study and experience as a student, teacher and scholar than of my particular religious affiliation. From my mentor, H. Richard Niebuhr, I learned that religious institutions are much influenced by non-religious factors and that religious impulses are expressed both inside and outside religious institutions. From both Mr. Niebuhr and another teacher, Perry Miller, I learned much about the vitality of religion in American history.

I have spent nearly all of my professional career in academic programs in religion in two state universities. During this time I have also engaged in close study of a variety of such programs in other state universities,[2] acted as a consultant to several state colleges and universities where departments of religion have been established, and had a brief courtroom experience as an "expert witness" in a case in which a state university course in the Bible as literature was challenged on constitutional grounds. From all this I have learned, among other things, the importance of distinguishing between the study and the practice of religion in a publicly supported institution. I have also long

[2]See Robert Michaelsen, *The Study of Religion in American Universities: Ten Case Studies with Special Reference to the State University* (New Haven: Society for Religion in Higher Education, 1965).

since concluded that the academic study of religion is both possible and, when carefully done, highly desirable in such an institution. These views, as they relate to religion and the public schools, are discussed briefly in the "positional postscript" at the end of this work. Possibly the reader might wish to begin at that point if he wonders where the author "comes out."

I do not think of the bulk of this work, however, as being primarily positional or advocatory in nature. I have intended and hoped to make the book primarily descriptive. In doing so I have attempted to write as much as possible according to the perspective of the time and people under discussion. Hence, for example, in defining and using "religion" I have attempted to follow common usage and prevailing practice. The interests and desires of many public schoolmen and civic leaders in the nineteenth century can be cryptically described in terms of "common religion" (Chapter III). "Common faith" does better for the schoolmen of the first part of the twentieth century (Chapter V). These designations have what I would call a contextual relevance about them. They are useful for descriptive purposes. But for purposes of analysis, as suggested above, I prefer the more general "public piety" to refer to the kind of phenomenon under discussion.

Chapters I and II consist of analyses of what might be called the foundation and framework of the rest of the study—that is, the meaning of "religion" in the American context, salient aspects of religion in America, the development and chief elements of American public piety, and the role which Americans assign to the public school, especially as that role relates to religion and public piety. The next six chapters consist of an historical analysis of significant trends and issues in the relationship between religion and the public school from the beginnings of that institution in the early nineteenth century down to yesterday. Obviously this survey is selective not comprehensive. The criteria for selection include my own judgment as to what is significant as well as the availability of materials. For example, I have devoted much more attention to Bible reading and prayer than to observances of religious holidays because the former have been more pervasive in public school history and more significantly contested in the courts and because they are also of greater symbolic import to public piety.

Much of the material on Cincinnati in Chapter III has appeared in my "Common School, Common Religion? A Case Study in Church-State Relations, Cincinnati, 1869–70," *Church History*, XXXVIII (June 1969), 201–17.

I wish to express appreciation to my former colleague at the University of Iowa, Professor Sidney E. Mead, who contributed much to my interest in this subject both through his writings and in personal conversations; to Professor David Louisell of Boalt Law School, University of California, Berkeley, who read Chapter VII in an early draft; and to my colleagues at the University of California, Santa Barbara, Professor Thomas F. and Mrs. Janet O'Dea who made helpful suggestions on portions of the manuscript. I, of course, assume sole responsibility for its contents.

ROBERT MICHAELSEN

I

Religion and Piety in America

"The prayer of each man from his soul must be his and his alone. That is the genius of the First Amendment . . ."
—Justice Hugo Black, following the U. S. Supreme Court's decision in the New York Board of Regents' prayer case, 1962[1]

"A cursory glance will show that the problem of the relation of religion and political society is less simple than our politicians half a century ago supposed."
—J. L. Diman in 1876[2]

The Meaning of "Religion" in America

CHURCH RELIGION

"When I mention religion, I mean the Christian religion; and not only the Christian religion, but the Protestant religion; and not only the Protestant religion, but the Church of England."
—Parson Thwackam in Fielding's *Tom Jones*

Few Americans would be comfortable with Parson Thwackam's pristine precision. "Religion" encompasses more for most Americans than the Church of England or the Church of Rome or Christianity or even an organized institutional structure. Nevertheless, in its most obvious usage "religion" does refer to recognizable historic institutions and belief structures. To the question "What is his religion?" an expected reply might be "Methodist" or "Catholic" or "Jewish." This would usually imply

[1] *The New York Times,* June 26, 1962, p. 16. The case was *Engel* v. *Vitale,* 370 U.S. 421 (1962).
[2] "Religion in America, 1776-1876," *The American Review,* CXXII (January 1876), 40.

not only an organizational affiliation but some sort of relationship with a system of beliefs and practices. In this connection, the word "faith" is sometimes used with the definite article, as in "the Christian faith" or "the Jewish faith." I refer to religion in this sense as church or institutional religion, using church in the generic sense.

NATURAL RELIGION

But "religion" may also be used in a broader sense to refer to something fundamental which is held in common by all men or to something which is a part of the natural order. Since the eighteenth century many Americans have assumed, and some have argued, that there is an elemental religion which is common to all mankind and is at the root or foundation of all particular religions, including Judaism and Christianity. This religion has often been referred to as the religion of nature or natural religion. In the eighteenth century it was contrasted with "revealed religion" and the assumption was made that through the unaided reason any man could discover the essential elements in this religion of nature. Such founding fathers as Franklin, John Adams, and Jefferson often appealed to this generic religion as containing all that was necessary to human well-being. Everyone knew that God existed and that God regarded doing good to one's fellow men as the most desirable form of worship. Anything beyond this was superfluous as far as the general welfare was concerned. If a person chose to believe more than this, that was his own business.

PERSONAL RELIGION

This suggests a third American understanding of religion as involving an essentially private or personal outlook and faith—hence personal religion. There is a strong tradition in America which protects and even encourages the "sanctity" of personal belief. This was evident in Jefferson's well-known remark to the effect that he never divulged his religion or required this of another.[3] It is popularly expressed by the assertion that a man's religion is his own business. It is formally supported by the constitutional provisions which assure the "free exercise" of religion and freedom from "an establishment of religion." Supreme Court Justice Hugo Black demonstrated this understanding of the private nature of religion in his remarks on *Engel*, quoted above. It is an understanding which is an important element underlying his church-state decisions and opinions.

This practice in America of categorizing religion as essentially private grew out of the context of the eighteenth century. Natural religion meant chiefly personal religion to such men as Franklin and Jefferson. While natural religion was common to all men— because of a common creator and the commonness of human nature—its practice required little beyond personal affirmation and action. Church religion might be all right for those who chose to affiliate with it; it might possibly enhance their personal faith. Furthermore, church religion might also help to elevate community morals. But it had no inherent grounding in nature and no necessary relation to public life. In fact, the commonweal was better served if church religion had no formalized relationship to public policy.

Religious leaders on the pietistic wing of eighteenth-century American Protestantism tended to share this understanding of religion as private, especially in relation to civil authority.[4] They also shared with Franklin, Jefferson, Madison, and others a common reaction against the formal alliance between church and state which existed in several of the colonies. Something of the European tradition of Christendom had been carried to American shores and planted in these colonies. This was a tradition in which the church played a large role in public life and church and state were two sides of one coin. The First Amendment to the federal Constitution was drawn and ratified by men who

[3]"I never told my own religion, nor scrutinized that of another. I never attempted to make a convert, nor wished to change another's creed." Letter to Mrs. Harrison Smith, August 6, 1816, as quoted in Norman Cousins, *In God We Trust: The Religious Beliefs and Ideas of the American Founding Fathers* (New York: Harper & Brothers, 1958), p. 147.

[4]See Mead, *The Lively Experiment*, ch. iii.

reacted against that tradition and practice—for the sake not of irreligion but of the essentially private nature of religion.

"COMMON RELIGION?"

Pre-eminent stress upon the personal nature of religion tends, however, to underplay the richness of the religious life generally and—in the context of our own national history—to overlook the complexities of the relationship between religion and public life. *Common* affirmations and ceremonials were essential to nationhood. As these emerged they exhibited some of the characteristics of religious phenomena. The affirmations of the Declaration of Independence constituted a kind of national confession of faith. The ceremonials associated with the annual public recollection of those affirmations took on a quasi-religious cast, as did other public ceremonials such as presidential inaugurations. There emerged also a body of shared memories which were akin to a sacred history. The mighty acts of God and of national heroes were recalled and celebrated. This phenomenon has been called variously "common religion," "civil religion," "societal religion," and "the religion of the Republic" by present-day scholars.[5] Such terms as "political religion" and "public religion" were used by some nineteenth-century figures in describing much the same phenomenon.[6]

In the context of our analysis of the meaning of religion, which relies to a considerable extent upon common usage, it is necessary to point out, however, that Americans generally have not used the word "religion" to designate this national phenomenon. They have used "faith" more commonly—as in such

[5]"Every functioning society," sociologist Robin M. Williams, Jr. points out, "has to an important degree a *common* religion." *American Society; A Sociological Interpretation,* 2nd. ed., rev. (New York: Alfred A. Knopf, 1964), p. 332. On "civil religion" and "the religion of the Republic" see Robert N. Bellah and Sidney E. Mead in footnote 1 of the Preface, p. x. J. Paul Williams distinguished between "private," "denominational," and "societal" religion in *What Americans Believe and How They Worship,* rev. ed. (New York: Harper & Row, 1962), p. 477.

[6]See the discussion of the Cincinnati Bible controversy in Ch. III, p. 89.

popular phrases as "the American faith," "the American democratic faith," or merely "our faith." Possibly "religion" has been
regarded as too strong or too definite a term to use in connection with the national affirmations and ceremonials. It has
often been associated with *ultimate* commitment, as indicated
below, and Americans have not been of a single mind in giving
their ultimate loyalty to the nation. Furthermore, such a
designation as "common religion" runs counter to much in
American experience. Diversity of religion—personal and institutional—has been fully as evident as commonality.

"PUBLIC PIETY" AND "COMMON RELIGIONIZING"

For these reasons I have chosen to use "public piety" as my
own designation of this significant process in American experience. By this I mean, as indicated in the Preface, the moral
and spiritual resources of the American community, especially
as they relate to the nation, and the attempted expression of
these in word, ceremony, and act.

The need to develop a national self-consciousness in the
context of a diversity of regional and ethnic factors and a
variety of churches and denominations heightened the urgency
of achieving and affirming some commonality of assumptions and
commitments and of devising ceremonies for expressing these.
Hence there emerged a self-conscious public piety which involved affirmations of loyalty to the Republic and to the
democratic ideal of faith,[7] and which was often buttressed
by appeal to the sanctions of both church and natural religion.

During that early period of national history in which the
need for common affirmations and ceremonies first become
evident there also occurred a significant upsurge of institutional
religion. This phenomenon complicated the elucidation and
affirmation of public piety. The emerging Protestant denomina-

[7]On "The Doctrines of the American Democratic Faith" in the context
of the early nineteenth century, see Ralph Henry Gabriel, *The Course of
American Democratic Thought,* 2nd. ed. (New York: The Ronald Press,
1956), pp. 12–25.

tions, for example, increasingly asserted concern for the total community, for the national welfare. Yet no single denomination, and so single religious group of any kind, could become the church of the nation because of the plurality of competing denominations and an American tendency to resist the overly-tight embrace of any religious institution.[8] It was this sort of complexity to which J. L. Diman alluded in his summary of the first one hundred years of religious history in the United States.

In the absence of a national church there occurred what I call "common religionizing"—that is, an attempt to identify an existing religious form, such as a generalized Protestantism, as the common religion of the Republic. In actuality, however, public piety was not easily assimilated into any kind of religion. It is true that many nineteenth-century Protestants, and a few more recent observers, understood the public piety of nineteenth-century America largely in terms of common Protestantism.[9] But, while the beliefs, symbols, and spirit of Protestantism did exercise great influence upon American public life, the attempt to make Protestantism America's common religion overlooked too easily the rising importance and dramatic growth of Roman Catholicism on the one hand, and the continuing vitality of the Enlightenment view of natural religion on the other. (See Chapter III.

Common Protestantism was not broad enough to be America's common religion. Common Christianity, even if it had been a viable possibility, also lacked sufficient inclusiveness to fill this need. Some hoped, as a consequence of these institutional complexities, to bypass institutional religion altogether in achieving "a common faith." (John Dewey, Chapter V.) Others called for a stress on the "moral and spiritual values" held in common by Americans. (Chapter VIII.) Such emphases tended to move

[8]On the emergence of denominationalism see Mead, *The Lively Experiment,* ch. vii. On denominational concern for total community see the suggestive essay by George H. Williams, "Church-State Separation and Religion in the Schools of Our Democracy," *Religious Education,* LI (September–October 1956), 369–77.

[9]This is evident, for example, in the description of our own period as the "post-Protestant era." See Mead, "The Post-Protestant Concept and America's Two Religious," cited in footnote 1 of the Preface, p. x.

to higher and higher levels of abstraction and in so doing to exhibit less and less the characteristics of religion. This seemed to be a necessity in America's pluralistic culture.

The apparent necessity of understanding public piety at high levels of abstraction, or in terms of broadly stated values such as "human personality,"[10] has not always been accepted with grace, however. Affirming the hegemony of Protestantism was one way of attempting to achieve a common religion. Another and sometimes closely related way was to religionize or sacralize the nation. Zealous patriots have often attempted to pour the moral and spiritual resources of the nation into a restrictive mold. They have sought to make a national religion of public piety. Where a form of church religion has not seemed to fit into their pattern of patriotism, that religion has been branded as alien and un-American. On the other hand, types of religion that have given some appearance of fitting have been eagerly seized upon and shaped so as to accord with the needs of an excessive nationalism. These patriots have sought to enforce the inculcation of their understanding of public piety in the public schools by such devices as requiring that all youngsters within certain age limits attend those schools and requiring that all students and teachers engage in public professions and acts of that piety.[11]

"RELIGION" AS ULTIMACY

The concept of religionizing the nation suggests an understanding of religion as something about which a man feels more strongly than anything else. Common usage in America often implies a deep involvement in or commitment to a cause or a position, an involvement of such a nature as to have an indelible effect upon one's public as well as private life. Often the adjectival form "religious" or the adverbial form "religiously"

[10]The "basic value" affirmed by the Educational Policies Commission of the National Education Association (NEA) in *Moral and Spiritual Values in the Public Schools* (Washington, D.C.: NEA, 1951), p. 18.

[11]This phenomenon is discussed in several places below, including chapters IV, V, and VII, and the Positional Postscript.

is used to suggest this degree of commitment. When so used these forms suggest zeal, rigor, and strong devotion, as in "he went about his job religiously." Such a phrase as "his business is his religion" also conveys much the same sense of totality.

This common usage is related to one of the roots of "religion" in the Latin *religare*, which means "to bind." Hence religion may be understood as a state of being bound—by certain obligations, to certain convictions, or to the Supreme Being. But the notion of obligation does not carry the full sense of the word "religion." One might be bound to something willingly or unwillingly, and "religion" more often conveys the former than the latter sense. Furthermore, "bound" may be understood not only as being tied to something but also as being held together. Hence "religion" conveys the notion of unifying. It is that which holds life together. It centers or orients the self or the group.

As that about which one feels strongly, which binds, which orients, religion may be understood in terms of ultimacy. The late Paul Tillich, one of the most influential Protestant theologians in America, reflected this American—and Western—propensity to identify religion with ultimacy when he defined religion as "ultimate concern" and "the state of being grasped by an ultimate concern."[12] Religion is that concern which conditions all other concerns, that obligation under which all other obligations stand, that orientation which conditions all swings of the compass. Chief Justice Hughes understood religion in these terms when he affirmed in his dissent in the *MacIntosh* case in 1931 that "the essence of religion is belief in a relation to God involving duties superior to those arising from any human relation." It is "a belief in supreme allegiance to the will of God . . ."[13]

The tendency to identify religion with ultimacy is a direct result of the American inheritance of a tradition of monotheism. This tradition has stressed singleminded loyalty to God above all else. It has also detected a human propensity to worship "idols"—

[12]*Theology of Culture* (New York: Oxford University Press, Galaxy Book, 1964), pp. 7–8, and *Christianity and the Encounter of the World Religions* (New York: Columbia University Press, 1963), p. 4.

[13]*United States* v. *MacIntosh*, 283 U.S. 605, 633–34.

that is, to attribute ultimacy to something other (or less) than the one supreme God. While the Tillichian definition does not depend directly upon the traditional language of monotheism, it does assume that man is prone toward having or being "grasped by an ultimate concern."

An understanding of "religion" in terms of ultimacy may provide the common element in the other definitions suggested above. Such an understanding raises difficulties with the notion of "common religion," as we have suggested. It is evident that Americans have not been commonly "grasped" by the same "ultimate concern," even though at times many have been caught up in intense patriotic fervor. It is also evident that quite a few Americans have not expressed their "ultimate concern" in terms of church religion. At the same time, however, many have done so. And finally it is clear, under this definition, that an understanding of religion as personal is especially apt since "ultimate concern" may be quite personal and may also fluctuate considerably. Religion, said Whitehead, is what a man "does with his own solitariness."[14] "Faith," suggested Wilfred Cantwell Smith, Harvard historian of religions, "is new every morning."[15] Still, what a man does in his solitariness is very likely to affect what he does as a member of a group and even a fluctuating faith is likely to be related to what Smith calls "cumulative tradition."[16] Were it not for such communal elements there would be no way of proceeding with an account of the developing relationship between religion and the public school or with any history or sociology of religion.

"RELIGION" AND THE PUBLIC SCHOOL

The most obvious way to write about religion and the public school in America would be to confine the designation "religion" to church religion. Much discussion of the subject does just that.

[14]Alfred N. Whitehead, *Religion in the Making* (Cambridge, England: Cambridge University Press, 1930), p. 6.
[15]Wilfred Cantwell Smith, *The Meaning and End of Religion; A new Approach to the Religious Traditions of Mankind* (New York: Macmillan, 1962), p. 187.
[16]Ibid., ch. vi.

Public educators who, understandably, wish to maintain a sharp distinction between religion and the public schools can do so by understanding religion in this sectarian or institutional sense. It is that which the churches do and represent. Hence, as it impinges on the public school it involves such onerous but specific issues as released time or baccalaureate services. On the other side, representatives of religious denominations often encourage a denominational understanding of the nature of religion as they seek to advance or protect their own causes.

Such a limited definition, however, does not fully capture the richness of the phenomenon of religion in America. There is much that can be and is labeled religious experience in America which is not initially or primarily institutional in nature. Furthermore, what can be called religious in American experience and what can be understood as national or cultural are so intertwined that it is difficult to separate one from the other and still do a measure of justice to reality. Deity, for example, is understood both in the traditional religious terms of the Western heritage and in more specifically American terms as the special guardian of the nation. Hence to treat the subject at some depth we must deal both with the traditional religious heritage—and its offspring in belief patterns and denominational structures—and with various expressions of public piety. In the rest of this chapter I deal with aspects of religion and public piety in America. Under the heading "Aspects of Religion in America" I discuss the results of the encounter between the assumptions, thought forms, and practices of the Western religious heritage and the American environment. This is an effort to present in a brief compass some of the chief elements in religious experience and practice in America. The last section, "Elements of Public Piety," presents the underlying assumptions and commitments of Americans as a separate people, or of American nationhood. These are not unrelated to the historical religious heritage. In fact, they are heavily influenced by that heritage. But they also depart from it at certain points and considerably modify it at others.

An examination of the history of the public schools bears out the importance of viewing religion as more than institutional or churchly and of taking the dynamics of American faith seriously. The public schools have been ambiguous in their treatment of traditional religious beliefs, forms, and practices. Schoolmen have wanted to exclude the particularities and peculiarities of religion—usually called sectarianism—while maintaining the general elements, those assumed to be held in common by all or most of the people. The former divide; the latter unite. And because the latter unite they are contributory to the fundamental purpose of the schools—the making of Americans. The public school has been, then, a favorite vehicle for engaging in "common religionizing." It is also the chief instrument for eliciting and inculcating public piety. These roles of the school are discussed specifically in Chapter II and generally throughout the book. Before giving more attention to this public school context, it will be helpful to have a closer look at American religious life.

Aspects of Religion in America

PERVASIVENESS

I see that in every way you are a very religious people.
—Paul to the Athenians, Acts 17:22

St. Paul, were he permitted to visit these shores, might see Americans as a very religious people. Astute foreign observers, from Tocqueville to Harold Laski, have noted the extent of American religiosity and the inter-mixture of religion with American life. The former concluded after his visit to America in 1831–32 that "there is no country in the world where the Christian religion retains a greater influence over the souls of men than in America . . ."[17] More than a century later Laski found that the impact of "the Christian tradition" upon "American

[17]*Democracy in America,* ed. J. P. Mayer and Max Lerner (New York: Harper & Row, 1966), p. 268.

life was, and, indeed, continues to be, in many aspects profound."[18]

The outward evidences of religion have been abundant. "There are churches everywhere, and everywhere equally," observed Lord Bryce in the late nineteenth century.[19] From inner city store front to elaborate "plant" in suburbia the buildings continue to appear. (It has been said that Americans suffer from an "edifice complex.") There is also the ubiquitous profession of faith—"In God We Trust"—on every coin and bill. Hence a kind of perpetual-motion piety is achieved by the constant flow of legal tender which all the prayer wheels and flags in Tibet cannot begin to match in magnitude. There are also the American ceremonials, the pledge of allegiance to the flag with its recently added "under God," and the solemn rituals and paraphernalia associated with the inaugurations of leaders of state, the opening of legislative and judicial assemblies, and most other public occasions.

There are other signs of American religiosity. There is, for example, the reverence and respect with which most Americans have regarded religion. Radical antireligious movements have not gained large followings in this country. Furthermore, until recently at least, some sort of religious attachment has been a near prerequisite for success in gaining public office or any position of "public trust." It has been assumed by many that being religious in some sense—however minimal—is a part of being American.

The cynic might write these signs of religion off as sham and the prophet as hypocrisy. The subtle analyst might see in them only surface evidences of more fundamental movements of economic motivation or an uneasy subconscious, and the up-to-date investigator might even find significant signs of a decline

[18]*The American Democracy* (New York: The Viking Press, 1948), p. 264. On the importance of religion in America, as noted by foreign observers, see also D. W. Brogan, *The American Character* (New York: Alfred A. Knopf, 1944) and Andre Siegfried, *America Comes of Age* (New York: Harcourt, Brace & Co., 1927).

[19]James Bryce, *The American Commonwealth* (Chicago: Charles H. Sergel & Co., 1891), II, 587.

in their importance. Undoubtedly there would be truth in the assertions of each. But the serious student of American life cannot afford to take these evidences lightly. They are significant indicators of American self-understanding and sense of direction. And their importance in the development of public education is yet to be fully fathomed.

GOD

Belief in God is a key element in American religious life. There appears to be an unbroken line running from the latest public opinion poll, which finds anywhere from 93 to 98 percent of the American people believing in God, back through Western history to Moses on Mount Sinai. "We are a religious people," Justice Douglas argued with some warrant, and our "institutions presuppose a Supreme Being."[20]

Faith in God gave steel to the Puritan will and tenderness to the Quaker heart. It served as an anchorage for the rights affirmed in the Declaration of Independence and as a prime motive force in the War of Independence. Revivalists offered eternal salvation in the name of an eternal deity and American missionaries carried word of God into every corner of the globe. The Mormons made their troubled way from New York to Missouri and from Nauvoo in Illinois to the basin of the Great Salt Lake under the certain direction of divine guidance. Black slaves looked with anguished hope to a transcendent power which was not owned by the white man. "Huddled masses" came to the promised land of America from Ireland and Italy, from Norway and East Europe, with the memory and the hope of providence in their hearts.

The atheist has been a rare bird in America. Tocqueville doubted whether man could "support complete religious independence and entire political liberty at the same time."[21] Whether his doubts were warranted or not, it is clear that

[20]*Zorach v. Clauson,* 343 U.S. 306, 313 (1952).
[21]*Democracy in America,* ed. Mayer and Lerner, p. 409.

democracy has not spawned unbelief in this country. If anything, as Tocqueville himself observed, it has been fertile ground
for luxuriant growth of belief.

Belief has been so pervasive in America that the avowed
atheist has usually attracted considerable attention. Tocqueville
reported the case of a witness who was not allowed to testify
in the Court of Common Pleas in Chester County, New York in
1831 because he professed not to believe in God. The presiding
judge remarked that he had not before been aware "that there
was a man living who did not believe in the existence of
God . . ."[22] In recalling his life in a small town in the midwest
in the late nineteenth century Roger Galer wrote that "there
was no doubt that God really existed and that he exercised a
fatherly care over his children. In all the history of the community through a period of perhaps sixty years there was but
one known atheist. He was a good man," Galer indicates. "But
he was regarded as decidedly odd . . ." It did not occur to
anyone in the community "to inquire into his reasons or to
argue with him. How any one could deliberately doubt God's
existence was beyond conception."[23]

This type of community experience of belief and rarity of
out-and-out unbelief has been reflected in the public school.
That institution has been closed to any teacher who has openly
professed atheism. Even such a profession by a student might
well create a minor crisis. Mary Antin reported such a crisis
which occurred when her fellow students at a Boston area school
around the turn of the century discovered that she was an
unbeliever. This profession stirred up adverse comment all around
and caused the teacher, in quieting the disturbance, to inform
Mary "that it was proper American conduct to avoid religious
arguments on school territory."[24] A half century later young
Terry McCollum achieved considerable notoriety among his
schoolmates in Champaign, Illinois, when he expressed his

[22]Ibid., p. 270, note 3.
[23]"Recollections of Busy Years," *Iowa Journal of History & Politics*, XLII
(January 1944), 17ff.
[24]*The Promised Land* (Boston and New York: Houghton Mifflin, 1912),
pp. 243–44.

doubts about the deity. On the witness stand in the case that bears his name, the ten-year-old boy testified that he wanted to keep the knowledge of his atheism from some of his fellow students "because I would get teased, because the majority believed in God . . ." However, he also indicated that he "felt no sense of shame about being an atheist." In fact, he confessed, he "sort of enjoyed being different from other people with reference to the matter of God . . ."[25]

Belief in a supreme being has been central to American understanding of religion and of life itself. Until relatively recently the United States Supreme Court has identified religion with belief in God.[26] Expressions of dissent from American political policies have been more readily tolerated if asserted in a context of belief in God than if maintained in a context of atheism. This has been especially evident in the case of conscientious objection to participation in war.[27]

The recent ripple on the theological ocean caused by reports of the "death of God" further illustrates the point. This discussion attracted nearly as much public attention as the famed "monkey trial" did in the mid-twenties. Shrewd journalists eagerly exploited the newsworthiness of this "issue." Indeed, one had the impression that the so-called "death-of-God movement" was more a figment of journalistic promotion than a substantial reality. Whatever was there, it did make for good copy. It had the right measure of sensationalism to attract public interest and even alarm. In America one might with impunity ignore God most of the time or patronize him endlessly or even profane his name, but one must not kill him. That is almost as serious as doing away with Uncle Sam himself.

While the confession "I believe in God" has been common

[25]*Transcript of Record, Supreme Court of the United States,* October Term, 1947, No. 90, pp. 183–85. Interestingly enough, two of Terry's fellow students testified that before the court case they had not known what "atheism" meant.

[26]*Davis* v. *Beason,* 133 U.S. 333, 342 (1890), *U.S.* v. *MacIntosh,* 283 U.S. 605, 633 (1931), and *Torcaso* v. *Watkins,* 367 U.S. 488 (1961). In *Torcaso* the Court pointed out that there are nontheistic religions in the U.S. and declared unconstitutional a Maryland requirement that all men assuming public office take an oath invoking the name of God.

[27]See *U.S.* v. *Seeger,* 380 U.S. 163 (1965).

among Americans, the nature and precision of that belief has often changed. There is considerable permissiveness and even nonchalance about the particulars of dogmatic assertion. While some Americans have spent much time and energy on the fine points of soteriology and eschatology, most have not been so precise. Nevertheless, there has been, by and large, an insistence upon certain "fundamentals"—at a minimum, God and the good behavior desired by God. Benjamin Franklin's "creed" illustrates the point. "I believe in one God, Creator of the Universe" who governs by Providence and "ought to be worshipped," Franklin wrote to President Stiles of Yale in summing up what had been his views over most of his mature life. The "most acceptable service" that man could render to God was "doing good." Finally, the "soul of man is immortal" and he "will be treated with justice in another life" respecting his conduct in this one. On further details of belief, Franklin hedged his bets. He regarded the "system of morals and . . . religion" of Jesus as "the best the world ever saw or is likely to see," but he had his doubts about the divinity of Jesus. He never dogmatized on that latter question, "having never studied it" and seeing no point in going into it at his late stage in life since he would soon discover the truth anyway. He could see no particular harm in the belief in the divinity of Jesus, especially if it had "the good consequence" of making the doctrines of Jesus "more respected and better observed . . ." In any case, he was not aware that "the Supreme takes it amiss" by visiting those who did not believe in this doctrine "with any peculiar marks of his displeasure." And he concluded with a personal testimony of assurance "that having experienced the goodness of that Being in conducting me prosperously through a long life, I have no doubt of its continuance in the next . . ."[28]

Franklin affirmed the three fundamentals of deism—God, morality, and immortality. These, and especially the first two, have pervaded so much of American belief that they can be described as typical. But, as was the case with Franklin, they leave a great deal of latitude for detail. Hence, while belief

[28]Quoted in Cousins, *In God We Trust*, p. 42.

in God has been and is pervasive among Americans, there has been no general agreement on the nature of the supreme being or the direction of his will and the proper manner of his worship. One man sought to reform common social practices in God's name while another justified the status quo in the same name. "Both sides pray to the same God," Lincoln observed with pathos in his second inaugural. And the name of God has been invoked by both the Ku Klux Klan and many in the civil-rights movement.

Concepts of God have ranged from stern judge to "sugar daddy," from prime mover to co-worker to junior partner, and from a transcendent and awe-inspiring mystery to a comforting presence. God "is an absolute sovereign," asserted a Puritan, Increase Mather. He "has a greater power over his Creatures, than the Potter over the Clay."[29] This conviction gave rise to a variety of sentiments among the Puritans, ranging from the graphic scenes of divinely initiated terror, destruction and "Vengeance . . . to all Eternitie . . ." pictured in Michael Wigglesworth's best seller *Day of Doom*, to the intimacy expressed in the poems of Edward Taylor.[30]

The greatest of the Puritans, Jonathan Edwards, is chiefly remembered for his vivid portrayal of the plight of "sinners in the hands of an angry God." But, like Taylor, he too experienced the possibility of an intimate relationship in which one could become transported beyond the confinements of this world. In his "Personal Narrative" he reports in detail his own experience of being suddenly "wrapt and swallowed up in God."[31] Of Sarah Pierepont, the young lady who was to become his wife, he wrote that she was greatly "beloved of that Great Being, who made and rules the world" and at times "this Great Being . . . comes to her and fills her mind with exceeding sweet delight . . ." so that "she hardly cares for any thing, except to meditate on him . . ." Finally she expects "to be

[29]As quoted in Perry Miller and Thomas H. Johnson, *The Puritans* (New York: American Book, 1938), pp. 335–36.
[30]Ibid., p. 605, for Wigglesworth; see pp. 650–56 for Taylor.
[31]In *Jonathan Edwards: Representative Selections*, ed. Clarence H. Faust and Thomas H. Johnson, rev. ed. (New York: Hill and Wang, 1962), p. 60.

received up where he is . . . being assured that he loves her too well to let her remain at a distance from him always. There she is to dwell with him, and to be ravished with his love and delight forever."[32]

"Sinners in the hands of an angry God" became something of a model for the "hellfire and damnation" sermon that characterized much of American evangelism after Edwards. Most evangelists, however, also stressed the graciousness of God—toward those whom he had chosen or those who chose him. In either case, the well-being of the individual was inextricably bound up with the power of deity.

Within Congregational Puritanism itself there developed after Edwards an increasing emphasis upon the benevolence of deity. As a consequence of this trend, the terrors of Hell subsided. Some even asserted that *all* men would be saved, thus disposing of Hell entirely. God became a kind of benign heavenly father who would do good to His creatures if given half a chance. Whitehead's progression from "God the enemy" to "God the companion" aptly describes this trend within Puritan history, and within American religious history more generally.[33]

The notion of a benevolent deity, and the whole American *Weltanschauung*, was dealt a rude shock by Darwinism. Creation, special providence, the whole concept of a transcendent being and a supernatural world—these and other ideas were severely challenged. Some denied Darwin and spun out an even more rigid supernaturalism than that of their predecessors. Others managed to find evidences of God himself in the evolutionary process. Evolution became "the way in which God makes things come to pass,"[34] or evolution became God: "Some call it evolution, some call it God."[35] Overlooking the "waste" and "brutality" that seemed evident in the process of evolution, these men brought the benevolent God down to earth and made him one with nature. In the doing of it nature itself

[32]Ibid., p. 56.
[33]*Religion in the Making*, p. 6.
[34]John Fiske, *Destiny of Man Viewed in the Light of His Origin* (Boston and New York: Houghton Mifflin, 1887), p. 32.
[35]W. H. Carruth, "Each in His Own Tongue" in *Each in His Own Tongue and Other Poems* (New York: G. P. Putnam's Sons, 1908), p. 2.

became benevolent. This *tour de force* laid the ground for a growing assurance that God is the provider of success and happiness in this world. In the words of H. Richard Niebuhr, "A God without wrath brought men without sin into a kingdom without judgment through the ministrations of a Christ without a cross."[36] "American religion," wrote D. W. Brogan, "was committed, more and more, to an optimistic view of God's purpose in the world and to an identification of that purpose with the purpose of man, especially American man."[37]

Some Protestant thinkers reacted sharply in the 1930's and '40's to this trend in belief about God. They reaffirmed, in a trend of thought dubbed "neo-orthodoxy," the justice of God and the sinfulness of man.[38] Other religious thinkers dismissed the notion of God entirely and affirmed a non-theistic humanism.[39]

In the meantime there emerged in the Jewish community a variety of concepts as the traditional belief in the God of Abraham, Isaac, and Jacob, and even the restatement of that belief by the articulators of Reform Judaism in the late nineteenth century, were subjected to serious erosion. By mid-twentieth century notions of God in the Jewish community ranged from Mordecai Kaplan's understanding of deity or "the God-idea" as a process that makes for human fulfillment within a given community to Abraham Joshua Heschel's revival of prophetic notions in the semi-mystical context of a neo-Hasidism.[40]

Hence the concept of God has undergone considerable change,

[36]*The Kingdom of God in America* (Chicago: Willett, Clark & Co., 1937), p. 193.
[37]*The American Character*, p. 66.
[38]The works of Reinhold Niebuhr and especially *The Nature and Destiny of Man*, first published in the early 1940s.
[39]"A Humanist Manifesto," *The New Humanist*, VI (May–June 1933), 1–4.
[40]Kaplan, *Judaism as a Civilization* (New York and London: Thomas Yoseloff, 1934), Part V, and other works, especially *The Meaning of God in Modern Jewish Religion* (New York: Behrman's Jewish Book House, 1937). For Heschel, see *Man is Not Alone* (New York: Farrar, Straus & Young, 1951) and *God in Search of Man* (New York: The Jewish Publication Society, 1955).

and some have even disposed of it entirely. But some form of affirmation about God continues to be of central importance to most American religious communities.

RELIGION IN MOTION

Throughout much of the development of the notion of God in America there ran a persistent theme of divine action—whether God was understood as judge, designer, mechanic, father, friend, or benign force. Aristotle's unmoved mover might have satisfied the philosopher but not the destiny- and movement-conscious American. God was mover, but active mover—dynamic, with concentrated energy and full of purpose and direction. And these qualities have been characteristic of his followers.

Generally religion in America has put a heavy emphasis upon action. Franklin believed that the most acceptable service to God was doing good. While this hardly constituted a complete system of religious ethics, it is a view that has been popular among Americans. Over the years, religion became in America, as D. W. Brogan observed, "a matter of conduct, good deeds, of works with only a vague background of faith."[41]

The doing has not been without pattern or context; it has not been random action for action's sake. There has been a sense of purpose and destiny in much religious action. There has been confidence that life has a goal and history a direction. Man's task has been seen as one of seizing the fullness of time, subduing the powers that deter him from his noble intention, claiming the promised land. Thus the American's assurance of a supreme being has given purpose to his ceaseless movement in space.

The American has had a sense of purposeful movement because his God has been understood as mover. This God was not only lord of the past; he is also lord of the future. Like the cloud and fire in the Sinai wilderness, he leads his people onward. While there is a strong strain in American religion

[41]*The American Character*, p. 102.

which affirms that God fully revealed himself in the past, this is counterbalanced by an equally strong assurance that, in the words of Pastor John Robinson to his Pilgrim followers who were poised on the edge of their long sea journey to the new world, "the Lord hath *more truth* yet to break forth out of his holy Word."[42] This future orientation has interacted in mutual reinforcement with many an immigrant vision - of America as the land of promise and with the pioneer's assurance that a new and better life awaits him at the end of the wilderness road.

There has existed in American religious history a tension between order and openness. This tension is rooted in the concept of God as one who, on the one hand, has disclosed his will—in a book or a person or an institution—and who, on the other hand, is living power with a continuing active will. Under the former assurance men have often sought to create what in effect have been closed or nearly closed societies. But the sense of present reality has caused others to break away from an established order and to strike out in new and uncharted directions. This latter propensity toward openness has been much reinforced in America by two additional factors—space and religious pluralism. One could always move—physically upon the face of the earth or in one's religious orientation.

The point can be illustrated well from the early history of the Massachusetts Bay Colony, a history which became something of a prototype of subsequent American communal experiences. Driven by a God-given sense of purpose and destiny, the Puritans who founded that colony endeavored to set up a state and a society which corresponded with God's revealed plan. They called it a "Biblical commonwealth" because God's plan was evident in that book. The primary leader, John Winthrop, also called it "A Modell of Christian Charity" because he, like most of his associates, was convinced that *this* godly order would become a pattern for all others. But within less than a decade after its founding this Puritan commonwealth experienced two

[42]Quoted by Cotton Mather, *Magnalia Christi Americana* (New York: Russell & Russell, 1967; reproduced from the 1852 ed.), I, 64. Emphasis in original.

major crises which almost destroyed it. Roger Williams challenged the leaders' understanding of God's revealed will. He found his fellow Puritans to be too sanguine in their assurance that they could build a godly society on earth and too authoritarian in their efforts to do so. Because of his dissent he was forced to leave the colony and to plunge into the wilderness of New England. Religiously, he became a seeker. This is not to say that he gave up his belief in God. On the contrary, God was so real to him that he was unable to discover a true godly order in this world. Two years after Williams' forced departure Ann Hutchinson was also exiled. Claiming access to the living power of God, Ann dissented from common religious practice and refused to follow the judgments of the community leaders. She and her followers were convinced that they were children of promise. But the Puritan leaders looked upon them as children of the devil and forced them to strike out into the wilderness on their own.

Both the Massachusetts Bay leaders on the one side and Williams and Hutchinson on the other were fully convinced that God gave man a mission and a destiny. They were prototypes of that kind of American religious man, who has had a sense of mission, who has felt himself sent, who has had an "errand into the Wilderness."[43]

As the Puritans came to establish a Biblical commonwealth, so the Quakers, under the leadership of William Penn, engaged in a "holy experiment" in their attempt to revive primitive Christianity. The Mormons sought, found, and built Zion. And countless individuals have been catapulted into space with a sense of urgency to tell others the good news or to build their own version of the Kingdom of God.

Faith was one of the first mass-produced and mass-distributed American commodities. Spanish friars set up outposts of production on the Pacific Coast in the eighteenth century. George Whitefield, that intrepid Anglican-Methodist evangelist, made five separate missionary trips up and down the Eastern Seaboard between 1739 and his death in 1770. One might claim him as the

[43]Ibid., II, 316.

first American citizen, despite the fact that he maintained his home base in England. He finally died in America and his remains were buried in Newburyport, Massachusetts. Francis Asbury, early American bishop, traveled over the colonies an estimated 275,000 miles—mostly on horseback. That old stormy-weather remark—"Nothing out tonight except ducks and Methodist preachers"—attests to the inveterate mobility of his kind. One Daniel Boone type, having set himself in motion once again in order to escape the confinements of civilization, was thoroughly disgusted to be approached at his new wilderness location by a Methodist minister. Both the itinerant and the trail blazer had errands; while the former used a more obvious language of faith and mission, the latter, if he spoke at all, spoke in terms of hope and promise.

Messengers of faith traversed the continent, accompanying and sometimes preceding the course of empire. Evangelists Jason and Daniel Lee reached Oregon in 1834 with one of the first groups to settle that region. They were followed two years later by the Presbyterian missionaries, Marcus Whitman and Henry Spalding, who were accompanied by their wives. Narcissa Whitman and Elizah Spalding were the first white women to cross the Rockies. The great Belgian Jesuit Pierre-Jean De Smet traveled those Rocky Mountains as extensively as any white man in the middle years of the nineteenth century. He established numerous missions among plains and mountain Indians, laid the groundwork for the establishment of others, and personally interceded as a peacemaker between whites and Indians on more than one occasion.

The revivalist tradition which was shaped and dominated by Whitefield and Edwards in the eighteenth century was carried on in the nineteenth by Charles G. Finney and Dwight L. Moody and in the twentieth by Billy Sunday and Billy Graham. In the early nineteenth century Finney lighted the greatest revival fire that the burned-over district of upstate New York had ever seen. Then, with the sound and pyrotechnics of an electrical storm, he swept into the sacred precincts of Boston, where he was reported to have laid the New Englanders into windrows. After a longer stay in New York City, where he was so successful that a special building had to be put up to accommodate his revival audiences, he moved to Oberlin College, where he kept the students in motion for another quarter century.

It was said of Dwight L. Moody, who used Finney's revival techniques with consummate skill, that "in his rage to save souls he traveled more than a million miles, addressed more than a hundred million people, and personally prayed and pleaded with seven hundred and fifty thousand sinners. All in all," it was concluded, Moody probably "reduced the population of hell by a million souls!"[44] The voice of Billy Graham, a present-day descendant of these earlier worthies, has carried much the same word to even greater numbers in the mid-twentieth century.

A product that good is worth exporting. And Americans have carried their faith into every corner of the world. In 1812 five students from Andover Seminary in Massachusetts set sail for India under the aegis of the American Board of Commissioners for Foreign Missions, the first such group to go from the United States. Thousands have followed in their stead since then, commissioned by great or small organizations, or even self-appointed, and all alike devoted to conveying their faith to others.

The distinguished historian of Christianity Kenneth Scott Latourette referred to the nineteenth as "the great century" because this was the age of "the most extensive geographic spread of Christianity."[45] And during this time of expansion, which was more Protestant than Catholic, "it was from the United States that the majority of the [Protestant] missionaries and more than half of the funds of the Protestant missionary enterprise . . . came."[46] Today the United States is the chief source of support for Protestant and Catholic missions all over the world.

This discussion of religion in motion is obviously conditioned by the context of the predominant religious tradition of Western

[44]Robert L. Duffus, "The Hound of Heaven," *American Mercury,* V (April 1925), 424, as quoted in Gamaliel Bradford, *D. L. Moody: A Worker in Souls* (New York: George H. Doran, 1927), p. 16.

[45]*A History of the Expansion of Christianity* (New York: Harper & Bros., 1941), IV, 1.

[46]Ibid., p. 75.

civilization, whether that tradition be called Christian or Judeo-Christian. This is not to suggest that there are no differences between the Judaic and the Christian heritages. Obviously there are. But both are rooted in an understanding of a God and a people in motion. Christianity has, however, given more of a missionary twist to this understanding, especially in modern times. Hence American Christians have generally been much moved in broadcasting the "good news." Jews and Christians alike have also put themselves in motion in various ways in affirming their own peculiar convictions and heritages. No one knows the full extent to which immigrants and migrants have been motivated by the quest for religious freedom, but the evidence indicates that this has been a factor of great importance. Furthermore, within the various religious communities there has been a continuing development somewhat analogous to that described above in connection with the early history of the Puritan colony of Massachusetts Bay.[47] Religious and nonreligious (ethnic, class, generational, etc.) factors have spun off new movements in old communities. The Americanism controversy that gripped the Roman Catholic Church for a decade and more at the end of the nineteenth century involved the interplay of a variety of religious and nonreligious factors and was significantly related to the founding of the Paulist order and the Catholic University as well as to "the school question" (Chapter IV). Masses of Jewish immigrants from central and eastern Europe ignored or rejected the Americanized Reform Judaism of the nineteenth century. Instead they stimulated the formation or activation of a variety of vital movements such as conservative Judaism, Zionism, and Reconstructionism, and these movements greatly influenced the development of Judaism in twentieth-century America.

Possibly what is being pointed out here is nothing more—or less—than a common sociological phenomenon in the history of religions—that is, that men do act under the impulse of religious as well as non-religious factors. Still I want to say somewhat more than that: The western religious heritage has put a pre-

[47]Pp. 21–22.

mium upon motion, whether as quest for the promised land or mission to other peoples. This has tended to give religious faith in America a peripatetic and thrusting quality. And, among other things, this quality has certainly been of significance in the history of the public school.

ORGANIZED RELIGION

The American has been pictured as a rank individualist; he is also an inveterate joiner. He might be so individualistic as to declare that his religion is his own business. He might also be a real religious organizational man. Generalizations about American religion have often stressed its individualistic nature.[48] But this kind of generalization does not do justice even to such indigenous American expressions as Mormonism, Christian Science, and Jehovah's Witnesses.

The church—using that term generically to refer to religious organizations generally—is the oldest and perhaps the most successful voluntary society in America. Life in this country required the fashioning of a mobile and adaptable organization, one that could follow the people, identify with them, attract their interest and command their loyalty and support. The pattern of being born into the church, into Christendom, that pattern which prevailed in Europe ⁴for a thousand years, never really worked on American soil. Here and there Christian states were attempted—as in Massachusetts Bay and Virginia—but it was impossible to maintain uniformity and to embrace a majority of the people. Religious pluralism is as old as America. And it has always given something of a market-place appearance to American religion. Thus the churches were forced relatively early to make their own way in a competitive world.

Over much of American history the majority of American people did not belong to a church. However, the steady trend has been toward increasing affiliation with religious denomina-

---

[48]For example, the late Willard Sperry, one-time Dean of the Harvard Divinity School, designated "individualism" as one of the most discernible characteristics of American religious life. *Religion in America* (New York: Macmillan, 1946), ch. i.

tions, and today well over 50 percent of the American population maintains such an affiliation.[49] In this process the church has tended to become an effective organization for recruiting and maintaining members. It has also become the prototype for the successful voluntary society. Political, fraternal, philanthropic, professional, and labor organizations have all benefited from the church's experience and success.

Today churches are among the most impressive American organizations in wealth of holdings and extent of organization—[50] a fact which, incidentally, can hardly help but have some implications for the public school. Few American institutions can compare in size and splendor with the Roman Catholic Church in the United States, or even with the United Methodist Church. These institutions not only engage in the one-hour-a-week Sunday morning service. They are also involved in educational, missionary, charitable, and humanitarian activities on a massive scale; and as organizations they are inextricably bound up with the fabric of American society.

The techniques of successful organization, once learned, have been appropriated by dissenters as well as the faithful. If one does not agree with his church he may join another. But if he finds none to his liking and if his convictions are strong enough he may start his own. No one knows today just how many separate religious denominations there are in the United States. The number certainly exceeds two hundred. Groups that do report to gatherers of church statistics range in size from the twenty-five members of the Independent Baptist Church to the over forty-five million Roman Catholics.[51]

One of the more typical American religious organizations— the denomination—has trod a thin line between openness and exclusiveness. This institution, which is most characteristically

[49]No government-conducted census of church membership has been taken since 1936. The National Council of Churches collects data annually from the religious groups themselves and reports these data in its *Yearbook of American Churches*.

[50]See Alfred Balk, *The Religion Business* (Richmond, Va.: John Knox, 1968).

[51]See *Yearbook of American Churches for 1968*, ed. Lauris B. Whitman (New York: National Council of Churches, 1968), pp. 198, 200.

found within Protestantism, has tended to be open to all comers; indeed, it has gone freely into the market place to augment its numbers. At the same time, it has also sought to maintain a distinctive if not unique emphasis or character. Claims to be the true church have been made in America, but some form of accommodation to the realities of religious pluralism (and modernity) has frequently occurred. Hence, instead of making exclusive claims the denomination has stressed its distinctiveness, its peculiar qualities, and has worked hard at instilling loyalty to itself. Somewhat in this spirit, one member of the Church of England in the eighteenth century is reported to have remarked that while there might be various ways of getting to heaven the Anglican was the most gentlemanly. This remark typifies what later came to be a generally accepted attitude among denominations: There are other ways, but ours has this or that to recommend it above them. Thus denominational loyalty came to be something like loyalty to one's school or service club. One knows that there are other schools or clubs, but out of pride and fellow-feeling one insists—often quite good-naturedly —upon the superiority of his own.

This is not to deny the existence of real interdenominational bitterness in American history. Parson Thwackam's remark that he'd rather Tom Jones become a blockhead than a Presbyterian could have been made by a nineteenth-century Anglican or even Methodist in the United States. It was such denominational hard feelings that plagued Horace Mann and led him to be so adamant in his insistence that this kind of sectarianism be kept out of the common school. Furthermore, the intensity of feeling was usually much greater across Catholic–Protestant lines than it was among Protestants. However, by and large the trend in this country has been toward a rounding off of the sharpest edges of denominational rivalry.

The denomination as a voluntary society stressing distinctiveness but not exclusiveness of claim to religious truth has generally not attempted to establish the elements of a separate culture. Instead it has tended to understand itself as moving between the poles of accommodation to and domination of the general culture of the American community. For example, denominations have generally relied upon the public school for the education of their young. At the same time, they have attempted to exercise influence upon that institution, often by working with other denominations in doing so. (See Chapter VI.) Interestingly enough, religious denominations have assiduously established colleges. For the most part, however, such educational institutions have not been used systematically to instill some form of religious or theological orthodoxy, and they have generally been open to all comers, regardless of belief.

The denomination is, then, a common form of organizational accommodation to the American environment. But many religious groups have not accommodated in quite the same way. Some have either maintained or virtually been forced into a near exclusiveness because of a combination of ethnic with religious factors. (Jewish and Negro or black religious groups, for example. Most Eastern Orthodox churches also define themselves along ethnic lines.) Some have achieved a marked distinctiveness by placing primary emphasis upon a particular religious belief or practice. (Groups that stress healing, pentecostal groups, and snake-handling cults, for example.) And some have clung with varying degrees of tenacity to exclusive claims on theological grounds. (The Roman Catholic Church and the Church of Jesus Christ, Latter Day Saints, for example.)

The claim to embody the true religion has sometimes driven groups into the wilderness in search of their own kingdom. One thinks of the Puritans, the Mormons, and the Amish in this connection. Such groups endeavored, in effect, to create their own separate cultures. Where geographical isolation from the general culture has not been possible, some groups have endeavored to create their own cultural enclaves and institutions within the more general culture.

The complex history of Roman Catholicism is interesting in this connection. In the first place, the Roman Catholic Church has had to deal with greater ethnic variety than any other American religious group. This has often involved a greater appearance of foreignness than that characterizing other religious groups. This ethnic variety has also exerted considerable centrifugal force upon the church. In the second place, this church has often been forced from the other side to affirm Americanness along with or over against general Protestant hegemony. In the midst of these realities the church has clung to its own asserted uniqueness as the One, Holy, Catholic, and Apostolic Church of Christ. Strength in numbers and vigorous determination have enabled the Roman Catholic Church to build many of the institutions of a separate American Catholic culture, including schools and colleges, hospitals, lodges, veterans' organizations, professional societies, and newspapers and journals. There have, however, been no significant attempts to found a Catholic political party or labor union. And although church leaders have argued that every Catholic child should be in a Catholic school, the actual enrollment of Catholic youngsters in such schools has never exceeded half of the total number.

The Roman Catholic Church, then, has gone an impressive distance toward the achievement of a separate Catholic-dominated culture. In recent years, however, a combination of circumstances—including the rise in the socioeconomic level of the Catholic population, the exigencies of religious pluralism, and liberalizing developments within both European and American Catholicism—has softened the claim to exclusiveness. What effect this will have on the separate institutions remains to be seen.

The efforts of Protestant exclusivists to establish their own institutions of culture have not been as obvious as those of Catholicism. This is true in part because their numbers are much smaller and in part because of the fact that in certain areas of the country—especially the South—they have managed to maintain a considerable hold on the institutions and ideology of the prevailing culture. For example, Protestant fundamentalism has often managed to keep the teaching of evolution out of the public schools (at least from a formal, legal standpoint) and the practice of prayer and Bible reading in. In areas where this has not been possible, some conservative Protestant groups have endeavored to establish their own schools.

Within Judaism, tensions between universalism and religio-cultural separatism have been especially strong. Reform Judaism in the nineteenth century clung to few distinctive marks of the historic community of Jews. Such Reform leaders as Isaac Mayer Wise and Max Lilienthal eagerly identified with the American community and were rhapsodic in their praise of this land. They stressed publicly what they shared in common with Americans of all faiths and tended to play down Jewish claims to uniqueness.[52] However, even these accommodating rabbis, and others of like mind, still held to a distinctive Jewish identity.

As masses of Jewish immigrants poured into the United States from central and eastern Europe at the turn of the century the problems of identity were aggravated. Some continued to hold to the traditional orthodoxies of central European Jewry. Others turned against religion entirely and attempted to find meaningful relationships with the most secularized aspects of American culture. But most Jews—whether traditional or moderate— looked to the public school as the crucial institution in the Americanization process. A few of the more orthodox did endeavor to establish their own full-time day schools. More commonly, however, an effort was made to maintain elements of Jewish culture and religious heritage through educational devices that were maintained in addition to the public school.[53]

In conclusion, it is worth noting that the religious groups that have stressed exclusiveness or some kind of uniqueness in their own position have sometimes exerted a strong influence in counteracting tendencies for the public schools to become either Protestant preserves or instruments of a sacralized nationalism.

[52]The American Jew, said Lilienthal, is "in creed a monotheist, in descent a Hebrew, Israelite or Jew, in all other public or private relations an American citizen." Quoted in David Philipson, *Max Lilienthal, American Rabbi: Life and Writings* (New York: Bloch Pub., 1915), p. 108.

[53]On trends in Jewish education, see Marshall Sklare, *Conservative Judaism* (Glencoe, Ill.: The Free Press, 1955), pp. 144–58. Also Kaplan, *Judaism as a Civilization*, Chapter XXXI on "The Meaning of Jewish Education in America." Kaplan, founder of the Reconstructionist movement, argued that the Jewish child should, in effect, be educated in two systems of education—the public school, on the one hand, where the child would develop certain basic skills and learn the elements of American culture, and Jewish education, on the other, where he would be saturated with the elements of "Judaism as a Civilization."

The activities of various Jewish and Roman Catholic organizations and of the Jehovah's Witnesses are especially noteworthy in this regard.

THE BOOK

The Bible might well be claimed as America's sacred book. Its influence upon American culture is beyond dispute. But the question of the nature, significance, and implications of that influence can easily be the subject of a thousand debates. This much is clear: Most American religious groups have regarded the Bible as the special source of divine disclosure, and most have affirmed Biblical roots for their faith. Many groups have claimed to represent or reproduce in modern times Biblical patterns of belief, action, and organization. In addition, American memory generally is liberally inhabited by images and myths of creation, Eden, fall, divine calling, exodus, wilderness wandering, and promised land. What follows from this?

Many Americans have regarded the Bible as the primary source book for spiritual inspiration and moral guidance. Not a few have attributed a sacred and even a magical quality to this book. It became for them, the fountainhead of all that is good, the source of all purity, and the reference book for all exemplars of virtue. In a paean of praise for the book Justice Hagans of the Cincinnati Superior Court wrote in 1870 that the Holy Bible impresses "on the children of the common schools, the principles and duties of morality and justice, and a sacred regard to truth, love of country, humanity, universal benevolence, sobriety, industry, chastity, moderation, temperance and all other virtues, which are the ornaments of human society."[54] A book of such quality must have a place in the public school— or so it seemed to many.

The Bible has also been a subject of great disagreement and

[54]From the opinion of Justice Hagans in the case of *Minor* v. *Board of Education of Cincinnati* (1870) as printed in *The Bible in the Public Schools* (New York: Da Capo Press, 1967), p. 371. (This Da Capo Press edition is an unabridged republication of the first edition published in Cincinnati in 1870 by Robert Clarke & Co.)

controversy. Men have divided, re-divided, and divided again over its meaning. Bitter antagonism has arisen between groups even over the matter of acceptable translations. And a few brave (or foolhardy) souls have even argued that the book might do more harm than good in its effects upon human attitudes and actions. It was really not so obvious, then, that such a controversial book did belong in the schools. Still its impact upon the religious and cultural heritage has been so substantial that it could be excluded from the public school curriculum only with the greatest of difficulty.

RELIGIOUS OUTLOOK

The American has been pictured as an optimist. He is that. His optimism, however, ranges from cautiously sober to wildly enthusiastic. In fact, American views of man and history vary from the highly pessimistic and apocalyptic certainty that things must get much, much worse before they get better to the assurance that whatever is is good. Many of the early Americans reflected what Perry Miller called the "Augustinian strain of piety," that is, a rather sober understanding of human sinfulness balanced by a faith in God's pervasive and prevailing sovereignty. Eighteenth-century men, influenced by both pietism and the Enlightenment, tended to be more confident in human ability and more sanguine about destiny than their forebears had been. Buoyed up by the hopeful experience and outlook of the young Republic, early nineteenth-century men dared to conclude that all human problems—with the possible exception of slavery— were capable of solution.[55] Realities of slavery, and all the ugly brood of offspring that accompanied and followed it, of economic depression, of urban slum and sprawl, and of world war did not entirely dampen that hope. Even in the twentieth century some Americans have expected the early arrival of the Kingdom of God in the form of the good (peaceful, prosperous, and perhaps even just) society. But the nature of American optimism underwent a subtle change which represents, to some

[55]See Sidney Mead, *The Lively Experiment,* pp. 90–103.

observers, a backing off from the harsher realities of human pride and greed and of American and world social problems. Now one's hope and assurance rested in a proper frame of mind. Evil was an illusion, "bad luck" a figment of the imagination. Right thinking made one like God and one's future divine.

William James referred to the religious expression of this kind of psychological optimism in the "New Thought" movement and in Christian Science as "a spiritual movement as significant for our day as the Reformation was for its time."[56] It was a movement which expressed itself institutionally in such religious groups or organizations as Christian Science and the Unity School of Christianity. But its strength was even more evident in the fact that it tended to dominate the thinking of a large number of Americans who belonged to more traditional religious denominations.[57]

"New Thought" is one of the more popular ways of reacting to the realities of the twentieth century while preserving something of a deeply rooted American optimism. Less popular but perhaps equally significant as a way of balancing reality with hope is the view of the radical apocalypticists. For these men— Jehovah's Witnesses, for example—the only hope lies in God's direct intervention in history in which He destroys evil and overcomes human sin and death and all problems associated therewith. Such intervention might bring catastrophe upon many —perhaps even the majority—but it will be worth the wait for those who survive. This view expects tomorrow to be better, at least for the selected few. "New Thought" claims that today already is the best if one but has eyes to see it. The majority of Americans find themselves between the two, neither expecting a dramatic divine intervention nor completely casting aside life's gloomier aspects, but generally future-oriented, confidently expecting that tomorrow will be better for most men, assured that man is basically good and that history—especially American history—is redemptive.

[56]As quoted by Charles S. Braden, *These Also Believe* (New York: Macmillan, 1949), p. 130.

[57]Note, for example, the enormous popularity of Norman Vincent Peale's *The Power of Positive Thinking* in the years following its publication at mid-century.

VARIETY

There is likely to be an exception to every generalization about religion in America. And there is always the possibility that the forest is more in the eye of the beholder than it is an actuality upon the American landscape. The trees are obviously there however; indeed in such profuse variety that possibly the only generalization that is really warranted is to note the variety. American religious groups range from the Shakers to the Peyote Cult, from Christian Science to the Jehovah's Witnesses, from the Unitarian Universalist Association to the Primitive Baptists, and from Reform Judaism to Syrian Orthodoxy. A study of the "varieties of religious experience" focused on the American scene might include examples ranging from the humanitarian spirituality of a John Woolman to the athletic showmanship of Billy Sunday, from the silent strength in the mystical contemplation of a Thomas Merton to the great onrush of revelations in the visions of Joseph Smith, from a Kentucky revivalist captured or captivated by the "holy jerks" to a Hassidic Jew raptly absorbed in the Torah, and from the prison conversion experience of a Malcolm X to the eager concentration of a novice engaged in zazen.

From this variety one might well conclude first of all, that it is a gross mistake to assume that there is a standardized American religion; indeed, it would appear to be "un-American" (as well as dehumanizing) to push for such in any aspect of public life, and especially in the public school. Pressures have been exerted upon that institution to produce a standardized product —even to the point of religion. But the best in the tradition, as forcefully expressed in the First Amendment, does not call for this; indeed, freedom from religious uniformity was and is a primary condition of the Republic.

Where or what, then, was the ground of unity in this diversity? One might even write the story of the relationship between religion and the public school in terms of a constant search for some kind of principled basis of unity, some kind of ideological sinew that would hold the body-politic together without unduly restraining its many members. This search will concern us throughout this account. What follows immediately in the concluding section of this chapter is a sketch of the main elements in the developing public piety in the United States. That public piety afforded some of the needed basis for unity.

Elements of Public Piety

America inherited the tradition of Christendom. For more than a thousand years, Europe had sought to embody the idea of a Christian society and culture. It was believed that: (1) God had revealed himself in Christ; (2) the Church was the guardian of that revelation; (3) there should be but one true Church in civil society; and (4) the pattern of Christian truth should be fundamental in the structuring and functioning of that society.

Early immigrants sought to claim America for Christendom. Missionaries set out to convert the natives. Puritans endeavored to build Biblical commonwealths in the wilds of New England. Quakers attempted to revive Primitive Christianity in and around the city of brotherly love. For each of these and other groups of Christians the pattern for society was to be found in the Bible. And for each that pattern included some degree of religious uniformity, ranging from the relatively mild requirement of belief in Jesus Christ for public-office holders in Quaker Pennsylvania to the more stringent restriction of the franchise to members of the Congregational Church in Puritan Massachusetts.

By 1776 the tradition of Christendom had lost much of its force in America. A multiplicity of Christian groups made it quite clear that no single one could reign supreme or claim uniformity of belief or practice in a particular colony or state. Furthermore, men now appealed to reason and nature with as much zeal and certainty as they once had to revelation and supernature. Now the pattern for society was evident in the bosom of nature herself.

What was seen in nature was not a society built along

specifically Christian lines but a society built upon the laws of nature and nature's God. What was seen was not an established Church to show the way but a relative degree of freedom in matters of religious belief, practice, and affiliation. The ship of state could sail without the fixed star of Biblical revelation and the rudder of ecclesiastical control to guide it. Nature afforded her own star and reason was a sufficient guide.

The founding fathers' understanding of this new society which replaced Christendom was succinctly expressed in the words inscribed on the reverse of the great seal: *novus ordo seclorum* —a new order for the ages. This new order or new society stood in contrast to the older *corpus Christianum*—that is, the Christian society or order.

The American nation was new. It began *de novo*. It owed its existence to nothing save the will and the work of the people in concert appealing to God and to nature. It was not dependent upon the will of any wordly or ecclesiastical sovereign. It did not stem in fixed manner from any previous historical pattern. There were lessons to be learned from the past, but the experiences of the past were more to be rejected than followed. "The representatives of this nation," John Adams pointed out, "frankly cut assunder the ties which had bound them . . ."[58]

The nation was to be of this world—or, one might even say, secular.[59] Its goals were not the kingdom of God or a Christian state and its means did not involve ecclesiastical control or even close cooperation between church and state. What was sought was the establishment of "Justice," the insurance of "domestic Tranquillity," provision for "the common defence," promotion of "the general Welfare," and the securing of "the Blessings of Liberty . . ." These ends were to be accomplished by the formation of "a more perfect Union" of states living together under a constitution which deals almost entirely with the means of government and which says of religion only that "no religious

[58]Inaugural Address, *The Presidents Speak: The Inaugural Addresses of the American Presidents from Washington to Kennedy,* annotated by Davis Newton Lott (New York: Holt, Rinehart & Winston, 1961), p. 9.
[59]*Saecularis, saeculum*—meaning age, or in Christian Latin, "the world," especially as opposed to the church.

Test shall ever be required as a Qualification to any Office or public Trust under the United States," and that "Congress shall make no law respecting an establishment of religion or prohibiting the free exercise thereof . . ."[60]

This is not to claim a complete disjunction between the colonial fathers of the seventeenth century and the revolutionary fathers of the eighteenth. The latter were men of faith also, even though their faith took a different form with regard to the ordering of life in this world. They were confident of divine providence, as we have seen. And their convictions about man and society were convictions of faith. The affirmation that all men are created equal and that they are endowed by their creator with certain inalienable rights are more statements of faith than statements self-evident to reason.

The revolutionary fathers, Lincoln recognized in his Gettysburg Address, were "dedicated to the proposition that all men are created equal." A proposition is not so much a statement of fact as it is an affirmation of truth to be demonstrated or proved. The American founding fathers, then, affirmed themselves to be committed to a particular idea about man and society. In declaring their independence they also opted for a certain type of existence. The *novus ordo seclorum* whose pattern was evident in nature was now to be made a reality in political life.

G. K. Chesterton once observed with perceptiveness that "America is the only nation in the world that is founded on a creed." He tells of his consternation upon being asked about his political and moral ideas and practices when he sought a United States visa. But then he decided that since American citizenship implies an affirmation of certain truths about man and society it was quite proper that visitors to the United States should be asked to state their own views. "So far as its primary ideal is concerned," Chesterton observed, America's "exclusiveness is religious . . ."—that is, based upon an affirmation of faith.[61]

The affirmation is both individual and communal, and both in

[60]Quotations from the Preamble, Article VI, and the First Amendment, Constitution of the United States.

[61]"What I Saw in America" in *The Man Who Was Chesterton*, ed. Raymond T. Bond (New York: Dodd, Mead, & Co., 1937), pp. 188–89.

the past and in the present. That is, there is a sense in which each American dedicates himself to the proposition and in which each generation renews the commitment. Even more basically, there is a sense in which each man "joins" the nation, becomes a citizen, renews the covenant, and in which each generation re-enacts the declaration of independence and commits itself anew to the embodiment of the *novus ordo seclorum.* Hence each individual American and each American generation lives contemporaneously with the fathers.

The revolutionary themes persist in the process of Americanization.[62] As the nation began *de novo* so did the people. Sailing across the Atlantic entailed a metamorphosis, a putting away of the old and a putting on of the new. Even in the eighteenth century Crèvecoeur wrote that "The American is a new man, who acts upon new principles; he must therefore entertain new ideas, and form new opinions."[63] The Atlantic crossing provided a release from the bondage of the past. In this new land, James K. Polk affirmed, "genius is free" and unhampered, and "the hand is free to accomplish whatever the head conceives . . ."[64] "We are the heirs of the ages," Teddy Roosevelt proclaimed, but "we have had to pay few of the penalties . . . exacted by the dead hand of a bygone civilization."[65]

Subsequent generations, "birthright Americans," have accepted their newness without the Atlantic crossing. They are "born free." At the same time, however, they too must undergo initiatory rites.

Americans have been called upon again and again to renew their dedication to what President Eisenhower called "the abiding creed of our fathers."[66] We are bound to those fathers, and to each other, by what Lincoln called "the mystic cords of memory"[67] and by our commitment to their promise. "Surely I do not misinterpret the spirit of the occasion," said Benjamin

[62]Chesterton observed that Americanization was what was really unique about America. Ibid., p. 193.
[63]Hector St. John de Crèvecoeur, *Letters from an American Farmer* (New York: E. P. Dutton & Co., 1912), p. 44.
[64]*The Presidents Speak,* p. 91.
[65]Ibid., p. 185.
[66]Ibid., p. 258.
[67]Ibid., p. 123.

Harrison of his inauguration, "when I assume that the whole body of the people covenant with me . . ."[68] In terms of practical politics perhaps Harrison did misinterpret the extent of his public support, but in the context of national ceremonial he did not misinterpret the spirit of the occasion. "This is not a day of triumph," said Woodrow Wilson after defeating Taft and Teddy Roosevelt. It was, he affirmed, "a day of dedication . . ." And he summoned "all honest men, all patriotic, all forward-looking men," to his side.[69]

The American creedal affirmation, Chesterton pointed out, involves "the pure classic conception that no man must aspire to be anything more than a citizen, and that no man shall endure to be anything less."[70] To be a citizen means to be on a par with everyone else, so far as public, civil life is concerned. There are and there must be no civilly initiated and supported special privileges. Citizenship is a platform upon which each and all men can stand and claim equal treatment, evenhanded justice—according to each his due. Citizenship is also a springboard from which one can affirm his rights as a citizen, the rights of "life, liberty, and the pursuit of happiness." The pledge of allegiance summarizes this twofold aspect of the American credo in the phrase "with liberty and justice for all."

The phrase in the pledge is, of course, more an affirmation than a description. Actual conditions of American life have continually fallen short of this ideal. Citizenship was denied to millions of black men until 1863, and its full rights have been effectively denied to most of their descendants since "emancipation." But the affirmation of the ideal has served both as a constant spur to the disadvantaged and disenfranchised to seize their rights, and as a constant goad to citizens to help others to gain those rights.

The founding fathers rooted their affirmations concerning equality and liberty in nature and nature's God. Hence *all* men were created equal and *all* were endowed with inalienable rights. Not only has this sense of inclusiveness made for an

[68]Ibid., p. 155.
[69]Ibid., p. 201.
[70]*The Man Who Was Chesterton*, p. 195.

enlargement of the ranks of citizens in the United States but it has also inclined Americans toward the mission of claiming equality and liberty for all men. The "blessings of liberty" were to be secured not only "to ourselves and our Posterity," as indicated in the Preamble to the Constitution, but to all the world. "Ask not what America will do for you," said John F. Kennedy in an evangelical appeal to all men, "but what together we can do for the freedom of man."[71] Hence the extension of liberty became an important aspect of public piety.

American democracy has been seen as a model, illustrative of fundamental truth and universally admired. "The eyes of all nations are fixed on our Republic," Andrew Jackson confidently affirmed in 1833.[72] Jackson's perspective was no more provincial and no less confident than that of John Winthrop, who had predicted more than two hundred years earlier that "wee shall be as a Citty Upon a Hill, the eies of all people are uppon us . . ."[73] This same sense of importance, of visibility, has continued—perhaps with more reason as the nation has advanced toward becoming a major power. If we fail in our democratic task, Teddy Roosevelt declared, "the cause of free self-government throughout the world will rock to its foundations . . ."[74] There is mustered here in this time, this place, this nation, confidently declared Woodrow Wilson in 1913, "the forces of humanity. . . . Men's hearts wait upon us. . . . Men's hopes call upon us. . . ."[75] "The faith we hold," said Dwight D. Eisenhower forty years later, "belongs not to us alone but to the free of all the world."[76]

The model could not be static. The example must be expanded; it must be carried to others. The "manifest destiny" of the United States was to expand territorially and in so doing to spread the good news of democracy. In response to Bryan's contention that expansion would undermine democracy, William

[71]*The Presidents Speak*, p. 271.
[72]Ibid., p. 62.
[73]"A Modell of Christian Charity," Miller and Johnson, *The Puritans*, p. 199.
[74]*The Presidents Speak*, p. 186.
[75]Ibid., p. 201.
[76]Ibid., p. 259.

McKinley confidently stated in words that carry a familiar ring almost three quarters of a century later: "Our institutions will not deteriorate by extension, and our sense of justice will not abate under tropic suns in distant seas." The American people take their love of freedom "with them wherever they go . . ."[77]

Even when the ardor for geographical expansion had cooled the sense of mission continued. Although Americans fought on European soil in World War I, no territorial claims were made by the United States after that war. But the war itself was fought "to make the world safe for democracy," that most precious of products which the United States exemplified, protected, and spread abroad. It was fought by a people who, in the words of President Wilson, were "provincials no longer," whose parish was the world and whose principles were those of a "liberated mankind . . ."[78] And today this outward thrusting mission has propelled us to the moon where Americans planted the American flag with the proclamation that they came in "peace . . . for all mankind."

As John Winthrop was confident that God had put him and his fellows in the limelight of history, so subsequent Americans have been sure that their system represented the ultimate, whether that ultimate was understood in terms of natural law, God, or the universal opinion of mankind. Providence would not suffer this, "the most perfect form of government . . . ever devised by man . . . to perish," said James Buchanan, ". . . until civil and religious liberty" shall have been extended "throughout the world."[79] Democracy "cannot die," exclaimed Franklin D. Roosevelt in 1941. It "alone, of all the forms of government, enlists the full force of men's enlightened will."[80] And President Eisenhower saw the American faith aligned with the forces of good in battle against the forces of evil, freedom against slavery, and "lightness against the dark." In this struggle Americans affirmed a position which was "governed by eternal moral and natural laws."[81] This national self-assurance was expressed in

[77]Ibid., p. 180.
[78]Ibid., p. 204.
[79]Ibid., p. 113.
[80]Ibid., p. 244.
[81]Ibid., pp. 258–59.

even more cosmic terms when American astronauts, returning from man's first walk upon the moon, were greeted by the President of the United States with the statement that what they had done was the most important event since creation. Confidence in the righteousness of our faith and its causes has often given rise to the conclusion that America is the vehicle of the divine will, God's new Israel. But the greatest of the statesmen and the most perceptive articulators of the American Credo have stopped short of this consummation. It was Abraham Lincoln who referred to the United States of America as "this almost chosen people."[82] The "almost" suggests a degree of humility. While Lincoln had no doubt about the high value of democracy—which he referred to as "man's last best hope of earth"[83]—he was acutely aware of the degree to which American practices fell short of demonstrating the American proposition. He also had a keen sense of a prevailing providence whose will was not always fathomable and whose ways could not easily be identified with human ways. "The almighty has his own purposes,"[84] Lincoln confessed near the end of the Civil War in a statement which refused to separate North from South as good from evil, godly from ungodly.

James Madison argued that "before any man can be considered a member of civil society, he must be considered as a subject of the governor of the universe." Thus "every man who becomes a member of any particular civil society" must do so in such a fashion as to reserve or maintain his "allegiance to the universal sovereign."[85] Here, then, was a point of appeal beyond the nation-state, a critical element which restrained public piety from sacralizing the nation.

This ultimate has been understood to be beyond not only in some metaphysical sense but also in a historical sense. Lincoln reminded his fellow Americans that the divine purpose is not

[82]Address to the Senate of the State of New Jersey, February 21, 1861, in Paul M. Angle and Earl Schenck Miers, *The Living Lincoln* (New Brunswick, N.J.: Rutgers University Press, 1955), p. 378.

[83]Ibid., p. 522.

[84]Ibid., p. 639.

[85]Saul K. Padover, *The Complete Madison* (New York: Harper & Bros., 1953), p. 300.

easily discerned in the movement of history. And at times his sense of providence bordered on divine determinism. But he was also confident in the plasticity of the historical process. One could determine to bind up the nation's wounds; the future held some promise of achievement of this and other human ends. In such a world education and the instruments of education were especially important.

II

The Public School as "Established Church"?

". . . of necessity the state in its public-education system is and always has been teaching religion. It does so because the well-being of the nation and the state demands this foundation of shared beliefs. . . . In this sense the public-school system of the United States *is* its established church."

—Sidney Mead[1]

"The work of public education is with us . . . to a large degree, a piece of religious work."

—Ellwood P. Cubberley, 1909[2]

"Today, education is perhaps the most important function of state and local governments."

—The Supreme Court of the United States[3]

It has become fashionable in some circles to advocate the "fourth r" in education—meaning religion. The phraseology is perhaps more clever than perceptive. American public education has never stopped with the three r's. And the fourth r has sometimes been first, has sometimes underlain the rest, and has sometimes, ambivalently, been both an "in r" and an "out r."

The pupil in the public school has been taught to read, to write, and to do his sums in order that he might *be* something —that he might be a pious person, or a moral man or a loyal citizen. The content of the reading and writing, and at times even the arithmetic, has usually reflected these ends. The early readers and spellers were saturated with religious, moral, and

[1]*The Lively Experiment*, p. 68.

[2]*Changing Conceptions of Education* (New York: Houghton Mifflin, 1909), p. 68. Cubberley was one of the most influential early-twentieth-century historians of American public education.

[3]*Brown* v. *Board of Education*, 347 U.S. 483, 493 (1954). This is the famous school-desegregation case.

patriotic materials. Content has changed but goals remain much the same.

Two things are explored in the brief historical survey in this chapter—the role of the public school in eliciting and instilling what I have called public piety and the ambivalent relationship between religion and public piety as evidenced in the public school. Americans have assigned the public school a dynamic communal role from its beginnings. It has been suggested that this is comparable to a religious role, that the public school can be understood as doing in the United States what the established church did in medieval Europe. This is a stimulating analogy that can be useful if not pushed too far. The established church of medieval Europe regarded itself as the receptacle and guardian of the true faith. Conformity to the essentials of that faith was understood to be necessary both theologically and politically, both for the individual's ultimate salvation and the community's immediate well-being. Some have viewed public piety and the public school in these terms, but others have demurred.

A blue-ribbon commission of the National Education Association affirmed a common American view in 1951 in stating that the development in children of devotion to the moral and spiritual values central to the American heritage specifically, and to mankind generally, "is basic to all other educational objectives." So important is this task, the commission held, that "there must be no question whatever as to the willingness of the school to subordinate all other considerations to those which concern moral and spiritual standards."[4]

In arguing that the school *should* be concerned primarily with moral and spiritual values the NEA commission assumed that the school *could* successfully instill such values. Furthermore, the commission, like most Americans, also assumed that the public school was the single most important institution for achieving this end. Indeed, that institution was understood to be not only primary but indispensable.

[4]*Moral and Spiritual Values in the Public Schools*, pp. 6, 54. The report was issued by the Educational Policies Commission of the NEA. Among the members of the commission which prepared this report were James Bryant Conant and Dwight D. Eisenhower.

The NEA's Educational Policies Commission stood in a line of succession which went back at least to the Continental Congress. The members of that body affirmed in 1787 that since "religion, morality, and knowledge" were "essential to good government and the happiness of mankind, schools and the means of education" should "forever be encouraged."[5] Present in that statement were all of the elements which went together to make up the story of public education in America: religion, morality, patriotism, knowledge—all induced through the public school. Knowledge was almost always seen in a context of religion, morality, and patriotism, and these three were usually understood as being inseparable. However, the three were not static, and it is especially evident that the meaning and function of religion changed.

Evangelical Religion, Republican Piety, and Formal Education

The common school arose in America out of a variety of factors, including the heritage of Europe—and especially England—transported to the new world; the exigencies of the new environment; and the desire to spread evangelical religion and republican politics. Bernard Bailyn has pointed out that among the earliest settlers the family, the community, and the church were the chief instruments of acculturation. While formal schooling played some role, it was by no means the most important institution in the educational process. By the end of the colonial period, however, this condition had changed radically: "Schools and formal schooling had acquired a new importance."[6] The openness of the new world required more formal provision for education than had the relatively more stable environment of the mother country. Without this, barbarism was a constant threat. The early settlers of Massachusetts Bay, "dreading to

[5]Article III, Ordinance of 1787, familiarly known as the Northwest Ordinance.
[6]Bernard Bailyn, *Education in the Forming of American Society* (Chapel Hill: University of North Carolina Press, 1960), p. 21.

leave an illiterate Ministery . . . when our present Ministers shall lie in the dust," as they put it, founded Harvard College.[7] And many a subsequent immigrant and migrant community endeavored to found some kind of school as a hedge against barbarism.

Openness not only posed the threat of barbarism; it also offered opportunity for change, for the development of a new man and a new society. "Where there had been deeply ingrained habits, unquestioned tradition, automatic responses, security, and confidence," writes Bailyn "there was now awareness, doubt, formality, will, and decision."[8] This transition is most evident religiously in the Great Awakening, that colony-wide movement of the eighteenth century which broke with the established order from New England to Virginia and which had an enormous effect upon the developing American society, not only in terms of religion but also in such areas as education and political life.[9] The awakeners sought to transform every man, to give birth to a new consciousness which was neither under the shadow of the institutions and orthodoxies of the past nor confined to the twilight of a narrow provincialism. Salvation was of God in Christ, not of man or his church or of mother England. Under His grace man was changed from a narrow, petty creature capable only of feathering his own nest into a new being who now could love all being. The church became a voluntary society of the saved, a company of divinely drafted souls who displayed all the zeal of the most enthusiastic volunteers. The world—meaning chiefly the developing American society and culture—became at one and the same time staging area, battleground, and enemy. Here the troops prepared for their mission, here they sought to effect the desired change in

[7]"New Englands First Fruits," as quoted in Miller and Johnson, *The Puritans*, p. 701.

[8]*Education in the Forming of American Society*, pp. 21–22.

[9]Standard monographs on the Great Awakening include: Edwin Scott Gaustad, *The Great Awakening in New England* (New York: Harper & Bros., 1957); W. M. Gewehr, *The Great Awakening in Virginia, 1740–1790* (Durham, N.C.: Duke University Press, 1930); and Charles Hartshorn Maxson, *The Great Awakening in the Middle Colonies* (Chicago: University of Chicago Press, 1920).

their fellow man, and here they endeavored to transform the
site itself; for they hoped, as a result of their labors, not only
to see newborn men, but to know at least the first fruits of a
new society—a new heaven and a new earth.

While it is well known that the Great Awakening was directly
or indirectly related to the founding of a number of colonial
colleges, the effects of this movement upon education at lower
levels have not been systematically studied. It is clear, however,
that most of the leaders of the movement, themselves well-
educated men, were keenly concerned for education at all levels.
This was not an obscurantist movement, as it has sometimes
been pictured. The greatest of the leaders, Jonathan Edwards,
who became president of Princeton for a short period late in
his life, urged, in his *Thoughts on the Revival,* that schools be
established and children of the colonies be raised up "in common
learning" as well as in "vital piety."[10] One student of the
Awakening has observed that education "was one plank" in the
revivalists' platform "for promoting the happiness of the American people" and that at the close of the Revolutionary War,
the clergymen who had been most active in the Awakening
"were the first to enter a plea for education in the new republic."[11] Another points out that the Great Awakening brought one
of the first major efforts to reshape education in America and
to use it with specific purpose in mind.[12]

The awakeners wanted a kind of schooling which would
produce men who were both learned and zealous. The springs
of motivation must be affected as well as the regions of intellect.
Conviction, purpose, dedication must result as well as knowledge.

This kind of product was sought first of all in the educating
of ministers—"sons of the prophets," as they were sometimes
called. But the awakeners' vision of education profoundly
affected the education of all. This is illustrated well in the case

[10]*The Works of Jonathan Edwards* (London: Ball, Arnold, & Co., 1865),
I, 426.
[11]Alan Heimert, *Religion and the American Mind: From the Great
Awakening to the Revolution* (Cambridge: Harvard University Press, 1966),
pp. 49, 187. See also pp. 14, 426, 528f.
[12]Thomas Jefferson Wertenbaker, *Princeton, 1746–1896* (Princeton:
Princeton University Press, 1946), ch. i.

of Princeton College. That institution was founded in 1746 by a group of "New Light" Presbyterian clergymen—all of whom were actively a part of the Great Awakening in the middle colonies. Convinced that no other college could be counted on to produce a properly converted and dedicated ministry, these founders set out to build such an institution. But as they moved toward the realization of their goal they concluded that what was a good education for prospective clergymen could also be a good "means of raising up men that will be useful in other . . . professions—ornaments of the State as well as the Church."[13] The combination of learning and piety, tutelage of head and heart, was as necessary and desirable for laymen as for ministers of the gospel.

With the passage of the years the focus of the piety shifted at Princeton. "If," writes Princeton's historian, T. J. Wertenbaker, "during the first two decades of the college, religion held the dominant place . . . in the next ten years patriotism became a strong rival."[14] But what occurred seems to have been more a case of partnership than rivalry. The Reverend John Witherspoon, president of Princeton from 1767 until his death in 1794, eagerly combined piety and patriotism in his life and work. Leaving Scotland to accept the presidency of the college, he was quickly caught up in the fast-flowing patriotic stream. He had not been in New Jersey a decade when he became one of the signers of the Declaration of Independence. Witherspoon early caught the vision of the new man and the new society that were aborning in this new world. His college, which had been founded to produce zealous converts to Christianity, could as easily also produce zealous citizens of the new republic.

Evangelical religion was, then, the primary factor in colonial America which gave rise to formal education; and the motivation and the means (including the schools) of evangelical religion were quite capable of being directed toward patriotic ends. Hence it was quite natural that after the Revolution

---

[13]Ibid., p. 19. The original charter of Yale (1701) specified that Yale would be a college "wherin youth . . . may be fitted for public employment, both in church and civil state."

[14]Ibid., p. 55.

graduates went out from the schools of evangelical origin and purpose to become teachers in all parts of the young Republic. These men, who were mostly clergymen, were determined to perpetuate in schools and colleges that combination of learning and piety which had been instilled in them at their alma maters. Princeton men exercised considerable influence, especially in the South, where they played a leading role in establishing educational institutions. Yale men, especially those educated under Timothy Dwight in the late eighteenth and early nineteenth centuries, played a similar role in the West. And others went out from such schools as Dartmouth and Brown.

This devotion of clergymen to education continued well into the nineteenth century as many gave themselves wholeheartedly to the cause and establishment of the common school. With the perceptive overstatement that characterizes many of his observations, Alexis de Tocqueville pointed out that in the 1830's the greater part of education in the United States was "entrusted to the clergy."[15] The richly fermenting juice of evangelical religion was poured into the wineskins of the common school by Methodist and Baptist clergymen; and the generally more educated Congregationalists and Presbyterians continued to prepare men for service to church and civil state.[16]

To Raise Up Moral Men

The habit of looking to the school to produce learned piety and patriotism became so deeply ingrained in the American mind that few questioned its validity. The common ground for achieving this combination came to be morality. A good man

---

[15]*Democracy in America,* ed. Mayer and Lerner, p. 272, note 4.

[16]See Timothy L. Smith, "Protestant Schooling and American Nationality, 1800–1850," *Journal of American History,* LIII (1966–67), 679–95; and David Tyack, "The Kingdom of God and the Common School: Protestant Ministers and the Educational Awakening in the West," *The Harvard Educational Review,* XXXVI (1966), 447–69. On developments at Harvard see the section on "Horace Mann's Common Religion in Massachusetts," Chapter III below.

was by definition both religious and patriotic. And few doubted that one of the school's primary goals should be the raising up of moral men.

The amalgamation of religion, patriotism, and education with morality is also well illustrated in the case of Princeton. John Witherspoon brought with him from Scotland a keen concern for what was called moral philosophy. This was that branch of learning which established the principles of morality on the basis of reason or common sense and religion. It was a convenient meeting ground for learning and piety, reason and revelation, the natural and the supernatural. It also brought the truths of religion to bear on private and public morals. And it was a subject upon which men of various religious convictions could agree.

Generations of Princeton men, from Witherspoon's early years as president well into the nineteenth century, were thoroughly schooled in his "Lectures on Moral Philosophy." They carried with them in their educational endeavors, then, a convenient system for directing their evangelical zeal into the practical channels of moral character and good citizenship. In this they exemplified an approach which was to become common in American education.

Most Americans have assumed that there is a close relationship between religion and morality. We are inheritors of a tradition which has stressed this sort of relationship since the days of Isaiah and of Socrates. The Puritans regarded man as a sinner who could act rightly only under the power of God's grace. For Jonathan Edwards true virtue consisted of love of being in general, a love characteristic of and made possible by the almighty and benevolent God. Religion and morality were so intertwined for the Quaker John Woolman that it is impossible to separate them in his approach to life. His religious sensibilities gave power and acuteness to his intense moral concerns. Benjamin Franklin, like other Deists, was convinced that the one thing that the deity required of man was a good moral life. Reinforcement of this requirement was to be found in the afterlife, where good acts would be rewarded and bad punished. American revivalists from Finney to Graham have called for a radical change in life, which has entailed some obvious moral ramifications. Even the American pragmatist philosophers have seen morality developing in and supported by a context of human loyalty and devotion which can in some sense be called religious.[17]

It is noteworthy that the NEA Educational Policies Commission linked moral with *spiritual* values in their statement cited above. This suggests, among other things, that the commission saw a close relationship between religion and morality. "Spiritual" was preferred to "religious," however, because it is broader in implication; it avoids denominational or sectarian connotations. But they appeared to be saying that something beyond the merely moral is needed for a sense of imperative and a depth of conviction, or that the moral cannot be understood merely in terms of code. The first value suggested by the commission is "the supreme importance of the individual personality . . . the inherent worth of every human being . . ."[18] This may be understood as an essentially religious statement, a statement of faith and of commitment, which lends depth and power to moral conviction.

Americans have not always agreed on the implications and implementation of the relationship between religion and morality nor on the nature of the religion required to stimulate and buttress the moral life. Some—those we might call the "particularists"—have insisted on a direct correlation between virtue and their own system of religious truth and have often called for an educational program controlled by that system. Others—the "generalists"—have been content to accept a generalized, nondenominational, nonsectarian religion as sufficient to morality and hence to the schools in pursuing their basic purpose.

In the common parlance of the eighteenth century "good" and "Christian" were often used interchangeably, the latter being understood in a broad, not to say vague, fashion.[19] It was

[17]See the treatment of Dewey below.

[18]*Moral and Spiritual Values in the Public Schools*, p. 18. See note 4, p. 46.

[19]The Virginia Declaration of Rights, which was adopted by the Virginia Constitutional Convention on June 12, 1776, affirmed that "it is the mutual duty of all to practice Christian forbearance, love, and charity towards

assumed that the principles of morality were both divinely inspired and evident in nature. Revelation reinforced reason; religion reinforced morality.

Horace Mann embodied these eighteenth-century "generalist" notions in his own approach to the common school. He regarded education as primarily a process of moral nurture in which a kind of generic religion was of central importance. This generic religion, which Mann sometimes called "the religion of heaven," clearly resembled the "natural religion" of the eighteenth century. Bible reading, without adulteration, was a primary vehicle for the inculcation of the ideals of this religion and thus for the cultivation of morals. At the same time, Mann was a vigorous opponent of what he regarded as sectarianism in religion. Sectarianism was not only not common, in Mann's view, it was also scarcely conducive to morality.

Mann's contemporary Archbishop Hughes of New York also looked to the school as being of crucial importance in raising up good men and women. Hughes even advised his fellow Catholics that they "must proceed upon the principle that, in this age and country, the school is before the church."[20] Contrary to Mann, however, Hughes was unconvinced that it was possible to achieve a nonsectarian religious approach in the school—or anywhere else, for that matter. To be religious was to be a Presbyterian or a Catholic or a Deist, and any one school would of necessity be Protestant or Catholic or antireligious. There was no generalized middle religious ground on which one could stand.

When Hughes contended that morality was dependent upon religion he understood religion primarily in a church or denominational sense. Hence the morality produced in the school depended substantially upon the specific religion which pre-

each other." In this context "Christian" was understood to mean that which was commonly accepted as good in human behavior. Quotation from Anson Phelps Stokes, *Church and State in the United States* (New York: Harper & Bros., 1950), I, 303.

[20]As quoted in James A. Burns, *The Principles, Origin and Establishment of the Catholic School System in the United States* (New York: Benziger Bros., 1912), p. 375.

vailed there. If the school were antireligious there was little chance that its products would be moral. If it were Protestant, there was some hope for an acceptable result. But one could be most certain of desirable moral results if the school were Catholic. Thus Hughes worked vigorously for the establishment of a denominational educational system and fought for public support of that system.

The contrasting positions of Mann and Hughes (discussed more fully in Chapter III) continued to attract supporters. On the one side, and very much in the majority, were those who looked to the public school to instill a religiously aided and sanctioned morality without succumbing to sectarianism or the direct influence and control of a particular religious institution. "For more than a century," Payson Smith rightly observed in the early 1940's, the people of the United States showed "a consistent determination to achieve two seemingly irreconcilable ends; one of them to keep sectarianism out of the public schools, and the other to keep religion in them."[21] Keeping religion in seemed essential to the achievement of the primary goals of the public school—the fashioning of good men and good citizens. This view was clearly expressed by the Pennsylvania State Superintendent of Public Instruction when he argued in his testimony in the *Schempp* case in 1958 that the practice of reading ten verses from the Bible was "one of the last vestiges of moral value that we have left in our school system."[22] His assumption that Bible reading without comment—a major symbol of generalized, nonsectarian religion—is directly related to moral virtue was exactly the same assumption which Horace Mann had made more than a century before.

On the other side were those who thought of religion in quite specific terms and were convinced that a proper moral education could occur only in a specific religious context. In effect, this was the position of the American Catholic hierarchy as

[21]"The Public Schools and Religious Education," *Religion in the Post-War World*, ed. W. L. Sperry (Cambridge: Harvard University Press, 1945), p. 32.
[22]*Abington School District* v. *Schempp*, 374 U.S. 203, U.S. Supreme Court Records, Briefs, 1962, Nos. 142, 119, p. 89.

stated formally in the Third Plenary Council of Baltimore in 1884: "Take away religion from a people, and morality would soon follow. . . . Hence education . . . must foster religion . . ." in the school as well as the church and the home. But since "it does not lie within the province of the State to teach religion . . ." the church must do so in its own schools. Hence the Council decreed that "near every church a parish school, where one does not yet exist, is to be built . . ."[23] This was also the position of some conservative Protestants.

While the "particularists" and the "generalists" disagreed on the nature of religion, they both assumed that there is a close relationship between religion and morality. In this they were typically American. However, occasionally it has been argued by an American that there is no necessary relationship between religion and morality. William Torrey Harris was one such person. A major figure in public education in the late nineteenth century and U.S. Commissioner of Education from 1889 to 1906, Harris called for the complete secularization of the public school. He agreed with the "particularists" in their view of religion. A "live religion," he held, "must take a denominational form . . ." But such a religion should be separated from the public school. For the public schools to attempt to teach religion would result either in a degeneration of the content "into mere deism without a living Providence," or in "changing the school into a parochial school and destroying the efficiency of secular instruction."[24] Hence religious education belonged in the church and the home, and the public school could not be expected to do the whole work of education.

Harris separated religion from morality, but he did not take

[23]*Catholic Education in America: A Documentary History,* ed. Neil G. McCluskey, S.J. (Classics in Education, No. 21; New York: Bureau of Publications, Teachers College, Columbia University, 1964), pp. 90–94.

[24]"Religious Instruction in the Public Schools," *The Independent,* LV (August 6, 1903), 1841–43. See also "Morality in the Schools," *The Christian Register,* January 31, 1889; Merle Curti, "William T. Harris, The Conservator," *The Social Ideas of American Educators* (New York: Charles Scribner's Sons, 1935), pp. 310–47; and Neil G. McCluskey, *Public Schools and Moral Education: The Influence of Horace Mann, William Torrey Harris and John Dewey* (New York: Columbia University Press, 1958).

the next step in denying to the school a role in inculcating the latter. While the school's role was definitely limited, in Harris' view, it still included giving some attention to the achievement of virtue. Harris' view was unusual in America. Still more unusual—in fact, rare—was that view which held that the school's task should not even include the instilling of morality.[25] On the contrary, Americans generally have looked to their schools to achieve an end which in its magnitude and depth borders on being religious in nature.

The Making of Americans

The school's role might be called religious not only in the goal of achieving moral character but also in the development of a sense of community, of a common identity as Americans. In a striking passage penned in 1908, John Dewey argued that the public schools, in bringing together those of diverse backgrounds and "assimilating them together upon the basis of what is common and public in endeavor and achievement, are performing an infinitely significant religious work."[26] This was written at a time when America was faced with the task of assimilating large numbers of immigrants and the public school obviously was needed in achieving this goal. But Dewey held to this point of view even after mass immigration had ceased, for there were still diverse elements in the population and there was still the necessity of developing a sense of community.

This stress upon the unifying role of the public school has persisted to the present time. Even though the "task of assimilat-

[25]This was the position taken by the liberal jurist and Hegelian philosopher J. B. Stallo of Cincinnati, discussed in Chapter III below. It was also espoused by Robert Maynard Hutchins in *Morals, Religion and Higher Education* (Chicago: printed for Kenyon College for private distribution only by the University of Chicago Press, 1950).

[26]"Religion and Our Schools," *The Hibbert Journal*, VI (July 1908), 796–809. Reprinted in *Characters and Events, Popular Essays in Social and Political Philosophy*, ed. Joseph Ratner (New York: Henry Holt and Co., 1929), II, 504–16. Quotation p. 514.

ing many strains of migration has been accomplished," observed President James B. Conant in 1952, "the job of nourishing the spirit of democratic unity continues . . ."[27] And some fourteen years later Supreme Court Justice William O. Douglas pointed out that "in America public schools have a unique public function to perform." They must transcend or go beneath all "parochial, sectarian, and separatist influences" that tend to divide men and seek to instill the heritage which "all groups have in common." This heritage, which Douglas called "civic and patriotic," "cements all in a common unity of nationality . . ."[28]

G. K. Chesterton, it will be recalled, concluded that the unique aspect of America was Americanization, the notion of turning many peoples into one. This concept has seemed essential to nationhood, for the oneness is nationalistic, not internationalistic.[29] And the public school has been the primary instrument of Americanization.

Some Americans have felt so strongly about the Americanizing role of the public school that they have wanted all children to attend that school. In 1922 more than 100,000 citizens of Oregon (a majority of those voting) supported a law requiring all youth between the ages of eight and sixteen to attend the public school. While this statute was declared unconstitutional by the U.S. Supreme Court in 1925,[30] many have continued to support the idea that all American children really should attend the public school. Early in the 1940's a group of leading educationalists who were members of the John Dewey Society proclaimed their "firm belief that all the youth of all the people

[27]*Education and Liberty: The Role of the Schools in a Modern Democracy* (Cambridge: Harvard University Press, 1953), p. 62.
[28]*The Bible and the Schools* (Boston and Toronto: Little, Brown & Co., 1966), pp. 58–59.
[29]"What I Saw in America" in *The Man Who Was Chesterton*, p. 193.
[30]*Pierce* v. *Society of Sisters*, 268 U.S. 510 (1925). On the Oregon law see Chapter V below. Two attempts were made in Michigan in the early 1920's to amend the state constitution so that all children between the ages of seven and sixteen years would be required to attend the public schools. Sister Raymond McLaughlin, O.S.B., *A History of State Legislation Affecting Private Elementary and Secondary Schools in the United States, 1870–1945* (Washington, D.C.: Catholic University of America Press, 1946), pp. 111–12.

should be educated together in the common public school . . ."
These men acknowledged the "legal right" of "any local group"
to organize a private school, but they saw such efforts as inherent threats "to the democratic process" if they became more
than local.[31] Professor Philip Kurland of the University of Chicago
Law School affirmed a similar position in the early 1960's when,
in commenting on the question of public aid to parochial schools,
he argued that such aid is not unconstitutional, "so long as it
takes a non-discriminatory form." But, at the same time, he urged
his own strong conviction that "the segregation of school children
by religion is an unmitigated evil."[32]

Dewey himself was most articulate in picturing the role of
the public school as being religious because of its crucial importance in Americanizing and democratizing the youth. Here
they achieved a sense of self-identity and group consciousness
as Americans and as human beings. And this was "an infinitely
significant religious work" because the public schools were
"promoting the social unity out of which in the end genuine
religious unity must grow." Under the proper conditions, Dewey
maintained, schools were "more religious in substance and in
promise without any of the conventional badges and machinery
of religious instruction than they could be in cultivating these
forms at the expense of a state-consciousness."[33]

Dewey consistently distinguished between "religion" and "religious." The former referred to something substantive, to a body
of beliefs and practices related to the supernatural and institutionalized in a church—hence to what we have called church
religion. The public schools, in his view, should have nothing
to do with this. Dewey used the adjectival form—"religious"—
to refer, on the other hand, to a quality of experience, a manner
of valuing, a range of attitudes, rather than to something substantial that could be separated off as a segment of life or as

[31]*The Public Schools and Spiritual Values,* ed. John S. Brubacher,
Seventh Yearbook of the John Dewey Society (New York: Harper & Bros.,
1944), p. 6. Contributors to this statement included Samuel M. Brownell
of Yale and John L. Childs and William H. Kilpatrick of Columbia.

[32]*Religion and the Law: of Church and State and the Supreme Court*
(Chicago: Aldine Publishing, 1962), p. 9.

[33]"Religion and Our Schools," p. 513.

superhuman or supernatural. That which unifies the self and enables it to aspire toward greater things could be called religious. "All that is significant in human experience," that is emotionally stirred "by possibilities as yet unrealized and with all action in behalf of their realization," can be called "religious."[34] In short, for Dewey the religious had to do with what is distinctively human. And this was the central concern of the school.

Realization of the religious quality of experience, Dewey held, came only through community. All the positive values which men prize have "emerged from . . . human associations . . ."[35] Hence it was the pre-eminent task of the school to be a community in and through which the elemental human potential for good could be nurtured.

Given Dewey's distinction between "religion" and "religious" it is quite evident how one could speak of the religious function of the public schools without involving an obvious relationship to the churches or even to the historic religious traditions of America. In fact, Dewey abhorred such a relationship because he regarded historic supernatural religion as untrue to human experience and institutional religion as divisive on the American scene. Therefore, the public schools must do what the religious institutions could never do.

Making a distinction similar to that made by Dewey, Ellwood P. Cubberley, the Stanford historian of education, referred to the "religious work" of the public schools while also pointing out that in the United States "a national religion is inconceivable." Presumably by a national religion he meant something akin to an established church. Since this was impossible in America, Cubberley argued, "we are thrown back . . . upon our systems of public education, the public press, and our political life as the great moulding and unifying forces in our most heterogeneous national life, and of these three the school

---

[34]*A Common Faith* (New Haven: Yale University Press, Yale Paperbound, 1964; 1st ed., 1934), p. 57. The distinction between religion and religious is made in ch. i.
[35]Ibid., p. 74.

easily stands first as the force which ultimately shapes the other two."[36] In Professor Lawrence A. Cremin's apt description, Cubberley's story of public education in the United States presents an "optimistic story of educational struggles waged and won, of educational enemies routed and destroyed, and of educational services extended and perfected . . ." It is a story in which the public school emerges triumphant as the primary Americanizing and democratizing institution.[37]

In a similar vein, the formulators of the influential Seven Cardinal Principles of Secondary Education affirmed in 1918 that "the school is the one agency that may be controlled definitely and consciously by our democracy for the purpose of unifying its people . . ."[38] This document was one of a number that articulated the idea of the comprehensive high school, an institution in which children from all classes and religious and ethnic backgrounds would live and study together in a kind of microcosmic democratic community.

The comprehensive high school, and the public school generally, was valued not only because it brought children of diverse backgrounds together in one place. The community that resulted was also seen as having redemptive qualities. It could transform those who participated in it from narrow and provincial youngsters into tolerant and dedicated citizens. This school-induced community also had enormous potential for accomplishing change in the larger community. It was a leaven which turned the potentially democratic dough into the genuinely democratic loaf.

Nineteenth-century Americans had been almost universally persuaded of the redemptive and reforming capacities of educa-

[36]*Public Education in the United States,* rev. ed. (Boston: Houghton Mifflin, 1934), p. 761.

[37]*The Wonderful World of Ellwood Patterson Cubberley: An Essay on the Historiography of American Education* (New York: Bureau of Publications, Teachers College, Columbia University, 1965), p. 2.

[38]Report of the Commission on the Reorganization of Secondary Education of the National Education Association, *The Seven Cardinal Principles of Education,* Bulletin No. 35 (United States Bureau of Education, Department of Interior, 1918), p. 22.

tion.[39] With Dewey, however, there occurred a subtle shift in emphasis. He narrowed the educational focus until it was centered almost entirely on the common, public school. In a society becoming rapidly industrialized, the home, the neighborhood, and the church were facing serious limitations in their educational role. Hence the school must take on the educational function almost singlehandedly. The progressive educators' concept of educating the whole child sometimes became confused with the idea of providing for the child's whole education.[40] An enormous weight of responsibility was rolled onto that institution: so much so that D. W. Brogan made the apt observation in the early 1940's that the public school was America's "formally unestablished national church."[41] With Dewey and his followers, then, the significant transition of the primary locus of education in America from church and family to public school was fully accomplished.

Participation in common activities—common learning, common problem solving, etc.—was the most important work of the schools for Dewey and other educators of like mind. Others turned to more obvious devices for making good citizens and achieving a redemptive community. Curricular and extra-curricular practices which were seen as directly promoting patriotism and good citizenship received the attention of both educators and legislators. Laws requiring the teaching of American history, state history, civics, government, and social studies were passed in abundance. The pledge of allegiance to the flag and other patriotic exercises came into common practice, often reinforced by legal sanction.[42] Thus the religious function shaded into the

[39]See Rush Welter, *Popular Education and Democratic Thought in America* (New York: Columbia University Press, 1962), pp. 3–6; and Bessie L. Pierce, *Public Opinion and the Teaching of History in the United States* (New York: Alfred A. Knopf, 1926), p. 13.

[40]Lawrence A. Cremin, *The Genius of American Education* (Pittsburgh: University of Pittsburgh Press, 1966), pp. 4ff.

[41]*The American Character*, p. 137.

[42]See Bessie L. Pierce: *Public Opinion and the Teaching of History in the United States; Civic Attitudes in American School Textbooks* (Chicago: University of Chicago Press, 1930); and *Citizens' Organizations and the Civic Training of Youth* (New York: Charles Scribner's Sons, 1933).

patriotic and the achievement of a broad objective of moral goodness into the nurturing of good citizens. "In the United States, education as a whole is directed toward political life," observed Alexis de Tocqueville.[43] He was using politics in the Aristotelian sense as that science having to do with the good life in the community. A century later D. W. Brogan pointed out that the American public schools "do far more than instruct students; they let students instruct each other in how to live in America." Thus "the political function of the schools is to teach Americanism," Brogan continues, and, in this connection, "the ritual of flag worship and oath taking in an American school is a religious observance."[44]

Textbook studies clearly show that such areas as history or social studies are deeply involved in the communalizing and Americanizing process.[45] Dewey's distinction between "religion" and "religious" is helpful in describing the drift in social-studies textbooks dealing with American history and society. Obvious references to religion—that is, the commonly recognized religious institutions and traditions—are confined largely to the colonial period, with possibly a nod here and there to the role of selected groups in westward expansion and the place of religious controversy in the elections of 1928 and 1960. Yet following Dewey's definition one could argue that most of these books tend to be quite religious. They seek to cultivate certain attitudes, highlight certain values, and encourage the development of a certain type of faith, whether that faith be understood in Dewey's terms or in terms of nationalism. While church religion drops by the wayside as apparently of little relevance to the developing American democracy, the virtues of that democracy and of fervent devotion to the nation are repeatedly extolled. Denominational religion is eschewed while

[43]*Democracy in America,* ed. Mayer and Lerner, p. 280.
[44]*The American Character,* pp. 135ff.
[45]See the works of Bessie L. Pierce cited in notes 39 and 42 above; E. H. Dance, *History the Betrayer; A Study of Bias* (London: Hutchinson of London, 196ʋ); *History Without Bias? A Textbook Study of Group Antagonisms* (London: English Council of Christians and Jews, 1954); and Ray Allen Billington, *The Historian's Contribution to Anglo-American Misunderstanding* (New York: Hobbs, Dorman & Co., 1966).

some kind of communal or national piety is stressed. Such works perform a catechetical function in instilling piety.

Distinguishing Between the Religious and the Patriotic

Definition has continuing importance in assessing ideal and practice in the public school and in judging what is and what is not legitimate under American law. When are civil ceremonials and loyalties "merely" civil or patriotic and when do they become religious? While I have often used the language of religion in describing the concept and role of the public school, the final guardians of legality in America—the Justices of the United States Supreme Court—have attempted to be more precise. The "mucilage" that holds our society together is "neither atheistic nor theistic" (not religious), contended Justice William O. Douglas; our common heritage is "civic and patriotic."[46] Douglas made this statement about a decade after he had penned the famous phrase in *Zorach:* "We are a religious people whose institutions presuppose a Supreme Being."[47] In the interim it had become necessary to make a sharper distinction between the religious and the patriotic.

The Court made such a distinction between the religious and the patriotic in *Engel,* the case which struck down as "an establishment of religion" the use of the New York Board of Regents prayer in the public schools of New Hyde Park, New York. The prayer—which was addressed to Almighty God and sought his blessings on school, parents, teachers, children, and country—was declared to be a religious ceremony, and hence prohibited under the "establishment clause" of the First Amendment. Such a ceremony was distinguished from "patriotic or ceremonial occasions" on which children might recite historical documents which "contain reference to the Deity" or sing

46*The Bible and the Schools,* pp. 57–59.
47343 U.S. 306, 313.

"anthems which include the composer's professions of faith in a Supreme Being . . ."[48]

In *Engel* and later in *Schempp* what had traditionally been done side by side in many American schools—that is, prayer and Bible reading on the one side and the pledge to the flag and singing of patriotic songs on the other—were carefully separated. The former were designated as religious ceremonies and hence as instances of "an establishment of religion." The latter were not challenged. Since the Court has the responsibility of interpreting the Constitution it will become involved in discussing what is religious when dealing with such First Amendment cases. This is not an easy task, however. What criteria will be used in distinguishing that which is religious from that which is not? The criterion of common practice or usage? Possibly. While Jehovah's Witnesses object to the pledge of allegiance to the flag on the ground that it is a religious practice, most people see it as patriotic and not religious. And while some school administrators might argue for the use of pray-prayer and Bible reading primarily on moral and patriotic grounds, most Americans regard these as religious practices. But there are elements of insight in the views of both the Witnesses and the administrators. A flag salute might become a religious ceremony—or like a religious ceremony—when it is used to bind people together in an act of ultimate devotion. And a prayer from the Bible might carry no more emotional freight than the recitation of one of Poor Richard's maxims. We have once again introduced ultimacy as a criterion for defining what is religious. It is a criterion which the Court itself has not entirely ignored.[49]

No Formally Established Church

In their considered judgments the justices of the United States Supreme Court have tended to preclude rigid uniformity

[48]370 U.S., 421, 424, and n. 21, 435.
[49]See Chapter VII, pp. 212ff.

and standardized ultimacy in the public school. If one prefers and can afford it, he can send his youngsters to a private school.[50] And even within the public school one might legitimately refrain from certain practices,[51] although the price in social pressure is likely to be great. While the public school has come to occupy a central place in American public life, it has not become America's *formally* established church.

In addition to the legal factor there are also certain social factors in American life which mitigate against the packaging of a standardized product in the public school. These include regional, class, racial, and ethnic differences in the population itself. There is also generally an abstract quality about such notions as moral and spiritual values and even good citizenship. And, at its best, there is an openness to the public piety inculcated.

The fact remains, however, that the public school enjoys an enormous importance in the United States for its socializing and Americanizing role. And the relationship of the "fourth r" to that role remains an ambivalent one, in part because of the complexity of that "r" and in part because of the comprehensiveness of the task assigned to the public school.

[50]*Pierce* v. *Society of Sisters,* 268 U.S. 510 (1925).
[51]*West Virginia Board of Education* v. *Barnette,* 319 U.S. 624 (1943).

I I I

Common School, Common Religion?

Issues and Trends in the Nineteenth Century

The Bible should be "devotionally read, and its precepts inculcated in all the common schools of the land . . ."

The teaching of "partisan or sectarian principles in our public schools is a violation of the fundamental principles of our American system of education."

> —Successive resolutions, national convention
> of the National Teachers Association, 1869[1]

No tax funds shall be used for "the support of any school . . . under the control of any religious or anti-religious sect, organization, or denomination, or wherein the particular creed or tenets shall be read or taught. . . . This article shall not be construed to prohibit the reading of the Bible in any school . . ."

> —From JAMES G. BLAINE's proposed amendment to the federal Constitution, 1875[2]

"Resolved, that religious instruction and the reading of religious books, including the Holy Bible, are prohibited in the common schools of Cincinnati."

> —Adopted by the Cincinnati Board of Education, November 1, 1869

"The chief danger which threatens the common school system is unquestionably [the] difference of opinion in respect to religious instruction."

> —DANIEL COIT GILMAN, 1876[3]

The drive to develop a common school, like the great westward thrust, affected nearly every aspect of American life as

---

[1]National Teachers Association, *Proceedings, 1869*, p. 19. This organization was the forerunner of the National Education Association.

[2]Stokes, *Church and State in the United States*, II, 69. The proposed amendment failed, but it became something of a model for action in several states.

[3]"Education in America, 1776–1876," *North American Review*, CXXII (January 1876), 205.

it picked up a powerful momentum of its own. The common school movement exerted a centripetal force upon the American community, discovering in it, pulling from it, and developing for it elements of commonality. Hence there occurred, as we have suggested, a common religionizing, an effort to find in the American experience a common religion that could be the binding force in the common school. By 1876 public support of the common school had been given the force of law at both the national and the state levels. By this time also the sectarian devil had been exorcised from the common school—to the satisfaction of many Americans, at least.[4] What remained was a kind of "nonsectarian" religion that was most commonly symbolized in Bible reading. But even the practice of Bible reading, which smacked of sectarianism to a growing minority, was challenged in some school districts. Hence the road to a common religion was not a smooth one; in fact, there was some reason to doubt whether such a road either existed or could be built.

The purpose of this chapter is to describe the varying fortunes of this search for a common religion for the common school by discussing developments in four significant instances: (1) the experience of Horace Mann in Massachusetts through his years as the first secretary of the state board of education (to 1849); (2) trends in Virginia from Jefferson to the Reverend William H. Ruffner, first state superintendent of schools (to 1870); (3) the controversy in New York in the early 1840's

[4]States admitted to the Union after 1876 were required by Congress to provide "by ordinances irrevocable without the consent of the United States and the people of said States . . . for the establishment and maintenance of systems of public schools, which shall be open to all the children of said States." This Congressional act also stated that the public schools must be "free from sectarian control . . ." (Enabling legislation for the admission of N.D., S.D., Mont., and Wash., 25 *Stat.* 676, 677, repeated in the Enabling Act for Utah, Okla., N.M., Ariz. Provisions in the constitutions of Idaho and Wyoming are equally explicit. See 333 *U.S. Reports* 203, 220 n. 9.) Most older states had adopted similar provisions, either constitutional or statutory, by 1876. To reinforce further the public nature of the task involved many states prohibited public aid for schools of a sectarian nature. See W. G. Torpey, *Judicial Doctrines of Religious Rights in America* (Durham: University of North Carolina Press, 1948), p. 234; Carl Zollman, *American Church Law* (St. Paul: West Publishing, 1933), pp. 78–80; and 59 *Corpus Juris* 211.

over the use of public funds for schools under sectarian control; and (4) the controversy in Cincinnati over the removal of Bible reading from the city's public schools (1869-70).

Like most educators of the nineteenth century, Horace Mann scorned sectarianism. By that he meant chiefly the sectarianism of the evangelical Protestant denominations. At the same time, he called forth from the resources of the eighteenth-century Enlightenment a common religion which was seen as underlying both particular or denominational religion and American self-understanding. This common religion bore a striking resemblance to Mann's own brand of Unitarianism. In what can best be described as a stroke of genius Mann hit upon Bible reading, without added comment, as the chief vehicle of this common religion in the common schools.

Thomas Jefferson's bold plans for a common school system in Virginia were finally effected, after much modification, by an essentially Protestant coalition. The Reverend Alexander Campbell helped form this coalition by arguing in the early 1840's for a common Christianity in the schools. While Campbell's common Christianity was actually a common Protestantism, it did represent an advance over bitter rivalry between denominations. To many Protestants, both in and out of Virginia, it also looked like an accurate description of reality. Common Protestantism was the common religion of America; this was what the Continental Congress had had in mind in its reference to religion in the Ordinance of 1787. Furthermore, Campbell's common ground offered a convenient and attractive rallying point for doing battle with Rome. In this cause most Protestants were willing to join with almost anyone excepting the most outspoken atheist.

Naturally, Roman Catholic leaders were not pleased with this common-Protestantism-equals-common-religion equation; and, in fact, they tended to be less than enchanted with the very idea of common religion. Bishop Hughes ably demonstrated this in blocking the flow of public funds to the schools of common Protestantism in New York City and in his Herculean efforts to establish a Catholic school system.

Others had doubts about common religion in the common

school. In Cincinnati, Jews and freethinkers joined with Catholics and a few Protestants to oppose Bible reading and hymn singing in the public schools. The resulting controversy with Pan-Protestant forces drew national attention and brought the basic theme of this chapter into sharp focus.

Horace Mann's Common Religion in Massachusetts

Developments in Massachusetts are often cited for their importance to the growth of public education in the nation as a whole. Massachusetts was the inheritor of a one-hundred-and-fifty-year tradition of concern for education from the elementary level through college. This tradition, which was one of the legacies of Puritanism, prepared the ground for a relatively early acceptance in Massachusetts of a system of free universal education. At the same time it also fixed upon the state a restrictive religious world-view from which builders of the public school system had to break away in their quest for a position around which the diverse elements within the state could rally.

The constitution of the Commonwealth of Massachusetts, adopted in 1780, provided in a section on religion and education, which was largely the work of John Adams, that

> As the happiness of a people, and the good order and preservation of civil government, essentially depend on piety, religion and morality . . . the legislature shall . . . authorize and require, the several towns . . . to make suitable provision, at their own expense, for the institution of the public worship of God, and for the support and maintenance of public protestant teachers of piety, religion and morality . . ."[5]

Under the provisions of this constitution, Massachusetts continued to support the Congregational Church and to inculcate

[5]Quoted in Stokes, *Church and State in the United States,* II, 53.

the truths of Puritan Protestantism in its schools. Within the first half of the nineteenth-century, however, there occurred a series of development which split Congregationalism and considerably reduced the public influence of the Congregational churches. This opened the way for the development of a system of public education realtively free from domination by a single religious group or a narrow theological orientation.

The growing strength of Unitarian sentiments within the established religious order was symbolized by the appointment of a man of known liberal theological predilections to the Hollis Chair of Divinity at Harvard in 1805 and by the decision of the Massachusetts Supreme Court in the Dedham case of 1820. The appointment of Henry Ware dramatized the departure of the college from the theological way of the fathers. The Dedham decisions had the effect of turning over the control of many of the more influential and fashionable Congregational churches of eastern Massachusetts to men with Unitarian sentiments. By 1825 Unitarianism dominated the establishment, in both a legal and a sociological sense. The old Puritan theological hegemony had been toppled and the defenders of the more orthodox theological points of view had, in effect, become the loyal opposition. Echoes of this often bitter Unitarian-orthodox controversy sounded repeatedly in the struggles for the achievement of a "nonsectarian" public school system.

The religious scene in early-nineteenth-century Massachusetts was complicated further by the growth of such "sects" as the Baptists, the Christians, and the Methodists; by the spread of Universalism; by the rise of Transcendentalism, which was a disturber of Unitarian peace; and by the accelerating influx of Roman Catholic immigrants. Hence by mid-century the religious complexion of Massachusetts bore little resemblance to that of 1780. An increasing religious pluralism accentuated the difficulties attendant to any attempt to catechize the particularities of Congregational-Puritan-Protestantism, or any other form of Protestantism. At the same time, some rationale was needed which would replace the common assumptions of the earlier Puritan establishment, and which would be acceptable to the various religious elements within the state. It was one of the chief contributions of Horace Mann to articulate and defend such a rationale in connection with his efforts to establish a sound system of public education in Massachusetts.

Legislative acknowledgment of the fact of religious pluralism and the desirability of the reduction of narrow theological influence in the schools of Massachusetts is evident in the act of 1827 which gave local school committees control over school-books and prohibited these committees from purchasing or directing the use of any books "which are calculated to favour any particular religious sect or tenet."[6] In this, the first provision of its kind in American history,[7] the state of Massachusetts took a significant step toward disentanglement of the particularities of religion from the public schools. The legal disestablishment of the Congregational Church in 1833 constituted a final formal disapproval of the public primacy of any single religious denomination; indirectly, it also amounted to a public acknowledgment of religious pluralism.

The act of 1827 which ruled out sectarianism in textbooks also affirmed that it was the duty of all in education to instill "the principles of piety, justice, and sacred regard to truth, love to their country, humanity, and universal benevolence, sobriety, industry, and frugality, chastity, moderation, and temperance, and those other virtues, which are the ornaments of human society, and the basis upon which the Republican Constitution is founded."[8] It is quite clear that the legislators wanted the best of religion and morality without the onus of particularism.

In 1837 the Massachusetts legislature took another significant step in setting up the first state board of education in the United States. The president of the Senate, who signed the bill for that body, was Horace Mann. He was employed as the first secretary of the board of education and for the next twelve years (1837–1849) he devoted full time to this work. This was a

[6]Ibid.
[7]According to William Kailer Dunn, *What Happened to Religious Education? The Decline of Religious Teaching in the Public Elementary School, 1776–1861* (Baltimore: Johns Hopkins Press, 1958), p. 104.
[8]*Laws of Massachusetts*, March 1, 1827, Chap. 143, Sec. 3. The non-sectarian provision is found in Sec. 7. See McCluskey, *Public Schools and Moral Education*, p. 34.

decisive period for public education in Massachusetts. It was also a period dominated by Mann, who advanced an approach to religion and public education which was to become common across the nation and the influence of which has continued more than a century later.[9]

Horace Mann was born in 1796 in Franklin, Massachusetts. There, early in life, he came under the influence of the Reverend Nathaniel Emmons, a thoroughgoing Calvinist who endeavored to push that theological system to its logical conclusion at every point. To the sensitive young Mann the Calvinist sage of Franklin appeared to dwell almost entirely upon the dark, somber, and even terrifying aspects of religion and life. Mann recalled with horror the graphic sermon Emmons preached at the funeral of his favorite brother, Stephen, who had drowned. The preacher had dwelt exclusively upon the dangers of "dying unconverted" and thus only deepened further the grief and anxieties of the Mann family. From that point on Mann had little patience with a religion which appeared to threaten rather than console at the time of death. The "consistent Calvinism" of the Reverend Mr. Emmons represented in stark form what Mann came to abhor as "sectarianism" and to fight as not being fit for the minds of the young.

Although he came under less stringent Calvinist influences later in his life—when as a law student in Litchfield, Connecticut, he was exposed to the preaching of the moderate Calvinist, Lyman Beecher—by the time he settled as a lawyer in Boston Mann had become a convinced Unitarian. Unitarianism, Mann believed, accorded best with true Christianity and with the religion of reason, nature, and heaven itself. It also conformed much better than Calvinism with Mann's developing

[9]On Mann see: Mary Tyler Peabody Mann, *Life of Horace Mann* (Boston: Walker, Fuller, and Co., 1865; reproduced in facsimile, Washington, D.C.: National Education Association of the U.S., 1937); *Life and Works of Horace Mann* (Boston: Lee and Shepard; New York: C. T. Dillingham, 1891), 5 Vols.; Raymond B. Culver, *Horace Mann and Religion in the Massachusetts Public Schools* (New Haven: Yale University Press, 1929); McCluskey, *Public Schools and Moral Education;* and Edward I. F. Williams, *Horace Mann: Educational Statesman* (New York: Macmillan, 1937).

views of the place of virtue in life, the moral educability of man, and the possibility for social reform and progress. "I have faith in the improvability of the human race," Mann confessed in his *Journal* in 1837. And, for emphasis, he added, faith "in their accelerating improvability."[10] No more was needed to declare his complete independence from the Reverend Nathaniel Emmons.

During his years as secretary of the board of education Mann was often embroiled in religious controversy and his correspondence and annual reports to the board frequently dealt with this subject. Two instances illustrate the tenor of that controversy and throw additional light on the context out of which Mann's views and actions emerged.

In his first report to the board of education (1838) Mann called attention to the provisions of the law of 1827 and pointed out the desperate need for textbooks that would instill "the beautiful and sublime truths of ethics and of natural religion" without appeal to sectarian doctrine or apparatus.[11] To help meet this need Mann urged the compiling of lists of recommended books which local school committees could follow in stocking those school libraries which had been encouraged by legislative action in 1837. With the support of most members of the board of education steps were taken to compile such a list and to encourage publishers to produce more works which might inculcate morality and natural religion without being sectarian. At this point Frederick A. Packard, editor for the American Sunday School Union, entered the Massachusetts public-education scene. In 1837 the union had prepared a "Select Library" of 120 volumes for use in public schools. Packard pointed out that his product was especially well fitted for raising up pious and moral youngsters. While acknowledging that the advancement in the books of such doctrines as "a future state of retribution" might be regarded as sectarian by some citizens of Massachusetts, Packard urged

[10]As quoted in Williams, *Horace Mann*, p. 132.
[11]*First Annual Report of the Secretary of the Board of Education, 1838,* pp. 61ff., as quoted in Culver, *Horace Mann and Religion*, p. 42.

that the propriety of using his openly evangelical library could be judged best by majority vote in each community.[12]

As something of a trial balloon Packard wrote to Mann asking whether Abbott's *Child at Home*, one of the volumes in the union's collection, would be admitted into the district school libraries of the state. The book appeared to Mann to be obviously sectarian and hence excluded under the law of 1827. He pointed out to Packard that the Universalists and Unitarians would find its open espousal of divine judgment in the after life completely unacceptable. In fact, Mann found this book so objectionable on religious, moral, educational, and legal grounds that he argued that it would be better for the schools to have no libraries rather than include literature of this type.

Rebuffed in this manner, Packard proceeded publicly to attack Mann and the board of education, arguing that their policies with regard to religion could only result in a condition of "godlessness" in the public schools. Packard assumed that true morality and piety were possible only within an evangelical Protestant context.

This controversy precipitated a considerable correspondence between Mann and Packard and was carried on by Packard in secular and church papers long after Mann had withdrawn from any direct encounter with him. It was a controversy which strongly reinforced Mann's own convictions regarding the insidious effects of sectarian influences in the schools.

Some years later, toward the end of Mann's tenure as secretary, he and the board were publicly attacked again, this time by the Reverend Matthew Hale Smith, a vigorous Calvinist who accused the board of removing the Bible, religious instruction, and all visible means of discipline from the public schools. By thus making the schools a direct "counterpoise" to the religious influence of the home and the "Sabbath Schools" the board, Smith argued, had contributed substantially to the precipitous decline in the morals of the youth and the rapidly accelerating incidence of juvenile delinquency.[13] Against the advice

[12]Culver, *Horace Mann and Religion*, pp. 55–56.
[13]Ibid., p. 205, for Smith's words.

of some friends, Mann responded directly to Smith by pointing out that the board had consistently attempted to get the Bible *into* rather than out of the public schools. Rather than respond to Mann on issues Smith shifted his attack to Mann's personal views. Mann responded by pointing out that he had always urged that "nonsectarian" religion had an essential place in the schools and he substantiated his reply by references to his annual reports to the board.

As a result of these controversies and other factors which shaped his mind Mann settled on the following convictions with regard to religion and morals in the public schools:

1. It is possible to raise up morally good children through the proper physical and intellectual environment. While it is true that there are base instincts at work in man, these can be ameliorated, if not overcome, through the cultivation of nobler propensities. (As a believer in phrenology Mann held that physical influences were as important to moral character as abstract teachings.)[14]

2. The times are especially ripe for the moral advancement of men. In "the providence of God a new series of events" has opened up new possibilities for human betterment. The period following the American Revolution formed "a new era" on the stage of human history. While recent events have not changed human nature they have "placed that nature in circumstances so different from any it had ever before occupied" that we can and "must expect a new series of developments in human nature and conduct."[15]

3. The common school is the one institution which can achieve this moral advancement. Whatever enhances it "will enhance individual and social well-being for generations to come." "The common school is the greatest discovery ever made by man." Let it be developed to the full and "nine-tenths of the crimes in the penal code would become obsolete, the

14On Mann's convictions regarding moral improvability see his "Prospectus of the Common School Journal" in *Life and Works*, II, 14ff. On Mann and phrenology see Curti, *The Social Ideas of American Educators*, pp. 110–11, 122.

15*Life and Works*, II, 14ff; IV, 8ff.

long catalogue of human ills would be abridged, man would walk more safely by day . . . [and] all rational hopes respecting the future [would be] brightened."[16]

4. The primary task of the common school is moral in nature. Virtue is more important in the work of the school than knowledge, although the importance of the latter is not to be slighted. Still, "the highest and noblest office of education . . . pertains to our moral nature."[17]

5. Religion is essential to the task of the common school. But this is common religion, not sectarianism. "That which belongs to a part, not to the *whole*," i.e., sectarianism, must be abjured. But that upon which all rational men of good will can agree, the common element shared by all religions, belongs in the schools. While they cannot teach all of the particularities of religion, the schools can teach the most essential elements, those having to do with morals and character development which "tend to create brothers rather than enemies."[18]

"Our system earnestly inculcates all Christian morals," Mann wrote in response to charges that the common schools contributed to delinquency because of their irreligion. So far from being irreligious, antichristian or even unchristian, the Massachusetts system is one "which recognizes religious obligations in their fullest extent . . ." It is a system which "invokes a religious spirit . . ." by inculcating "the great commands upon which hang all the law and prophets . . ."[19] This much of religion is certainly in keeping with constitutional and legislative provisions as well as with sound educational principles. More would be unconstitutional, confusing, and divisive.

6. The moral and religious goals of the school may be achieved through a variety of means, including use of certain books. Among those approved by Mann was Paley's *Natural Theology*, a late-eighteenth-century work purporting to establish the existence and nature of God on natural and rational grounds

[16]Ibid., II, 30; IV, 2; Horace Mann, *The Common School Journal*, III (January 1, 1841), 15.
[17]*Life and Works*, V, 73; cf. IV, 283.
[18]Ibid., IV, 326.
[19]Ibid., IV, 311, 335.

and chiefly by appeal to evidence of design. Paley systematized for the common man of the early nineteenth-century much of the thought of the natural theologians of the eighteenth.

However, for Mann, the Bible was by far the most important single work for the school to use in achieving its noble end. To this book, read without comment, Mann ascribed an almost magical quality. Perhaps a more appropriate analogy would be that of the traditional Roman Catholic view which regards the Sacraments as being efficacious *ex opere operato*, that is, by virtue of the act performed and without any dependence on the disposition of the administrator. Hence for Mann the reading of the Bible had an efficacy in and of itself, apart from comments or explanation by any teacher. The word from the book alone had the capacity to elicit the desired moral response in the pupil.

In reply to criticism from more orthodox circles Mann affirmed that the schools welcomed the Bible and therefore welcomed "all the doctrines which the Bible really contains"; indeed, the schools welcomed "the religion of the Bible." In encouraging the reading of the Bible without added comment the school allowed the Bible "to do what it is allowed to do in no other system,—*to speak for itself.*"[20] And in his supreme optimism Mann believed that the Bible speaking "for itself" would say just what he heard it say.

These convictions reflect the Unitarianism which Mann had come to embrace and were rooted in and had affinities with the liberal religious and theological ideas of such founding fathers as Franklin, John Adams, Jefferson, and Madison. To the more orthodox of Mann's time—the Packards and the Smiths—Mann's point of view seemed to be a prime example of infidelity or deism. Nevertheless, Mann's convictions furnished a number of planks in the ideological platform upon which it was possible to erect a public school system. By stressing Bible reading in the school Mann detonated the heaviest bombs of his conservative critics. Few Protestants opposed that practice. The Bible, then, became a major symbol for common religion

[20]Ibid., IV, 311–12.

around which liberal and conservative Protestants could rally. And rally they did, especially when they became acutely aware of the mounting surge of Catholic immigrants into the state of Massachusetts.

Hence for Mann religion was a convenient mucilage for holding together reason, nature, patriotism, morality, and education. The Bible was a significant container of that mucilage and the common school was its chief dispensor. Mann's motto might well have been, "Common religion for the common school."

From Natural Religion to Common Protestantism in Virginia

While sentiments in support of public education were not universally held among the founding fathers, the majority recognized its importance to the future welfare of the nation. Thomas Jefferson, one of the most articulate on this issue, saw education as being so important that this was the one area in which he consistently urged the expansion of governmental activity. During his adult life Jefferson worked hard for the establishment of public education. As a member of a committee of the Virginia assembly to revise the laws of the new state Jefferson drew up a series of bills which embodied a comprehensive plan for a system of public education. These included a Bill for the More General Diffusion of Knowledge, a Bill for Amending the Charter of William and Mary, and a Bill for Establishing a Public Library. The first of these called for an extensive system of elementary and grammar schools which would be available to children without regard to financial condition and circumstance of birth. Such a system, Jefferson believed, would reduce the threat of tyranny, improve the possibilities for just laws, and generally contribute to the public happiness. This bill was the only one of the three to achieve any degree of legislative success when, in 1796, seventeen years after its initial proposal, the part of it relating to the common schools was adopted by the assembly. The effectiveness of the bill was practically destroyed, however, by an amendment which left institution and implementation of the provisions of the bill up to the court of each county. Since these courts were generally controlled by men of wealth who did not relish taxing themselves and their associates for support of the education of all, the measure had little chance of success. The problem was one of finding a system of support for universal education while maintaining a large degree of local control.

Shortly after his retirement from public office, at the end of his second term as President, Jefferson returned to the struggle for public education in Virginia. By this time he had become convinced that William and Mary could not be successfully transformed into a public university—the basic idea given formal expression in his proposed bill of 1779. He was now persuaded that a new state university must be erected, and he devoted much of his energy to this task. In 1817 he sent to his friend Joseph Cabell, who was a member of the Virginia senate, a Bill for Establishing a System of Public Education which included provisions for elementary schools, district colleges, and a university. This bill won little support in the legislature. However, Jefferson's proposal did manage to stimulate sufficient efforts on behalf of a state university that a bill authorizing the establishment of the University of Virginia was enacted early in 1819. Jefferson became the architect and first "rector" of that institution.

For Jefferson the chief end of education was the raising up of moral men who would be attuned to the workings of nature and nature's God, devoted to republican principles, and ready to assume their role as responsible citizens. This end he believed could be achieved only through a system of public education. The schools available in the Virginia of his day were few in number, spotty in quality, open for the most part only to the offspring of people of means, and chiefly under the control of denominational interests.[21] What was needed was a

---

[21]On early educational conditions in Virginia see Sadie Bell, *The Church, the State and Education in Virginia* (Philadelphia: Science Press Printing, 1930), pt. 2.

system which would be publicly supported, open to poor as well as rich, and free from sectarian control and influence. The sects could not do a proper job of education. They quarreled among themselves and diverted the attention of their adherents from important public questions to private and—to Jefferson— largely irrelevant matters of theology. But while he strenuously opposed sectarianism, Jefferson's approach to education was neither antireligious nor nonreligious. In fact, in producing moral men the schools would perform an essentially religious function, since morality was the fundamental element in natural religion. To achieve the chief end of education, then, Jefferson advocated a public school system which could produce an orientation which he regarded as true, available to reason, in accordance with Nature and the public good, and in no sense sectarian.[22]

When Jefferson died in 1826 the University of Virginia was in its infancy and his proposals for public education at other levels had made very little headway. Taxation for general education was often resisted by powerful local commercial and ecclesiastical interests. Charges of infidelity greeted efforts to reduce the obvious religious content in the curriculum— as at the University of Virginia, for example. In Virginia, as elsewhere, there occurred throughout the first half of the nineteenth century a struggle between religious groups and public figures with sentiments similar to Jefferson's over the control and content of education. By the middle of the century a compromise was taking shape. While it might not have satisfied Jefferson and did not satisfy some of the more determined religious groups, this compromise did point the way for the further development of public education. Under this compromise the schools were to instill a generalized or common Christianity, chiefly through the use of the Bible, and to avoid anything more obviously sectarian.

[22]Professor Robert M. Healey concluded that "the kind of religion which Jefferson believed had a place in public education corresponded exactly with his own beliefs." *Jefferson on Religion in Public Education* (New Haven: Yale University Press, 1962), p. 17. Healey's work is very useful on Jefferson's views relating to religion and public education. On Jefferson and education see also *Thomas Jefferson and Education in a Republic*, ed. Charles Flinn Arrowood (New York: McGraw Hill, 1930).

Horace Mann came to this kind of compromise in Massachusetts, mcre from the Jeffersonian than the Protestant side. The Reverends Alexander Campbell and William H. Ruffner, who were instrumental in achieving this compromise in Virginia, favored the Protestant side. But both were admirers of Jefferson and both, in the interest of the common welfare, sought to reduce the influence of Protestant sectarianism.

On September 8, 1841, Alexander Campbell, chief founder of a movement which claimed to restore New Testament Christianity (the Disciples of Christ), told a convention of educators at Clarksburg that what was needed in the state of Virginia was a system of common education permeated by the principles of "common Christianity." There were "certain great fundamental matters . . . in which all good men of all denominations are agreed . . ." Campbell pointed out. These "great common principles and views" formed "a common ground" on which all Christians could "unite, harmonize and co-operate in one great system of moral and Christian education." There was reason to hope that even the Roman Catholics might join in support of this "common Christianity."

The Bible and moral instruction, which were "made part of every day's education in every good school," constituted the chief expression of and means to this "common Christianity" in the common schools. The school which attempted to educate without these, Campbell warned, was "a curse to each and every community." To seek to develop the intellect without giving adequate attention to moral and religious culture was "only giving teeth to the lion, claws to the tiger, and talons to the eagle to seize and devour their prey."

Campbell's optimism concerning possible Roman Catholic support of "common Christianity" was based on his experience in 1837 with the bishop of Cincinnati, John Baptist Purcell. Campbell had the pleasure, he reported, of seeing

> even the Catholic bishop of Cincinnati, with all the clergy
> of all denominations—episcopal, presbyterian, baptist and
> methodist—then present at a meeting of the college of
> teachers in that city, voting in favor of my amendment of

a resolution to give the Bible to every school in the country, without one sectarian note or comment . . .

And this had occured only one year after he and Bishop Purcell had engaged in public debate on "romanism."[23]

Campbell's positive appraisal of Bishop Purcell's reaction was not without foundation. The bishop also reported on the same meeting with similar hopefulness. Perhaps "all good men of all denominations" could join in advancing the cause of what the bishop referred to as "our public schools" which could "be a great benefit for this country . . ." But this moment of hope was followed by years of bitterness. There was no easy escape from the animosities which had intermittently simmered and boiled for more than three centuries. Even the Bible, Campbell's sure symbol of common Christianity, became an object of controversy. And after a brief period of optimism concerning the public school Bishop Purcell turned away from that system and toward the development of one in which true religion—in his view—could prevail.[24]

Hence Campbell's "common Christianity" was less than common. But with its Bible and moral-instruction planks it was still a platform upon which Protestants and Jeffersonians might stand together in support of the public schools. From the former it required sublimation of some details of theological belief and of narrow denominational loyalty. For the Jeffersonians the platform contained more of Christianity than the master would have liked, but it was solid in support of public morality.

[23]Campbell's speech can be found in the *Journal of the House of Delegates of Virginia*, 1841–42, Document No. 7, pp. 36–38. Portions of the address are contained in Bell, *The Church, the State and Education in Virginia*, p. 347. The Campbell-Purcell debate of 1836 was published in 1837, and in several subsequent editions, under the title *A Debate on the Roman Catholic Religion*.

[24]The meeting to which Campbell referred was discussed by Purcell in a letter to the Society for the Propagation of the Faith, Lyons, France, dated October 27, 1837. The occasion was the annual meeting of the Western Literary Institute or College of Teachers. It was also attended by two other Protestant leaders, Lyman Beecher and Calvin Stowe. Excerpts from Purcell's letter can be found in Anthony H. Deye, *Archbishop John Baptist Purcell of Cincinnati; Pre-Civil War Years* (Ph. D. dissertation, University of Notre Dame, 1959), p. 197.

Furthermore, it did seem to offer hope for the actualization of the master's vision of universal education; for, as one historian of education in Virginia has pointed out, "the propaganda in favor of giving a religious tone to schools had been so successful" by the time Campbell delivered his address to the teachers "that it is hardly likely that schools of any other character would have been tolerated by the people at large."[25]

The first state superintendent of schools in Virginia, William H. Ruffner, built on this platform. Ruffner had become a Presbyterian clergyman after studying theology at Union Seminary in Richmond and Princeton Theological Seminary. He served briefly, 1849–51, as chaplain at the University of Virginia. There he studied under the well-known educator William Holmes McGuffey, who, according to Ruffner, "resolved my intellectual forces into common sense . . ."[26]

Shortly after his appointment as superintendent of schools in 1870 Ruffner wrote a treatise titled "The Public Free School System" in which he responded both to critics who claimed that there was too little religion in the public schools and to those who argued that state schools should have no religion in them. The state, he argued, "may formally teach the recognized morality of the country, and the will of God as the standard and ultimate authority of all morality, but distinctively religious teachings shall be left to volunteer agencies. . . ."[27] Mindful of the possible charge of undue sectarian influence in his own case, Ruffner demitted from the ministry when he became superintendent.

Altogether Ruffner issued eleven annual reports and various miscellaneous writings during his tenure in office. His writings reveal a consistent philosophy of public education which stressed the centrality of the common school and emphasized moral education buttressed by the fundamentals of religion. He is sometimes referred to as the Horace Mann of the South, and,

[25]Bell, *The Church, the State and Education in Virginia*, p. 344.

[26]"William Henry Ruffner," *Dictionary of American Biography*, XVI, 218–19.

[27]Quoted in Bell, *The Church, the State and Education in Virginia*, p. 438.

like Mann, his motto might also have been "Common religion for the common school."

Roman Catholicism Confronts Protestantism in New York

The state of New York took action as early as 1795 for the support of public schools. Ten years later a permanent school fund was created and shortly thereafter a state system of schools was authorized under a state superintendent. Some of these early schools were operated by religious denominations; most of the others had a distinctively Protestant coloration. The colonial practice of linking evangelical religion with public education was carried into the new publicly authorized and financed system.

Developments in New York City are especially relevant to our discussion. Denominational schools in that city received support from state funds until 1825 when the use of such funds was restricted to such "nonsectarian" bodies as the Free School Society. Shortly thereafter direct grants from the state were discontinued. Officials of the Free School Society then changed their organization to the Public School Society and this new organization was permitted to levy a tax for schools under its care. The Public School Society provided religious instruction which was "nonsectarian" in the sense that it was generally acceptable to Protestants of various points of view. But in certain practices—such as the use of the King James version of the Bible and certain other literature—the society gave a definite Protestant and even anti-Catholic tone to education under its direction.[28]

By 1840 New York City had become a major center of growing Roman Catholic strength in the United States. Augmented by

[28]On early-nineteenth-century and subsequent developments in New York see John Webb Pratt, *Religion, Politics, and Diversity: The Church-State Theme in New York History* (Ithaca, N.Y.: Cornell University Press, 1967), ch. vii.

the rapidly accelerating influx of immigrants from Ireland and Germany, the church had become an institution to reckon with in this place where 150 years earlier a Catholic priest entered at risk of death and where the state constitution of 1777 referred to "wicked priests." The church experienced its greatest period of formative growth under the vigorous leadership of John Hughes, who came to New York City as coadjutor bishop in 1838 and immediately assumed control of the diocese although he was not appointed Bishop of New York until 1842. Hughes, who had emigrated from Ireland in 1817 and had been ordained in 1826, had already proved himself to be an able administrator and a strong fighter for the church in Philadelphia, where he had served in the Chancery office, and where he had entered the lists against nativists and Protestants who had attacked the faith and the church. Once in New York he devoted all of his impressive skills to the advancement of the faith and that institution which embodied and preserved it. He early recognized the importance to the faith of education of the young. It was he who delivered the revealing manifesto that the day had come, and the place, when the school was more necessary than the church.[29] Imbued with this conviction Hughes sought every means at his disposal to advance the parochial school.

Hughes and his coreligionists in New York City became convinced that the Public School Society was using public funds for sectarian purposes. To the argument that the schools of the society did not teach the particulars of any religious faith but stressed instead a "nonsectarian" or "common" religion, Hughes and his supporters replied that this kind of approach was

[29]In "this age and country," Catholics "must proceed on the principle," he declared, "that . . . the school is before the Church." Quoted by Burns, *The Principles, Origin and Establishment of the Catholic School System in the United States,* p. 375. See also M. J. Considine, *A Brief Chronological Account of the Catholic Educational Institutions of the Archdiocese of New York* (New York: Benziger Bros., 1894), pp. 18–19. On Hughes see John R. G. Hassard, *Life of the Most Reverend John Hughes, D. D., First Archbishop of New York; With Extracts from His Private Correspondence* (New York: D. Appleton, 1866). Hassard reports Hughes' remark as follows (p. 338): "I think the time has almost come when it will be necessary to build the school-house first, and the Church afterward."

actually sectarianism in disguise. Removal of all distinctive dogmas—whether of the Catholics, the Baptists, the Methodists, or any other Christian group—actually left the way open for deism, and this also added up to sectarian teaching. Neither "common Christianity" nor "common religion" were viable options for the bishop.[30] If children were to be educated "promiscuously"—that is, those of various faiths under one roof— then "let religion in every shape and form be excluded," Hughes argued. But he much preferred a system in which public funds would flow to various denominational schools and hence each denomination would be "in full possession of its religious rights over the minds of its own children."[31]

Under the leadership of Bishop Hughes the Catholics of New York City carried their cause to the people and to their representatives in the state capital. There in 1840 Governor Seward—a Whig who sought to dislodge some of the almost unaminous Catholic support of Democrats—proposed that religious groups might be encouraged to assist in meeting the problem of educating the children of immigrants. What was needed, the governor argued in his proposal to the legislature, was the establishment of schools in which the children of foreigners could be instructed by teachers speaking the same language with themselves and professing the same faith . . ."[32] This suggestion that the state support secretarian and more specifically Catholic schools immediately brought forth, on the one hand, appeals from Catholic officials for such support, and, on the other, outraged protests from Protestants.

When they were rebuffed by various officials in their efforts to secure public aid for their schools the Catholics of New York City, under the leadership of Bishop Hughes, took the fateful step

[30]Hassard, *Life of Hughes*, p. 226; "Petitioners' Protest Against the Public School Society," *Catholic Education in America: a Documentary History*, ed. McCluskey, p. 68; Dunn, *What Happened to Religious Education?*, p. 254.

[31]Burns, *The Principles, Origin and Establishment of the Catholic School System in the United States*, p. 372.

[32]Pratt, *Religion, Politics and Diversity*, p. 175. The language question was hardly at issue. Apparently Seward mentioned this in order to divert some attention from the real issue of religion.

of entering directly into the political arena by presenting a Catholic slate in the 1841 election for the state assembly. Hughes promised that if Catholics stood up for themselves "public men" would soon come to their aid. Although this tactic achieved some immediate success, it also surfaced all of the Protestant and nativist forces in the city and the state. There ensued a raging public battle between Catholics on the one side and officials of the Public School Society and other Protestants on the other, with the apparently hapless politicians caught in the middle. However, the politicians beat a strategic retreat to the high ground of separation of church and state and from there denied state aid to both parties in the dispute. After involved maneuvering the state legislature enacted a law in 1842 which gave power over school funds and operation to locally elected ward commissions and prohibited the granting of public funds to any school in which "any religious sectarian doctrine or tenet shall be taught, inculcated, or practiced."[33] The act effectively brought the career of the Public School Society to an end, thus accomplishing one of Bishop Hughes' goals. But, as one observer has put it, this was "a pyrrhic victory for Bishop Hughes" since the act also excluded any aid to his own school system. Hence, "without intending it," Bishop Hughes by his campaign for tax funds "opened the way" for a greater secularization of the public schools and also helped to bring Protestants together in support of these schools and in opposition to the use of public funds for schools directly under religious control.[34]

For the next half century Protestants and Catholics of New York continued to engage in a running battle over public aid to Catholic schools. Following the Civil War, Catholics, with the aid of such political leaders as Boss Tweed of Tammany Hall, were successful in securing from the public treasury subventions for the parochial schools. This, however, once more helped to galvanize Protestants and nativists into action and New York experienced another outpouring of anti-Catholic sentiment. Finally, the constitutional convention of 1894 adopted an amendment which prohibited public tax aid to any school "wholly or in

[33]Ibid., p. 187. See pp. 176ff. for the full account.
[34]Dunn, *What Happened to Religious Education?*, p. 254.

part under the control or direction of any religious denomination or in which any denominational tenet or doctrine is taught."[35]

From mid-century on, in almost every instance where Catholics and Protestants engaged in conflict over educational issues there resulted increasing secularization of the public schools, more determined Catholic efforts to strengthen their own schools, constitutional and legislative prohibition of tax aid to church schools, and a practical diminution of intra-Protestant differences. While in Jefferson's day sectarianism had meant strongly held differences among Protestants, by the second half of the century Protestantism was managing to put up a relatively smooth public front. Protestant parochial schools were almost entirely given up. Generalized Protestantism could manage quite well in the public schools as long as school boards were in the control of Protestants and such potent symbols as the King James Bible were duly acknowledged within those schools. By now Protestantism itself, with its King James Bible, its prayers, and its hymn singing, had become sectarian—particular, distinctive, different from Catholicism or Judaism or unbelief.

Common Religion Challenged in Cincinnati

The proposition—common religion for the common school—was most directly and severely challenged in Cincinnati in 1869–70. The board of education of that city, in an unprecedented act, voted to exclude religious instruction, Bible reading, and hymn singing from the public schools. The action split the board and the city into two feuding camps. One group—largely Protestant—strongly maintained that "common religion" was indispensable to morality, essential to the welfare of the country, clearly

[35]Pratt, *Religion, Politics and Diversity*, p. 252; Constitution of 1894, Sec. 4, Art. 9. See Pratt, ch. ix for a discussion of the compromise under which some supporters of the Catholic claim to public aid for Catholic schools agreed to this amendment in exchange for an agreement by some of their opponents that public aid to institutions operated under the state board of charities—including church-controlled and -operated institutions—would not be discontinued.

acknowledged by the constitution of Ohio, and crucial to the task of the common schools. The other group, a temporary coalition of Jews, Catholics, freethinkers, and a few strong-minded Protestants, pointed to the religious pluralism of Cincinnati and the country and argued that the schools, for this reason and in keeping with constitutional principles, must be secularized—i.e., divested of all obvious religious content. The controversy between these two positions was fully aired in the Superior Court of Cincinnati, in local public discussion, and in the press throughout the nation. The board decision was over-ruled in the Superior Court of Cincinnati but later upheld by the Supreme Court of Ohio, which found that "the constitution of the state does not enjoin or require religious instruction, or the reading of religious books, in the public schools of the state."[36] This decision of the Cincinnati Board of Education embodied a position which was not formally acknowledged nationally until almost a century later when the U.S. Supreme Court excluded devotional Bible reading and school sponsorship of the Lord's Prayer from the public schools.[37] The story of the conflict in Cincinnati is of sufficient significance that it is worth telling in some detail.

Ohio was the first state admitted to the Union in the nineteenth century and the first state from the Northwest Territory. Its constitution of 1802, drafted at the time of admission to the Union, was one of the most comprehensive up to that time in its provisions for religious freedom. At the same time, in the language of the Northwest Ordinance, it acknowledged the role of religion, morality, and knowledge in relation to good government and the happiness of mankind and called for legislative provision—"not inconsistent with the rights of conscience"—for the perpetual encouragement of "schools and the means of instruction." In keeping with this provision governmental subsidies were granted in the early years of Ohio history to both schools and religious groups in the form of lands or proceeds

[36]23 *Ohio Reports,* 211 (1873).
[37]*Abington Township* v. *Schempp,* 374 U.S. 203 (1963). Writing for the Court, Mr. Justice Clark quoted from the minority opinion of Judge Alphonso Taft, who was one of the three Cincinnati Superior Court judges who had heard the case.

from lands originally set aside by the Continental Congress under the Ordinance of 1787.

Following these provisions the state of Ohio, in its first half century, pursued an oscillating course seemingly directed by two pole stars—on the one side, very liberal provisions for religious freedom, and on the other side a persistent assumption that the common welfare required the support of "common religion." And that "common religion," because of the nature of the population, took on a distinctively Protestant hue. This oscillating course continued in evidence in the 1850's. The section on education in the revised constitution of 1851 provided for a common school fund to be created and expended under general-assembly direction for securing "a thorough and efficient system of common schools throughout the state . . ." But, the provision continued, "no religious or other sect, or sects, shall ever have exclusive right to, or control of, any part of the school funds of this state."[38] Enabling public school legislation in 1853 brought the state even closer to the full establishment of a public school system. This legislation was greeted with strong opposition by Roman Catholics in Cincinnati and especially by Archbishop John B. Purcell—who had been ordinary of Cincinnati since 1832 and was to continue in his position well past the controversy of 1869–70. Like his counterpart in New York, Purcell desired a system which would channel tax funds into his own already quite substantial parochial school system. And like Bishop Hughes also, he contended that the public schools themselves were actually sectarian in prevailing atmosphere as evident in textbooks, in the use of the King James Bible, and Protestant prayers and hymns in opening exercises, and in the religious orientation of the teachers.[39] The archbishop did have some grounds for complaint. The Protestant version of the Bible was freely used in the public schools of Ohio in that day and the teachers were, according to one Ohio historian, "almost invariably Protestants and quite often Protestant ministers or former ministers." On occasion the public school "even aided the local churches in their revivals." Furthermore, the

[38]Art. VI, Sec. 2.
[39]See Deye, *Archbishop John Baptist Purcell of Cincinnati*, pp. 362ff.

state teachers' association had taken action urging school authorities "to insist on the daily use of the Bible in the classroom."[40]

Archbishop Purcell's opposition to public school legislation stirred up strong anti-Catholic sentiment in Cincinnati and was one of the contributing factors to a virulent outburst of nativism. This nativist fire, reduced to smoldering embers during the Civil War, burst into flame once again in the school controversy of 1869–70. By this time Catholic political power had grown significantly, as is evident, for example, in the fact that one-fourth of the members of Cincinnati's board of education were Catholics. However, Catholic power alone was not sufficient to bring down the Protestant establishment. In fact, in the final analysis, it was other forces—neither Catholic nor Protestant in any formal sense—which played the major role in this successful challenge to common (Protestant) religion.

Cincinnati was the major commercial, cultural, and religious center of the West in 1869. Its population of approximately one quarter of a million included many immigrants from all areas of Europe and migrants from all regions of the United States. The largest single ethnic element was German. But, while these people spoke a similar language, they differed considerably from each other in religious orientation and cultural outlook, including in their numbers a large group of Roman Catholics, a substantial number of Protestants, and sizable minorities of Jews and freethinkers.

This diversity among the German-speaking population was typical of the religious diversity of the whole population of Cincinnati. Conservative and liberal Protestants, Roman Catholics, Jews, and freethinkers lived side by side. On the four corners of the busy intersection of Eighth and Plum Streets there stood the city building, the Catholic Cathedral, Temple Benai Yeshurun, and the "new and radical Unitarian Church"—with a Presbyterian Church standing right next to it.[41] The city's more

[40]*The History of the State of Ohio*, ed. Carl Wittke, Vol. IV, "The Civil War Era, 1850–1873," by Eugene H. Roseboom (Ohio State Archaeological & Historical Society, 1944), pp. 177ff.

[41]The description of Eighth and Plum is found in an editorial by Isaac Mayer Wise in *The American Israelite*, October 15, 1869.

than one hundred congregations represented more than twenty-five religious denominations. The strongest single religious denomination was the Roman Catholic, with twenty-three churches and a substantial number and variety of humanitarian and educational enterprises, including a privately supported parochial school system which enrolled between 12,000 and 15,000 children.[42] All of the major and many of the minor Protestant denominations were represented in the city.[43]

The professional religious leadership of Cincinnati included such prominent clergymen as Archbishop Purcell, who was the senior prelate in the American hierarchy and one of the most influential ordinaries in his day; Isaac Mayer Wise and Max Lilienthal, two of the most influential rabbis in America; and two well-known religious liberals, Amory Dwight Mayo and Thomas Vickers.

The board of education reflected the religious heterogeneity of the city. According to one contemporary account its membership of forty included two Jews, eighteen Protestants, ten Roman Catholics, and ten "others."[44] The liberal Protestants, Mayo and Vickers, were the only clergymen on the board.

The controversy under discussion had its immediate inception in the summer of 1869 in an abortive effort to bring the parochial and public schools together under the control of the board. Discussions to this end, involving several board members and the Reverend Edward Purcell, vicar general of the archdiocese, chief editor of the Catholic *Telegraph*, and brother of the archbishop, aroused nativist fears. On the other

[42]According to an account in the Cincinnati *Commercial*, September 10, 1869. There were 22,280 pupils enrolled in the public schools according to the annual report of the superintendent of schools as reported in the Cincinnati *Enquirer*, December 14, 1869.

[43]On the religious make-up of Cincinnati see James Parton, "Cincinnati," *The Atlantic Monthly*, XX (August 1867), 229–46; Henry A. Ford and Mrs. Kate B. Ford, *History of Cincinnati, Ohio* (Cincinnati: L. A. Williams & Co., 1881), pp. 168ff.; and the *Directory of Cincinnati* for 1869.

[44]"The Bible in the Schools," a pamphlet containing the "Proceedings and Addresses at the Mass Meeting, Pike's Music Hall, Cincinnati, September 28, 1869, with a Sketch of the Anti-Bible Movement" (Cincinnati: Gazette Book & Job Printing House, 1869), p. 1. (Hereafter referred to as "The Bible in the Schools," 1869.)

side, when these discussions were brought formally to the attention of the archbishop he stoutly maintained that Catholics could not give to the state control over the education of their children and openly hinted that the only solution to "the vexed school question" was to be found in public support of church schools.[45]

It was during the course of discussions concerning a possible rapprochement between public and parochial schools that board member Samuel A. Miller, lawyer, geologist, and a man with no obvious institutional religious commitment, moved that "religious instruction and the reading of religious books, including the Holy Bible . . ." be prohibited in the common schools of Cincinnati, and that the regulation calling for Bible reading and "appropriate singing" at the beginning of each school day be repealed. In explaining his reason for this proposal Miller specified that "the true object and intent" of the new rule was "to allow the children of the parents of all sects and opinions, in the matters of faith and worship, to enjoy alike the benefit of the common-school fund." Miller, who was neither a Protestant nativist nor a Roman Catholic, was obviously searching for a way in which the school could fairly serve all the elements in Cincinnati, including the Roman Catholics.[46]

The Miller resolutions polarized the community and the board. Protestant preachers "thundered . . . against excluding the Bible from the free schools."[47] Mass-protest meetings drew overflow crowds. The board was bombarded with protest resolutions containing thousands of signatures. All opponents of Miller's resolutions extolled the virtues of America, the Bible, the common schools, and the common (Protestant Christian) religion. They warned against the sinister conspiracy of the "Romanists" and the nonbelievers to remove the Bible from the schools and they saw in this move an effort to undermine the public school

[45]Ibid., p. 3.

[46]The full text of the Miller motion is printed in *Board of Education of Cincinnati* v. *Minor et al.,* 23 *Ohio* 211 (1873). On Miller see *The Biographical Encyclopedia of Ohio of the Nineteenth Century* (Cincinnati and Philadelphia, 1876), p. 526; and obituary in the Cincinnati *Commercial Tribune,* December 19, 1897.

[47]Headline, Cincinnati *Commercial,* September 13, 1869.

system and even the country itself.[48] On the other side, the Miller resolutions received their strongest support from religious and political liberals, chiefly those who stood in the Jeffersonian tradition and/or in the tradition of the German Enlightenment. They were also supported by lay Catholics (but not noticeably by the Catholic clergy), by the Jewish religious leadership of the city, and by a few courageous Protestant evangelicals. Despite the disparate religious and theological orientations of this group, during the course of the controversy they achieved an operational consensus regarding the issues at stake. I have labeled this consensus the *civil view*. It was a view which was not, and in the minds of those who expressed it could not be, articulated in the precise language or represented in the symbols of any particular historic religion. It rested on the fundamental assertion that the state is secular. Hence the instruments of the state, such as the public schools, should also be secular.[49]

The Miller resolutions were adopted by a vote of 22 to 15 at midnight on November 1, 1869. The affirmative voters included all the Catholics on the board, most of the "others," one of the Jews, and perhaps a Protestant or two. The fifteen who voted against the resolution included the other Jew and a majority of the Protestants. Most of those who voted no could have been found on any list of prominent citizens. The two liberal clergymen split, Vickers voting for and Mayo against.

Following the adoption of the Miller resolutions, thirty-seven citizens immediately sought a court injunction preventing the

[48]Details in "The Bible in the Schools," 1869. Also the Cincinnati *Commercial*, September 14 and 20, 1869. See Harold M. Helfman, "The Cincinnati 'Bible War,' 1869–1870," *Ohio Historical Quarterly*, LX (1951), 369–86, especially p. 373.

[49]Miller articulated elements of this view in support of his resolutions before the board. Reports of these arguments can be found in a pamphlet entitled "Arguments upon the Secularization of the Public Schools" (Cincinnati, 1870). The civil view took further shape in the fall of 1869 under the influence of such spokesmen as the freethinking German druggist Herman Eckel, who was a member of the board; the Reverend Thomas Vickers; the two prominent Jewish rabbis; and the German-born liberal philosopher and attorney Judge Johann Bernard Stallo. See the Cincinnati *Commercial*, September 13 and October 16, 1869, and the *Enquirer*, September 27, 1869. Also an editorial by Rabbi Wise, "The Bible in the Schools," *American Israelite*, October 8, 1869.

board from implementing the vote of the majority. Thus for a week late in 1869 action in the controversy centered in the Superior Court of Cincinnati, where the best legal minds of the city argued the case. The lawyers for the challengers of the board, the plaintiffs, were led by Rufus King, product of a distinguished family, Harvard graduate (where he had studied under Justice Story), long-time Episcopalian vestryman, member of the board of education from 1853 to 1867 and president of the board during his last ten years of membership. Lawyers for the board included Judge J. B. Stallo, who was probably the most widely read man in the city if not in the whole West; Judge Stanley Matthews, whose role in the case was especially noteworthy since he was a Presbyterian elder; and Judge George Hoadly, great-grandson of Jonathan Edwards, also a one-time student under Story at Harvard, and a man who "leaned toward Unitarianism religiously . . ."[50]

The three judges before whom the case was heard included Bellamy Storer, a man described by Rabbi Lilienthal as being "strongly tainted with theological proclivities"; Marcellus Hagans, a Methodist Sunday-school teacher; and the Cincinnati patriarch Alphonso Taft, who was "the pillar of the radical Unitarian Church of the Rev. T. Vickers" for whom, according to Lilienthal, the trial was suited "to the very core."[51]

[50]On Stallo, see *Dictionary of American Biography*, XVII, 496–97, and Lloyd D. Easton, *Hegel's First American Followers* (Athens, Ohio: Ohio University Press. 1966), chs. ii, iii. Brief biographical accounts of King, Matthews, and Hoadly can be found in *The Biographical Encyclopedia of Ohio*. Hoadly is also treated in *Dictionary of American Biography*, IX, 84–85. Stallo later became ambassador to Italy; Matthews was for a short time U.S. Senator from Ohio and spent his last years as an Associate Justice of the U.S. Supreme Court; Hoadly became governor of Ohio. Interesting contemporary descriptions of some of the participants in the trial, including Stallo, Matthews, Hoadly, and the three judges of the Cincinnati Superior Court, can be found in Rabbi Lilienthal's report to the *Jewish Times* of New York, December 1, 1869, and reprinted in *The Bible in the Public Schools; Opinions of Individuals, and of the Press, and Judicial Decisions* (New York: Schemerhorn, 1870; hereafter referred to as *The Bible in the Public Schools*, 1870), pp. 62–71. Quotations are from that account.

[51]*The Bible in the Public Schools*, 1870, p. 67. Alphonso Taft was the father of William Howard Taft. See *Dictionary of American Biography*, XVIII, 264–65.

The attorneys for the plaintiffs argued that the constitution of Ohio required that religious instruction be encouraged in the public schools, such instruction being essential to morality and good government. They also maintained that the Bible was the chief source of this "political religion." The attorneys for the board responded that while religious instruction might be "necessary and indispensable" to good citizenship, the constitution did not require that it take place in the public school. Furthermore, any public school in Cincinnati must acknowledge the religious pluralism of the citizenry, which included "Israelites" who accepted only the Old Testament, some citizens who did not believe in the Bible at all, and a large number of Roman Catholics for whom the King James version was incorrect and incomplete and who also held that the Bible should not be read indiscriminately.[52]

The Cincinnati Superior Court, by a two-to-one decision, made permanent the injunction preventing the implementation of the Miller resolutions. Hagans and Storer found for the plaintiffs, arguing that Christianity was "the prevailing religion in the State," that the "religion" referred to in the Ohio Constitution was the "revealed religion . . . made manifest in the Holy Scriptures . . ." and that this religion was to be taught in the common schools. Taft dissented, arguing—in language that was to be cited by the U.S. Supreme Court almost a century later—that in its attitude toward religion "the government is neutral." Before the state all religions were equal, none were to be preferred and none to be disparaged.[53]

The board appealed the Superior Court decision to the Supreme Court of Ohio, which, almost three years later, overturned the ruling. By this time Cincinnati had apparently ceased to have much interest in the controversy. This is not to suggest that the case made no difference or that its only significance

[52]Arguments of the attorneys and the opinions and decision of the Cincinnati Superior Court are printed in *The Bible in the Public Schools* (Cincinnati: Robert Clarke & Co., 1870; reprinted, New York: Da Capo Press, 1967); hereafter referred to as *The Bible in the Public Schools,* 1967.
[53]*Minor* v. *Board of Education of Cincinnati* (1870), as printed in *The Bible in the Public Schools,* 1967, pp. 371, 379, 415.

lay in the exclusion of Bible reading from the schools of Cincinnati. The case is significant in at least two ways: (1) It
brought into sharp focus two opposing positions which were to
continue in conflict—philosophical, political and legal—for the
next century. One of these positions—in support of the "common
religion" of the Bible—had been articulated frequently before.
The other—the civil view—had not previously received as clear
and forceful an articulation as it did in the Cincinnati case.
This position became the rallying ground for nearly all those
elements in Cincinnati's heterogeneous population who found
themselves in opposition to the generalized Protestantism of
most of the supporters of common religion. In this view we
can catch a glimpse of some of the elements which were to be
more fully stated almost a century later in the church-state
views of a majority of the Supreme Court of the United States.
(2) The whole series of events made it quite evident that there
was no acceptable *modus operandi* which could bring together
the Catholic and public schools of Cincinnati. In this regard the
controversy signaled what was becoming a pervasive trend all
over the country. We turn now to a fuller examination of these
two points.

"COMMON RELIGION"
IN THE COMMON SCHOOL

The common religionists held that both "common religion"
and the common school were essential to the common welfare.
Rufus King argued that since there was no established church
in the United States the public school was "the only means left"
in which "the simple tenets of political religion" could be spread.
The Bible, which "for two hundred years" had lain "at the
very foundation of that great American institution—the Public
School . . ." was obviously essential to this task. But now an
"extraordinary coalition" of Catholics and "Nullifidians" (non-
believers who happened also to be mostly foreign-born)
threatened to tear down that foundation and hence to violate

the constitution of Ohio and the will of every patriotic American.[54]

King's "political religion" clearly resembled common, native American Protestantism. The Reverend A. D. Mayo, the most articulate defender of "common religion," hoped to draw a more inclusive circle.[55] He spoke with utmost confidence in the name of what he called variously "public religion," "religion itself," and "universal religion." This was a religion above sectarianism, "as old as Adam," and capable of uniting "all men." It was not common Protestantism, Mayo pointed out. In fact, it was "older than Protestant or Catholic, than Christian or Hebrew, than Mohammedan or pagan faith." All "special forms and creeds" were merely the offspring of this common religion.

The people of the United States, Mayo confidently asserted, were the "first of all peoples" to affirm this religion "that is not a sect" and to found their institutions upon it. The Ordinance of 1787 and the constitution of Ohio maintained that this "common religion" was necessary to public well-being, and hence that it must be taught in the common school.

In performing its task as "a politico-educational institution," the common school, this most public of American institutions, acknowledged "the universal obligation to worship God, and do good to man, as the condition of republican life." Hence this institution was neither sectarian nor atheistic but was "and shall be, religious."

Mayo's "common religion" resembles the "natural religion" of eighteenth-century deism, with its stress on belief in one God and service to men. However, Mayo stressed the Bible more

[54]King's address to an anti-Miller resolution assembly, September 29, 1869, as reported in "The Bible in the Schools," 1869, pp. 11–13, and his argument before the Superior Court, as contained in *The Bible in the Public Schools,* 1967, pp. 289–349, especially 310f., 341.

[55]The summary of Mayo's views which follows is based largely on three lectures he delivered in October 1869, which were published in pamphlet form as "Religion in the Common Schools" (Cincinnati: Robert Clarke & Co., 1869); quotations are from pp. 4, 26, 46. Mayo's lectures were reprinted in pamphlet form, together with three lectures delivered by the Reverend Thomas Vickers, under the title "The Bible in the Public Schools" (New York: Schemerhorn, 1870).

than such deists as Franklin or Paine had. The Bible was for Mayo *the* book of "public religion." Thus a threat to it in the schools was both a threat to the essential role of the schools and to "public religion" itself. While Mayo was far from being a Biblical literalist, he did have a general reverence for the book which was not uncommon among men of his religious persuasion. In fact, his position was very similar to that of Horace Mann, whom he revered.[56]

COMMON CITIZENSHIP
IN THE COMMON SCHOOL

The *civil view* emerged in the heat of the battle when men of varying ethnic background and religious affiliation discovered or reaffirmed that what they held in common as Americans was citizenship (actual or potential). This common citizenship did not require agreement on any particular religious doctrine, membership in any particular historic religious tradition, or acceptance of any particular religious book. At the same time, it clearly acknowledged the plurality of religious and irreligious positions in America.

The civil view was articulated most eloquently and in slightly differing form by the two liberal jurists, Stallo and Taft. Samuel Miller also voiced it in formulating and supporting his resolutions, as did his most vocal supporters on the board, Eckel and Vickers. The liberal rabbis, Wise and Lilienthal, reiterated it whenever they spoke or wrote on the Bible and the schools. The jurist of Protestant evangelical persuasion, Stanley Matthews, also spelled out this view in his court arguments and in an address favoring the secularization of the schools.

Stallo stressed the secularity of the state. In his view, the

[56]On Mayo's admiration for Mann see his address on "The Scholar's Vocation in the New Republic," delivered before the Union Literary Society, Antioch College, June 30, 1863 (Cincinnati, 1863). For a more general statement of his religious views see "Liberal Christianity: The Religion for the South-West," a sermon preached at the formation of the Ohio Valley Conference of Unitarian and other Christian Churches, February 22, 1867 (Louisville, 1867).

state was "as godless as a steam engine." It was not Christian or Protestant; it had no religion of its own, not even the "nondescript, asexual, graceless creature" which Mayo called " 'absolute, neutral unsectarian religion.' " Under this secular state "all forms of belief and unbelief" had equal rights, so long as they did not engage in overt acts of hostility to the laws of that state.[57]

Taft used a lower-key word—"neutral"—in describing the state vis-à-vis religion. But the effect was much the same. Both men understood that religion is manifested in definite, historical, even sectarian forms. In the United States the government could ally itself with none of these forms. Its relationship toward them must be one of neutrality and equal treatment.[58]

Matthews found the "broad Christianity" which the Miller opponents identified as the common religion to be nothing more than "broad humbug." As a "Calvinist Protestant" who believed "in the doctrines of election and predestination," in the "perseverance of the saints," and that the Bible was the word of the living God, he knew that the Christian religion was not this vain and unmeaning generality. It was, in fact, a definite and positive reality—a "supernatural scheme of salvation"—which did not belong in the public schools and did not need the aid of the state. While he prized his religion "as highly as any man," Matthews did not "ask for it any favor at the hand of the law." His religion could "stand on its own legs," and if it could not, "then it ought not."[59]

Others also urged that religion is a definite, historical, doctrinal, and ritual reality which should neither be affiliated with the state nor taught in the schools in the United States, both for constitutional reasons and because of the fact of religious

[57]From Stallo's argument before the Cincinnati Superior Court as found in *The Bible in the Public Schools*, 1967, pp. 102–04, and his lecture "Our State Gospel and Its Clerical Exponents," reported in the Cincinnati *Commercial*, April 4, 1870, and published as a pamphlet under the title "State Creeds and Their Modern Apostles" (Cincinnati, 1872).

[58]Stallo in *The Bible in the Public Schools*, 1967, p. 65; Taft, pp. 392, 411, 415.

[59]Matthews' argument before the Cincinnati Superior Court, *The Bible in the Public Schools*, 1967, pp. 207–87, especially 228, 240ff., and address as reported in the Cincinnati *Commercial*, March 31, 1870.

pluralism. Americans did not agree on religion, Rabbi Wise pointed out. Hence, in this country, "the state has no religion" and the public schools must be "secular."[60] The *Prostestantische Zeitblaetter,* organ of the German League of Liberal Christian Churches in the United States, asserted that "general religious instruction" without any sectarian tincture in which all might alike participate "belongs to those pious wishes that are never realized." Therefore, religious nurture was the task of the churches and the parents, not the public schools.[61] The free-thinking druggist and board member Herman Eckel affirmed that it was the intention of Miller and his supporters to make the schools "models to all the world . . ." To this end the schools must be "wholly devoid of sectarianism and religious influence . . ."[62]

All supporters of the civil view agreed that the Bible was a religious book and hence that its use in the public schools violated constitutional provisions. Furthermore, most argued that its influence could be divisive. Where they parted company was on the more general question of whether reading from the Bible was, in fact, conducive to morality. Most of them found such reading beneficial and thus a practice to be recommended at home and in the church. Some of the more radical proponents of the civil view, however, argued that Bible reading might be as conducive to immorality as to morality. Since the Bible contained stories of fratricide, the drowning of all mankind, fraud perpetrated upon a blind father, adultery compounded by murder, and others of a similar nature, it did not necessarily encourage sound morals, Stallo argued.[63] And the pamphlet supporting "secularization of the public schools" lists a whole series of Biblical passages which "probably should not be read on all occasions."[64]

What, then, remained for the public schools? Chiefly the development of a common citizenship according to the constitution and laws of the state and through a common living and working

[60]The *American Israelite,* October 8, 1869.

[61]As reported in the Cincinnati *Commercial,* October 6, 1869.

[62]From an address reported in the Cincinnati *Enquirer,* September 27, 1869.

[63]*The Bible in the Public Schools,* 1967, p. 67.

[64]Cited in note 49 above, pp. 10–11.

together in which religious differences were tacitly acknowledged but not played up. It should be the aim "of every true American," one pro-Miller resolution held, "to make the Public School a thorough and efficient means of Americanizing" the people. What the American situation required was a system which would produce out of "the several peoples that reside in the United States a homogenized nation."[65]

Stung by bitter and persistent attack which cast doubts upon their patriotism, the board members who had voted for the Miller resolutions argued that

> they thought it more important to educate all the children of our city in common, so that they may grow up together in our schools and thus learn by daily intercourse to love and respect each other and to work in harmony for the common weal, than to continue a practice, itself of doubtful utility, the practical effect of which was, and is, to separate our children into opposing factions, and thus leave them to grow up in suspicion and distrust of each other.[66]

Rabbi Lilienthal dramatically put his convictions regarding the importance of this common-citizenship motif when he told a pro-Miller resolution rally that he operated on the principle. "The State first, and the Church afterward." He was "first an American, and then a Jew," and he hoped that others were first Americans and then Christians.[67] The common school, then, afforded access to a civil identity which encompassed or transcended religious identity and difference.

THE "IRREPRESSIBLE CONFLICT" BETWEEN COMMON SCHOOL AND CATHOLIC SCHOOL

It is noteworthy that what looked at the beginning like another Protestant-Catholic confrontation actually took on a de-

[65]Resolution adopted by a meeting supporting the Miller motion to discontinue Bible reading in the Cincinnati public schools, the Cincinnati *Enquirer*, September 27, 1869.
[66]The Cincinnati *Commercial*, March 31, 1870.
[67]Ibid.

cidedly different complexion as the controversy proceeded. Many of the opponents of the Miller resolutions continued to see Rome as the ultimate villain. But it was difficult to pin the label "Romanist" on such articulate spokesmen as Stallo, Taft, Matthews, Vickers, Lilienthal, and Miller himself.[68] Obviously something new was emerging in the city, something that represented neither pan-Protestantism nor Roman Catholicism. And as the controversy proceeded, official Catholic spokesmen played a decreasing role.

While Miller initially drew up his resolutions with the hope of reconciling Catholics to the public schools, it soon became evident that this objective would not be realized. A century removed, this attempt by Miller and some other members of the board of education to reach a happy compromise between Catholic and public schools seems naïve. However, they must have had some reason to hope for positive results. Undoubtedly some—perhaps most—of the Catholic laymen on the board earnestly longed for a way to bring themselves and their children into closer relationship with others in the community and at the same time to lessen the financial drain on the resources of Catholics. Some of the non-Catholic members of the board hoped to be fair to their fellow citizens by making available to Catholic children the resources and advantages of education in a public school open to all elements in the population. Perhaps these hopeful board members were encouraged by conversations with some Catholic clergymen. But what remains in the printed word consists largely of either the sharpened edge of controversy or a restatement of the official position calling for church control of the education of Catholic children.

Throughout the controversy Archbishop Purcell seems to have held firmly to a position calling for public aid to schools under church control. In one contemporary account the archbishop is

[68]The Cincinnati *Commercial* commented editorially that "the charge that Thomas Vickers, Stanley Matthews, J. B. Stallo . . . Judge Taft, and others among the most eminent Protestants and liberals in the city belong to a 'Catholic party,' shows a fanatical infatuation in raising up enemies where friends might be had, that is only accountable upon the theory of the fusion of Puritanism in religion, and Know Nothingism in politics, at an intense heat." April 1, 1870.

described as "that gentle, benignant, and patriotic man."[69] He was also an able controversalist and a vigorous upholder of the cause of his church. During his long tenure in Cincinnati he entered into public controversy with such vocal Protestants as Alexander Campbell, Lyman Beecher, and, shortly before the Bible in the schools controversy, the Reverend Thomas Vickers.[70] During that tenure he also presided over the establishment of one of the most flourishing Catholic educational systems in this country. He was firmly critical of the public schools—"this plausible, but most unwise system"[71]—and consistently stated the official Catholic position in his public utterances. He is reported to have suggested to a committee from the board of education early in the controversy under discussion that he would speak with the Pope about modifying this position in the hope of moving toward the rapprochement which these board members sought. However, the committee's own report appears to be the only record of that suggestion. Furthermore, the archbishop was deeply involved in other matters in Rome during the winter of 1869–70. (There, at the First Vatican Council, he remained to the end a member of the minority of bishops who opposed the formal, dogmatic affirmation of papal infallibility.) He returned to Cincinnati in July of 1870 in ill health and soon became embroiled in a financial catastrophe which was to plague him to the end of his days. Thus there appears to have been little suggestion in the archbishop's public pronouncements or little occasion in his busy life for the achievement of an acceptable compromise with the board of education short of an actual division of the tax funds.[72]

[69]James Parton in "Cincinnati," *Atlantic Monthly,* XX (1867), 244.

[70]See note 23, above; and John B. Purcell and Thomas Vickers, "The Vickers and Purcell Controversy" (Cincinnati, 1868).

[71]Words from the Pastoral Letter of the Third Provincial Council of Cincinnati, 1861, as quoted in John Henry LaMott, *History of the Archdiocese of Cincinnati, 1821–1921* (New York and Cincinnati: Frederick Pustet, 1921), pp. 276–77.

[72]The president of the board of education appointed a committee of five, including two Catholics, one Protestant, and Miller and Eckel, to discuss the possible rapprochement with the archbishop early in September 1869. This committee's report can be found in "The Bible in the Schools," 1869, p. 5. According to the committee the archbishop stated that he

In his annual report for the year ending June 30, 1870, the president of the board observed that it had been a stormy year. In retrospect it seemed desirable to him to put the schools in such a position on the Bible and religious-instruction question that they would be "invulnerable to the attacks of all who desire to make them subserve any religious doctrines." Comparing attendance figures for 1857 with those for 1868 he noted that the percentage of Cincinnati youngsters in church schools had increased from 24 to 34 while the percentage in the public schools had declined from 63 to less than 61. (In the same period the percentage in private schools had dropped considerably.) "These facts," the president suggested, "would seem to indicate that a greater effort should be made to make the Public Schools less objectionable to Catholics if we desire to avoid an irrepressible conflict."[73] But, while the events of 1869–70 did reduce the level of obvious Protestant content in the schools of Cincinnati, the feared "irrepressible conflict" was scarcely avoided, if the president meant by that the continuing growth of Catholic parochial schools and the widening of the gulf between those schools and the public schools.

No "Common Religion" for the Common School?

In summarizing educational developments during the first century of the nation, Daniel Coit Gilman, the distinguished first president of both the University of California and Johns Hopkins University, pointed out that the "difference of opinion with respect to religious instruction" was "the chief danger" which threatened "the common-school system."[74] Such common Protestant practices as reading from the King James version of the

---

would "use every effort whilst in Rome, to procure such modification of the rule as may remove all obstacles . . ." to the attendance of Catholic children at schools under the board's control.

[73]*Annual Report and Hand-Book,* Common Schools of Cincinnati, 1870–71, p. 19.

[74]See note 3.

Bible, singing of hymns, and repeating of the Lord's Prayer (a Protestant version) were accepted as standard fare in the common schools of the early part of the nineteenth century. Protestants dominated most school systems, constituting clear majorities among teachers and boards. In many localities, then, Protestantism was the "common religion" of the common schools. But this Protestant hegemony was challenged, first and most consistently by Roman Catholics, and then also by Jews and nonbelievers. In some communities, like New York City, Catholic pressure was strong enough to bring about a toning down of Protestant volume but not strong enough to achieve a consistent pattern of public support for Catholic schools. In fact, while here and there Catholic school systems did receive public support, the general trend was toward legislative and constitutional prohibition of such support. In the meantime, a struggle continued over just how much and what kind of religious influence should exist in the common schools. This struggle produced the kind of coalescing of Protestant denominational religion and the natural religion of the eighteenth-century deists evidenced in the views of the Reverend Amory Dwight Mayo. Following the Bible controversy in Cincinnati in 1869–70 the Reverend Mr. Mayo continued his campaign for the common school and "common religion." At the invitation of Commissioner of Education William Torrey Harris he wrote, toward the end of the century, a detailed history of the common school in America, in which he celebrated the mutually reinforced triumphs of that institution and "the Gospel of American Democracy."[75] But Mayo's "common religion"—like that of many others—still had too much of Protestantism in it for some Americans. Catholics continued to challenge it—by testing the constitutionality of Bible reading in the public schools, for example. Some free-thinkers, who regarded themselves as primary inheritors of the tradition of the eighteenth-century fathers, disavowed any alliance with Protestants which gave the Bible and other instru-

[75]Cremin, *The Wonderful World of Ellwood Patterson Cubberley: An Essay on the Historiography of American Education*, pp. 15–17. Mayo spent twenty years in a "ministry of education to the South" where he endeavored to extend the common school.

ments of Protestant piety a prominent place in the schools. And a few sober analysts, such as William Torrey Harris, acknowledged the particularity of religious commitment and called for the complete removal of religious elements from the public school system. Perhaps, then, there was no common religious ground for the common school.

IV

Church Religion or No Religion?

*The Religious Context of the Common School
at the End of the Century*

"The attempt to find a common religious ground cannot be said to have succeeded. The question for the present remains unsettled—but it is a growing opinion that the common school, to be preserved, must be placed upon a distinctly secular basis."
—Francis Adams, secretary of the National Education League of England, 1875[1]

"The great majority of American schools are religious without being sectarian . . ."
—Philip Schaff, Protestant church historian, 1887[2]

"There is and there can be no positive religious teaching where the principle of non-sectarianism rules."
—Archbishop Ireland to the National Convention of the National Education Association, 1890

"Thank God, the public spirit in this country is fundamentally religious . . ."
—Cardinal Gibbons to Pope Leo XIII, 1890[3]

What Common Ground?

Under the title *The Secularization of American Education* Samuel W. Brown pointed out early in the present century that it was practical necessities which had brought about the "secu-

[1]*The Free School System of the United States* (London: Chapman and Hall, 1875), p. 6.
[2]*Church and State in the United States* (New York and London: G. P. Putnam's Sons, 1888), p. 75.
[3]Quoted by John Tracy Ellis, *The Life of Cardinal Gibbons* (Milwaukee: Bruce Publishing, 1952), I, 664.

larization" of the common school.[4] Rapid growth in population, increasing religious diversity, and the enlarged role of the state in the educational process brought about increasing centralization and uniformity in the common school. That uniformity, Brown assumed, was in no sense religious; it was "secular."

Brown's title is somewhat misleading. Church religion was neither generally routed from the common-school arena nor did it engage in any full-scale retreat. Furthermore, even where religious diversity and court decisions tended to reduce the influence of church religion, irreligion or "secularism" scarcely secured the field. Actually the field came to be occupied mostly by the temporizers, the moderates who sought neither to advance nor to destroy church religion but to subordinate it to other ends. Whether these ends could be labeled "secular" depends upon one's definition.

Brown used "secularization" in a formal—almost legal—sense to refer to obviously religious or "sectarian" practices and control. Used in this sense, it is clear that American education did become increasingly "secularized" in the nineteenth century. Church religion, in its Protestant forms, almost universally discontinued direct operation of elementary and secondary schools. Increasing religious diversity posed a serious threat to the hegemony of the Protestant ethos. As we have seen, a coalition of lay Catholics, Jews, liberal religionists, and nonbelievers succeeded in removing what were essentially Protestant practices from the schools of Cincinnati. Later in the century some lay Catholics in Wisconsin successfully challenged the practice of Bible reading in the public schools.[5] In both of these cases the courts moved in the direction of "secularization" in the sense in which Brown used that term.

The Ohio Supreme Court denied that Christianity was "a part of the common law of this country . . ." The constitution of Ohio did not mention the *Christian* religion, nor did the state's laws

[4](New York: Columbia University Press, 1912; reissued, New York: Russell and Russell, 1967), pp. 1–4.
[5]*Weiss* v. *The District Board of Edgerton, 76 Wisconsin Reports 177* (1890). A similar challenge was successful in Illinois early in the twentieth century: *People* ex rel. *Ring* v. *Board of Education, 245 Illinois Reports 334* (1910).

specify any sanction to uphold Christianity in preference to any other religion. Hence the notion of "legal Christianity is a solecism, a contradiction of terms." The court went even further in denying that there was any "religion of state" at all. All that was "comprehended in the word 'religion' . . ." in the Ohio constitution, the court affirmed, and all that could "be the subject of human 'instructions', must be included under the general term 'knowledge.'" Hence nothing further was enjoined by the constitutional provision relative to "religion, morality, and knowledge" than the increase of knowledge.[6]

In a concurring opinion in the Wisconsin case Justice Harlow South Orton, one-time Baptist "boy preacher" and later dean of the Wisconsin Law School, maintained that the state and all its civil institutions must be completely divorced from "all religions . . . and . . . everything of a religious character or appertaining to religion . . ." Thus the common schools were "as completely *secular* as any of the other institutions of the state . . ." To the charge that this made the public schools "Godless" Orton replied that they were indeed "Godless, in the same sense that the executive, legislative, and administrative departments" of the government were "Godless." The purpose of all of these agencies of the state "must be exclusively *secular*," Orton concluded.[7]

These two cases were significant, both for Brown's analysis and for ours, in securing some grasp of developments in the late nineteenth century. It would not be correct to conclude, however, either that they were typical of court decisions or even that they were clear instances of a fully "secularized" position. Brown himself dealt with a number of state supreme court decisions which were favorable toward what he called "the religious ideal of education."[8] Furthermore, while the Wisconsin Court in

[6]*Board of Education of Cincinnati* v. *Minor*, 23 *Ohio Reports* 211, 238ff. (1872).

[7]76 *Wisconsin* 177, 218f.

[8]*The Secularization of American Education*, ch. xii. "Since 1850," Brown pointed out, 'the supreme courts of no less than twenty-one states have been called upon to decide at least thirty cases involving in some form the question of the proper relation of religion and public education. Of these, seventeen cases, in fifteen states, have been decided in favor of the secular view; thirteen cases, in nine states, in favor of the religious view." 1967 reissue edition, p. 120.

its 1890 decision ruled out Bible reading as an instance of "sectarian instruction," the majority of that court had no thought that this entailed removing from the school all elements of a religious nature. Justice William Penn Lyon, who wrote the court decision, based that decision upon a definition of "sectarian instruction" as that which consisted of "religious doctrines which are believed by some religious sects and rejected by others." But he went on to suggest that to teach what is believed and taught by all religious sects would not be sectarian and hence, one could conclude, could be done constitutionally within the common school. Lyon even went so far as to point out that the two chief elements in this nonsectarian credo were "the existence of a Supreme Being, of infinite wisdom, power and goodness, and the duty of all men to adore, obey, and love Him . . ." This language, which is reminiscent of that of the "natural religion" of the eighteenth century, could hardly be labeled secularistic.[9]

In his discussion of the "secularization" of the American public school Samuel W. Brown tended to equate "religious" with "sectarian." His book consists chiefly of an examination of antisectarian provisions of state constitutions and legislation and of state court decisions striking down sectarian practices in the common schools. For this reason a more appropriate title might have been "The Desectarianization of American Education." The book does not support a conclusion that Americans had come to favor either irreligion or even no religion at all in their schools. "Secularization," understood in a philosophical or theological sense as involving a this-worldly orientation coupled with a distinct neglect of religious institutions and thought, had not gained the general support of the American people. While sectarianism was generally eschewed, there were few Americans who called forcefully for the excision of all religious elements from the public sector generally and the public school in particular.

President Ulysses S. Grant articulated the prevailing view of

[9]77 *Wisconsin* 177, 194. Lyon found that there was "much in the Bible" which could not "justly be characterized as sectarian." He had in mind especially the moral elements. "No more complete code of morals exists," he argued in Jeffersonian fashion, "than is contained in the New Testament . . ." And he optimistically concluded, "Concerning the fundamental principles of moral ethics, the religious sects do not disagree." Ibid., p. 195.

his time when he urged in 1875 that "every child growing up in the land of opportunity" should have access to "a good common school education" which would be free from "sectarianism" on the one hand, and unmixed with "pagan or atheistical dogmas" on the other.[10] "Secular" was not quite the proper designation to apply to this kind of education. That word implied to many paganization and the "exclusion of God," and that definitely was not what most Americans wanted in the public school. In assuming that there was a common ground which was neither "sectarian" nor "pagan or atheistic" and on which all Americans could stand, Grant stated a view of continuing popularity.

The common ground which Grant alluded to was the object of search by a host of Americans, including both educators and religious leaders. William Torrey Harris, Hegelian philosopher and believing Christian, sought that common ground in "secular instruction" in fundamental subjects in the common school. These fundamentals were grammar, literature and art, mathematics, geography, and history. The list did not include religion. "Common religion" was out. Harris' common ground might be called spiritual but not religious. The schools could seek to develop a sense of what later came to be called "spiritual values" —that is, an appreciation for things aesthetic, cultural, and intellectual. Harris did not deny the role of religious education in the life of the individual, but this was a role which he assigned exclusively to the home and the church.[11]

Harris' notion of "secular instruction" was too antiseptic for the American people, just as his notion of "spiritual" was too archaic. A livelier option was needed, one that caught up the dynamic character of the American approach to the common school and the forcefulness of American communal strivings. Such an option was offered by John Dewey. Before turning to Dewey's common ground, however, I propose to test more fully the winds of doctrine that swirled around the common school in the last two or three decades of the nineteenth century. In that period of its approaching adolescence, various evangelists sought to win over

[10]Address to the Army of the Tennessee at Des Moines, Iowa, as quoted in Stokes, *Church and State in the United States,* II, 68.
[11]On Harris see note 24, p. 56, Chapter II.

this fast-growing institution. In their competition with each other
they were forced to compromise their message or to turn back
into their own camp while perhaps condemning the strapping
youngster to perdition.

Church Religion and the Common School

As the century drew to a close almost all Protestant denominations had gotten out of the business of elementary and secondary
education while the Roman Catholic Church was struggling
valiantly to build a school system which would accommodate all
the faithful. Some observers have implied that formal Protestant
withdrawal from education represented a retreat from the high
ground of principle.[12] Whether or not this judgment is correct,
it is clear that most Protestant denominations had no alternative.
Only those groups with a strong ethnic and/or religious identity
could muster sufficient support for their own school systems.[13]
The other Protestant denominations—those which gave up on
separate religious schools and those which had never even seriously considered this option—tended to make a virtue of the
necessity confronting them. They labeled the common school
"religious"—not "sectarian" but "religious"—after the manner
of the distinguished church historian Philip Schaff, who is quoted
at the opening of this chapter. Like Justice Lyon of the Wisconsin
Supreme Court, they supported a "nonsectarian" religion upon
which all could agree. And when some Americans did not agree,

[12]This is a consistent undertone in Francis X. Curran, S.J., *The
Churches and the Schools: American Protestantism and Popular Ele-
mentary Education* (Chicago: Loyola University Press, 1954). See also
Dunn, *What Happened to Religious Education?*

[13]On Protestant parochial schools in the nineteenth century see Curran,
cited above; Lewis Joseph Sherrill, *Presbyterian Parochial Schools* (New
Haven: Yale University Press, 1932); Walter H. Beck, *Lutheran Elementary
Schools in the United States: A History of the Development of Parochial
Schools and Synodical Educational Policies and Programs* (St. Louis:
Concordia Press, 1939); and Theodore C. Blegen, *Norwegian Migration
to America* (Northfield, Minnesota: Norwegian American Historical As-
sociation, 1940), II, 242ff.

the more hard-line Protestants hinted that these people might be something less than one-hundred-percent American. But some of the more liberal Protestant leaders took America's religious diversity seriously. If necessity demanded, they were even willing to give up the notion of a "nonsectarian" religion common to all. They could settle for something less than a common religion in the common school; common morality and common civil identity might be sufficient.

There was no Catholic enthusiasm for "common religion." Archbishop Ireland's dismissal of nonsectarianism, quoted at the opening of this chapter, was typical. The real dividing issue in the Roman Catholic community was whether there could be any rapprochement at all with the common school. Was this institution so Protestantized or so secularized that it must be condemned out of hand? Or was there some common ground upon which Catholics and non-Catholics might stand together in support of some kind of common educational system? Papal decisions embodied in the encyclicals on Americanism (1899) and Modernism (1907) indirectly supported those who denied that such ground existed and who consequently took a hard line in opposition to the common school. Rapprochement failed and the public school was left largely to the Protestants, and to the progressive educators.

PROTESTANTISM AND "COMMON RELIGION" IN THE COMMON SCHOOL

As we have seen, the controversy in Cincinnati over the discontinuation of Bible reading in the schools of that city attracted nationwide attention. Articles and editorials appeared in newspapers from New York to San Francisco and in many journals, including the church press.[14] It is evident from these accounts and comments that there were some Protestants outside of Cincinnati who supported the majority decision of the board of education to discontinue Bible reading in the public schools. An

[14]*The Bible in the Public Schools,* 1870, contains an excellent sampling of these. Cited in note 50, page 96, Chapter III.

"evangelical Protestant" argued in the *Advance,* leading journal of Western Congregationalism, that a basic distinction must be made between religion and morality. The former did not belong in the common schools; morality, on the other hand, was seen as essential to the very structure of society.[15] The *Herald,* a Presbyterian journal published in Utica, New York, admitted that "in a cosmopolitan sense" the reading of a particular version of the Bible was "sectarian." Hence why not "disarm our opponents" (obviously the Roman Catholics) by "waiving" this practice in "our schools . . ."? Only then would "our common-school system" be secure.[16] Catholics and Protestants should agree as citizens, argued the Reverend Samuel T. Spear in the Congregational *Independent,* "to omit the reading of any version of the Scriptures in our public schools." Supporting the "voluntary principle," Spear pointed out that it was "best for the state and best for religion" if the two were in no way "organically connected . . ." He concluded by questioning the "practical wisdom" and "consistency as American citizens" of those Protestants who proposed "to fight this thing through to the bitter end . . ."[17]

Henry Ward Beecher, one of the most widely known Protestant preachers in the latter half of the nineteenth century, was possibly as open as any Protestant leader of his time to the realities of religious diversity. Where all agreed, he argued, Bible reading might be continued in the schools; but where religious diversity prevented such agreement, Beecher was willing that the practice be discontinued. At the time of the Cincinnati controversy this one-time resident of the city argued that while the common schools were essential to the welfare and unity of the nation, common "technical" religion (chiefly dogma) was not essential to the common schools. The essential elements in those schools were "intelligence," "fellowship and common feeling," and what Beecher called "Practical Christianity." By this last designation he meant essentially "morality and true virtue . . ." While the state needed these in its citizens, Beecher argued, "it

[15]Ibid., pp. 73–77.
[16]Ibid., pp. 90f.
[17]Ibid., pp. 37ff., and "The Bible and the Public Schools," *The Princeton Review,* I (1878), 361–94.

is not indispensable that . . . citizens [of the state] should be Calvinists or Arminians, Protestants or Catholics, or even Christians of any sect." Hence, the "free common school" should be "*unsectarian.*"[18]

By the turn of the century other liberal Protestants were calling for the elimination of such obvious religious elements in the common school as Bible reading.[19] It is quite clear, however, that they did not speak for the Protestant majority. In fact, that majority voice spoke for a kind of Protestant establishment, embracing the public schools both as mission territory and as part of the Protestant preserve.

THE COMMON SCHOOL AS PROTESTANT MISSION

Protestant voices were far more vocal in opposition to the action of the majority of the Cincinnati board of education, and to similar actions, than in support. The Honorable Gerrit Smith, Presbyterian philanthropist and reformer, argued as an "old abolitionist" that the move to take the Bible out of the schools in order to mollify Catholics might "prove a much more losing one to the cause of truth and righteousness . . ." than the compromise on slavery proposed by Henry Clay. Smith confessed that he would rather see the common school fall than have the Bible removed from it.[20] The Episcopalian *American Churchman*

[18]"The Common School as an Element of National Unity," a sermon preached on Thanksgiving Day, 1869, and printed in *The Christian Union*, December 4, 1869. Reprinted in *The Bible in the Public Schools*, 1870, pp. 3–14. Another Protestant leader, Horace Bushnell, had evidenced earlier a similar irenicism respecting religious diversity in the common school. See "Common Schools," a sermon delivered in North Church, Hartford, March 25, 1853, and published in *Building Eras in Religion* (New York: Charles Scribner's Sons, 1903), pp. 71–105.

[19]For example: Shailer Mathews, "The Use of the Bible in the Public Schools," *Biblical World*, XXVII (January 1906), 59–62; Washington Gladden, "Religion and the Schools," *Atlantic Monthly*, CXV (June 1915), 57–68; and Joseph H. Crocker, "Religious Instruction in the Public Schools," *Westminster Review*, CXLIV (August 1895), 203–13.

[20]*The Bible in the Public Schools*, 1870, pp. 51–52. Smith was the author of *Religion of Reason*, published in 1864. There is a biographical account in *Dictionary of American Biography*.

asked: What will happen to our common schools "if we propose, in Cincinnati fashion, to expurgate English literature to suit German infidels, Frankfurt Jews, and Maynooth priests?"[21] And in a similar vein the Dutch Reformed *Christian Intelligencer* denounced the Cincinnati board's action as a move to "hand the public schools over to Pope, Pagan, and Satan" and urged that the reign of Jesus Christ must not "be voted out of the public schools in the name of American liberty . . ."[22]

In response to the Cincinnati controversy the Methodist State Convention of Massachusetts adopted a resolution which labeled the Bible "the palladium of our liberties" and warned that any attempt to remove it from "our public schools" would be "a blow at the foundations of republicanism."[23] And in 1872 the General Conference of the Methodist Episcopal Church resolved to (1) "co-operate in every effort . . . to make our Common Schools more efficient and permanent . . ." (2) oppose the division of common school funds among religious denominations as "wrong in principle and hostile to our free institutions and the cause of education . . ." and (3) "resist all means employed to exclude from the Common Schools the Bible, which is the charter of our liberties and the inspiration of our civilization."[24]

By 1870 Protestants generally had arrived at the conclusion that the public school system was best for America, that sectarianism—as they understood it—had no place in that system, but that religion—"nonsectarian," "common" religion—was essential to the school. As the primary *modus operandi* of this nonsectariansm the Bible became a crucial rallying point for Protestants.

Protestantism was pushed toward these positions by the growth of the public school system, with the increasing sense of national identity symbolized in that system, and by the dramatic increase

[21]December 16, 1869, as in *The Bible in the Public Schools*, 1870, p. 79.
[22]Ibid., p. 98.
[23]Ibid., p. 115. See also the *Western Christian Advocate*, December 8, 1869.
[24]*Journal of the General Conference of the Methodist Episcopal Church*, 1872, p. 44.

in the strength of Roman Catholicism.[25] This latter development galvanized Protestant forces into a paroxysm of anti-Catholic nativism.[26] The public school offered them the most convenient common ground where they could advance their own cause in a general way while attempting to fight off Roman Catholic growth.

The common school also came to be a convenient point of convergence for the powerful emotions of patriotism and religion. Criticism of or failure to support that institution was often regarded as a sign of questionable loyalty to the nation. In the midst of a bitter controversy within Norwegian Lutheran circles over support of church-run elementary and secondary schools, for example, one of the editors of *Skandinaven*, a Dano-Norwegian weekly published in Chicago, went so far as to suggest that opposition to the public school might be regarded as treason. And R. B. Anderson, first professor in Scandinavian languages at the University of Wisconsin, for some years carried on his stationery the following words: "Whosoever directly or indirectly opposes the American common school is an enemy of education, of liberty, of progress. Opposition to the American common school is treason to our country."[27]

This prevailing Protestant evangelical-patriotic approach to the common school was forcefully articulated in the best-selling *Our Country*, written by the Reverend Josiah Strong, peripatetic Congregational minister, home missionary, social gospeler, and

[25]In the forty years between 1830 and 1870 the number of Roman Catholics in the United States had increased from considerably less than one million to over four million. Major Protestant groups experienced similar phenomenal growth. However, no Protestant denomination even began to approach the Roman Catholic Church in total members in 1870. In fact, the total number of Methodist and Baptists combined—and these were the two largest Protestant groups—fell considerably short of the total number of Roman Catholics. See Edwin S. Gaustad, *Historical Atlas of Religion in America* (New York: Harper & Row, 1962), pt. 2.

[26]For a keen sense of the challenge and supposed dangers of Roman Catholic growth see Daniel Dorchester, *Christianity in the United States* (New York: Hunt & Eaton, rev. ed., 1895), pp. 614–23, 756–60.

[27]Laurence M. Larson, "*Skandinaven*, Professor Anderson, and the Yankee School," in *The Changing West and Other Essays* (Northfield, Minnesota: Norwegian-American Historical Association, 1937), pp. 125, 133.

worker in the Evangelical Alliance—an early "ecumenical" movement among Protestants.[28] Something of the mood of Strong's
work is evident in his use of the word "perils" in eight of the
fifteen chapters. One gains the impression of a country and its
major religion facing catastrophic threats to their well-being.
(The "perils" included "Immigration," "Romanism," "Mormonism," "Intemperance," "Socialism," "Wealth," and "The City.")
Two great "perils" confronted the public schools, according to
Strong: "Secularism" and "Romanism." "Secularism" was defined
by Strong as the view that "the province of the State is wholly
secular," that "its true attitude is that of absolute neutrality
toward all forms of religious belief and unbelief . . ." Even
though those holding this view might include "many Christian
men," as well as Jews and agnostics, it was, Strong contended,
a wrong view. The "secularists" erred in their failure to dis-
tinguish between "*church* and *religion*." Separation of church
and state did not mean separation of religion and state. While
the principle of "the separation of Church and State undoubtedly
forbids sectarian instruction in the State schools," it did "not
forbid undenominational religious teaching." Indeed, such teaching was essential to the welfare of the state. "Popular morality"
could not "be secured without the sanctions . . ." of this kind of
religion; "reverence for law" sprang "only from reverence for
God." Hence it was incumbent upon the state to teach in its
school what Strong called "the three great fundamental doctrines
which are common to all monotheistic religions," that is "*the
existence of God, the immortality of man* and *man's account-
ability*." These were not sectarian; they were, in fact, held in
common by "all Protestants, Catholics, and Jews." When it came
to the agnostics, atheists, and others who did not accept these

[28]First published in 1886, over 175,000 copies of *Our Country* had sold
by 1916 and individual chapters had been reprinted in newspapers and
magazines and published separately in pamphlet form. The chief librarian
of Congress compared its influence with that of *Uncle Tom's Cabin*.
The Belknap Press of the Harvard University Press republished *Our
Country* in 1963 under the editorship of Jurgen Herbst. See Herbst's
Introduction for an evaluation of the influence of the work.

doctrines, Strong dismissed them with the statement that "the necessities of the State" were "above individual rights . . ."[29]

Strong might have hoped to express a point of view which would gain the support of all monotheists, but what he came out with was noticeably Protestant—and even Anglo-Saxon Protestant—in character. He deplored "the cleavage of population along religious lines" and regarded it as "un-American." He also fixed that same label on "Romanism," which represented, he said, an "alien civilization" because of such things as the official position of the Catholic Church on education. And he remonstrated with Jews and agnostics for their "secularism."[30]

Strong was commissioned by the Congregational Home Missionary Society to do his book as a campaign document. In keeping with this purpose, his attitude toward the public schools bore a clear resemblance to missionary motivation. While the schools were not to be used to convert people to sectarian religion, they must be used to salvage that large percentage of the children (Strong estimated the number at one-half) who did not come under direct religious influence at home or in Sunday school. Without the public schools these children would grow up godless and immoral. With it they might become decent citizens.

In addition to a civilizing and religionizing role, the common school had the peculiar function of Americanizing the children of immigrants, Strong maintained. It was "the principal digestive organ of the body of politic." By means of it "the children of strange and dissimilar races" which came to America would be "in one generation assimilated and made American." And again, one might assume, without it they would remain "strange and dissimilar . . ."[31]

Hence the public school became a major plank in the evangelical Protestant missionary platform. Protestants heaped paeans of praise upon it as God's chosen instrument for

[29]*Our Country* (Cambridge, 1963), ch. vi and pp. 96ff. Emphasis in original.
[30]Ibid., pp. 93–96.
[31]Ibid., pp. 89ff.

religionizing and Americanizing the youth, and they roundly castigated those who opposed it—chiefly the Roman Catholics. "We can take the ground explicitly, and clear of all ambiguity," Horace Bushnell had pontificated in 1853, "that those who exclude themselves [from the common schools] are not Americans . . ."[32] A generation later this Protestant dominant note was sounded more clearly than ever. Strong accused "Romanism" of being "un-American" chiefly because its leaders claimed "that the only way to make a good Catholic out of a child is to keep him out of the public school and separate him from American children . . ."[33] The Reverend Daniel Dorchester, prominent New England Methodist clergyman and author, argued extensively in his book *Romanism versus the Public School System*, published in 1888,[34] that all children must be *required* to attend the public schools if the health of the republic was to be maintained. Thus the deep-seated emotions of the sixteenth and seventeenth centuries lingered on and the public school became a major arena for the continuation of the Protestant-Catholic conflict.

CATHOLICISM AND THE COMMON SCHOOL

While they openly vented an anti-Catholic bias, these avid Protestants were not alone in their sensitivity to the acute difference between the official Catholic position on education and the majority American view of the public schools. This "irrepressible conflict" was noted and its implications discussed by others who were not obviously grinding the Protestant ax. After surveying the American public school system in the early 1870's, Francis Adams, secretary of the National Education League of England, concluded that "there is one thing, and one thing only, which appears to threaten the common school— that is, the Catholic question."[35] In a survey of religion in

[32]*The Christian Review*, XVIII (1853), 455. As quoted by Curran, *The Churches and the Schools*, p. 103.
[33]*Our Country*, p. 94.
[34](New York: Phillips and Hunt).
[35]*The Free School System of the United States*, p. 95.

America from 1776 to 1876, J. L. Diman, professor of history and political science at Brown University, wrote that the papal encyclical of 1864 which had branded secular education in a secular environment as a thing *"reprobatam, proscriptam atque damnatam"* ["rejected, proscribed, and condemned"] had put the Roman Catholic Church in the United States in irrevocable "conflict with a part of our public system which, by the great majority of our people, is regarded as absolutely essential to the perpetuity of our free institutions."[36] Sensitive Catholic observers were also acutely aware of this problem. In a letter to Pope Leo XIII, Cardinal Gibbons, the most prestigious of the American hierarchy, explained that the divisions between Catholics and other Americans "are caused above all by the opposition against the system of national education which is attributed to us . . ." This, "more than any other thing, creates and maintains in the minds of the American people the conviction that the Catholic Church is opposed by principle to the institutions of the county and that a sincere Catholic cannot be a loyal citizen of the United States."[37]

Throughout the nineteenth century it was universally held by American officials of the Roman Catholic Church that education was the right and responsibility of parents and the church, not the state. Members of the hierarchy consistently urged that the church must exert every effort to advance education under its control. At the same time, state schools—those under the primary control and authority of civil officials—were at best questionable in the eyes of the prelates and at worst infidel, atheistic, and antithetical to the interests of the church and of Christian civilization. Many warnings were issued to the faithful regarding the dangers of these public schools. If tax monies were to be used in support of popular education they should be turned over to the churches for the support of schools under their direct and sole control or at least some system should be worked out whereby the churches could have a

---

[36]*North American Review,* CXXII (January 1876), 205.
[37]Quoted by John Tracy Ellis, *The Life of James Cardinal Gibbons,* I, 664.

major voice in the selection of teachers and curriculum and could engage in religious instruction.[38]

In 1884 the Third Plenary Council of Baltimore decreed that "near every Church" a parish school must "be built and maintained *in perpetuum* within two years" of this promulgation, "unless the bishop should decide" that circumstances necessitated delay. The council decreed further "that all Catholic parents are bound to send their children to the parish school" unless these children received "a sufficient training in religion" in their own homes or in other Catholic schools; "or, when because of a sufficient reason, approved by the bishop, with all due precautions and safeguards, it is licit to send them to other schools."[39] A proper religious education was necessary, the fathers of the council argued, for preparing the laity for "the great coming combat between truth and error, between Faith and Agnosticism . . ." Furthermore, without education in religion morality would decline and the people would "degenerate into corruption which breeds decrepitude . . ." while what they did attain intellectually would serve only "to guide them to deeper depths of vice and ruin. . . . A civilization without religion," the Council concluded in the coming language of the day, "would be a civilization of 'the struggle for existence, and the survival of the fittest,' in which cunning and strength would become the substitutes for principle, virtue, conscience and duty."[40]

The council of 1884 followed by nine years the instruction to the American hierarchy from the Congregation de Propaganda de Fide dealing with the dangers confronting Catholic children who attended the public schools. The American hierarchy had sought some reinforcement from Rome in their efforts to secure lay support for parochial schools and to reduce the

---

[38]Pronouncements of the Plenary Councils of Baltimore, 1852, 1866, and 1884. The first council urged the establishment and support of Catholic schools and warned against "the evils of an un-Catholic education . . ." *Catholic Education in America: A Documentary History*, ed. McCluskey, p. 80. The relevant pronouncements on education are found on pp. 78–94.

[39]Ibid., p. 94.

[40]Ibid., pp. 89–90.

supposed loss to the Church occurring among those attending public schools. Propaganda obliged in strong language. The public schools were "most dangerous and very much opposed to Catholicity." Children who attended them were "fearfully exposed to the danger of losing their faith" and their morals were not "properly safeguarded." Such schools could not "in conscience be used" unless considerable change could be made in them. Hence those in authority must "use every means in their power to keep [the faithful] from all contact with the public schools."[41]

While there was general consistency on formal official policy, there was also considerable variation in practice and point of view. Catholic attendance at public schools obviously occurred in noticeable numbers and was, under certain circumstances, acknowledged to be a necessity. In some communities experiments were attempted in achieving some rapprochement between parochial and public schools.[42] The most widely publicized experiments were those conducted in Poughkeepsie, New York, and Faribault and Stillwater, Minnesota, where, for a nominal fee, parochial school buildings were rented to public school boards during school hours and teachers nominated by the local priest and approved and paid by the boards taught the regular public school curriculum to the parochial school students. Before and after school hours the buildings were used for religious exercises and instruction.

Liberal Catholic officials, such as Archbishop Ireland and Cardinal Gibbons, encouraged such experiments. Gibbons was confident that "a practical method of reconciling the general diffusion of elementary education with a proper regard for the sacred rights of conscience" could be worked out by the American people who were "so resourceful in solving perplexing social and religious problems."[43] But such compromises were

[41]Ibid., pp. 121–26.

[42]A contemporary observer, Father Thomas Jefferson Jenkins, pointed to some thirty-two communities in which such "compromises" had been made. See Robert D. Cross, *The Emergence of Liberal Catholicism in America* (Cambridge: Harvard University Press, 1958), p. 139.

[43]In *The Ambassador of Christ*, as quoted by Cross, *Liberal Catholicism*, p. 139.

vigorously opposed by conservatives who wished only to promote their own institutions and wanted nothing to do with the evil public schools.[44]

There is evidence that many lay Catholics desired some type of arrangement which would enable them to send their children to public schools and still not be unfaithful to their church. According to Professor Cross, the *Catholic Citizen* of Milwaukee, stronghold of German conservatism, admitted that the laity favored the public schools. Laymen willingly and even eagerly served on school boards where the opportunity presented itself (as we have seen in the case of Cincinnati). One such individual, a member of the Boston school board, called the establishment of church schools "a most serious mistake, if not a great misfortune, especially to those who attend them."[45] Catholic laymen also supported, and in some cases even initiated, board and court actions to force the discontinuance of readings from the King James Bible in the public schools (as in the Wisconsin case examined above). They also promoted the appointment of Catholic teachers and engaged in other activities for making public schools more acceptable. In predominantly Catholic communities the inch of exception to the parish school ruling suggested by the Third Plenary Council, and other evidences of official permissiveness vis-à-vis public schools, was eagerly stretched to a foot. Where school board and teachers were primarily Catholic, why bother to establish parish schools? Such permissiveness must also have been welcomed by many Catholics who were in a minority in their home community.[46]

One constant factor which faced all within the church was an anti-Catholic bias among a sizable segment of the American population. While some outside the Catholic community were sympathetic to the dilemma confronting Catholics with regard to public education, others kept this ever-present anti-Catholic sore in a constant state of inflammation. The American Pro-

[44]See Cross, *Liberal Catholicism*, ch. vii.
[45]Ibid., p. 135.
[46]See Timothy L. Smith, "Parochial Education in American Culture," *Religion on Campus* (published by the Council of Religious Advisors at the University of Minnesota), I (Fall 1965), 5–8.

tective Association, formed in 1887, included among its primary aims the "protection" of the nation from foreign, and especially Catholic, influences, and the preservation of the purity of the American public schools. This and other Protestant nativist movements instigated and supported legislation designed to compel all children to attend public schools or allow exceptions only with the permission of public school authorities.

It seemed to some Catholic spokesmen that the best way to fight such virulence was with equally strong counterattacks. But there did emerge in this period a significant group of leaders, liberal in outlook, who were confident that the voice of Protestant nativism did not represent the majority of Americans, who were hopeful of appealing to the good sense and fairness of this majority in attempting to advance the cause of education in a direction acceptable to both Catholics and non-Catholics, and who were fully persuaded that the Catholic Church in particular and America in general needed the fostering of a vigorous intellectual life from which greater tolerance and freedom would spring. These Catholic leaders sought to present to their fellow Americans a vision of a common endeavor in popular education for the good of all. They stressed what a later generation was to call "moral and spiritual values," but they used the more definite language of historic religion. They held that the connection between religion and education was necessary to the welfare of both the individual and the community. All Americans could agree on the noble goal of producing faithful, loyal, and morally upright youngsters; the question at issue was one of means.[47]

Cardinal Gibbons and Bishop John J. Keane, rector of

[47]Cross, *Liberal Catholicism*, offers the best treatment of this group, which included most prominently Gibbons, Ireland, Bishops John L. Spalding and John J. Keane, and Father Isaac Thomas Hecker, founder of the Paulist order. In 1876 Father Hecker called for a new "phase of Catholicity in the United States" which would be marked by a "higher" and "more elaborate" mental culture, one in which Catholics would prove themselves equal or superior to Protestants in intellectual achievement. "The Next Phase of Catholicity in the United States," *The Catholic World*, XXIII (August 1876), 577–92. One of the most succinct statements of this liberal view can be found in John L. Spalding, "Religious Instruction in State Schools," *Educational Review*, II (July 1891), 105–22.

Catholic University, spoke such language to the annual convention of the National Education Association in Nashville in
1889. "To keep the social body within its orbit," the cardinal
asserted, "the centripetal force of religion should counter-
balance the centrifugal motion of free thought." Bishop Keane
assured his audience that there was no incompatibility between
being a Christian and being an American. Indeed, he urged,
"the best Christian is sure to be the best American." One
could count on "a good Christian" being "fully trustworthy
and self-sacrificing and faithful as a citizen . . ." It followed,
then, that the schools of America "ought to be the most truly
Christian schools in the world."[48]

Gibbons and Keane spoke primarily on behalf of "denominational schools." A year later Archbishop Ireland dramatically
caught the attention of his listeners and startled many of his
fellow Catholics when he forthrightly declared before the
meeting of the National Education Association in St. Paul:
"I am a friend and an advocate of the state school. . . . The right
of the state school to exist is . . . a matter beyond the stage
of discussion." The state school was not only necessary, but
its work in "imparting secular instruction" was, the archbishop
enthusiastically confessed, "our pride and glory. . . . Withered
be the hand," then, that would be "raised in sign of its destruction."

While praising this "wonderful edifice which Americans have
raised," Archbishop Ireland was clearly critical of the public
school system for not giving adequate religious instruction. To
the argument that "the state school teaches morals," he replied:
"Christians demand religion," not a vague, "nonsectarian"
religion, not even "Common Christianity," but the distinctive
teachings of the various religious groups. To achieve the goal
of adequate religious instruction Ireland suggested two alternative procedures: (1) permeate the regular, existing state school
with the religion of the majority, "be it as Protestant as
Protestantism can be . . ." and "pay for the secular instruction

[48]"Should Americans Educate Their Children in Denominational
Schools?" National Education Association, Nashville, July 1889, pp. 5, 9,
10.

given in denominational (chiefly Catholic) schools . . ." or
(2) inaugurate a system akin to the Poughkeepsie plan.[49]

In keeping with his own suggestion Archbishop Ireland
encouraged and approved the institution of a plan in two
communities in his archdiocese, Faribault and Stillwater,
Minnesota, which incorporated most of the provisions of the
Poughkeepsie plan, as indicated above. Added features included an agreement that no textbooks would be used to
which the archbishop objected, and both teachers and students
in the parochial schools would be subjected to examination by
the public school boards.[50]

The archbishop's St. Paul speech and his promotion of the
Faribault Plan unloosed what Professor Merle Curti has described as "one of the most bitter and dramatic controversies
in the history of the Catholic Church in America."[51] Ireland
expected to be attacked by Protestants, but he was greatly
bothered when his fellow Catholics objected strenuously to his
approach.[52] Conservative priests and prelates, especially in
New York and among the Germans in the Middle West, argued
in alarm that the archbishop was undermining their hardwon
gains in the parochial school system. Furthermore, he was far
too positive in his attitudes toward the twin devils of
Protestantism and the public school.[53] Ireland maintained in a
letter to Cardinal Gibbons that either his Catholic opponents did

[49]"State Schools and Parish Schools: Is Union Between Them Im-
possible?" *Journal of the Proceedings and Addresses of the NEA*, 1890,
XXIX (1890), 179–85. Reproduced in *Catholic Education in America: A
Documentary History*, ed. McCluskey, pp. 127–40.

[50]Burns, *The Growth and Development of the Catholic School System
in the United States*, p. 232.

[51]*The Social Ideas of American Educators*, p. 352. On this controversy
see Cross, *Liberal Catholicism*; Thomas Timothy McAvoy, *The Americanist
Heresy in Roman Catholicism, 1895–1900* (Notre Dame; Ind.: University
of Notre Dame Press, 1963); and Daniel F. Reilly, *The School Controversy, 1891–1893* (Washington, D.C.: Catholic University Press, 1943).

[52]Ireland wrote Gibbons: "I have found myself in a singular predica-
ment on this whole Faribault matter. I am between two enemies—one
Catholic; one Protestant. If I placate one I arouse the other." Reilly,
The School Controversy, 1891–1893, p. 86.

[53]The most vocal objectors included Bishop McQuaid of Rochester,
New York, Archbishop Corrigan of New York City, and some of the
priests and hierarchy of Wisconsin. Cross, *Liberal Catholicism*, pp. 22–50.

not understand his St. Paul speech or their opposition sprang
"from hatred of the American state."[54] In supporting his own
position against his Catholic critics Ireland appealed to such
Catholic writers as Thomas Bouquillon, Belgian-born theologian
at the Catholic University, who advanced the position that in-
herently the state had a right to insist upon certain educational
standards and levels of achievement among the population, and
hence challenged the traditional Catholic view that the state's
right was only substitutional in nature.[55]

Some of Ireland's opponents appealed to Rome for support.
He was fully conscious of the possible effects of a statement
from that source adverse to his own position or to the Faribault
Plan. "A public condemnation from Rome of the address would
set America in fury," he reminded Gibbons, because it would
appear to Americans to be an attack upon principles which
they "will not give up . . ."[56] The cardinal was as mindful as
Ireland of the possible effects of Roman condemnation of either
the speech or the plan. Thus he took pains to enlighten Pope
Leo on how Americans regarded their public schools and of
the general lack of sympathy among non-Catholic Americans
for Catholic views on education and the parochial school
system.[57]

In May of 1892 the Pope acted upon what had come to be
called "the school question" by reiterating "the sound decrees"
of the Third Plenary Council of Baltimore "as to parochial
schools" and indicating that the Faribault-Stillwater arrangement, "all the circumstances being taken into consideration, can
be allowed" (*tolerari potest*). Instead of resolving the growing

[54]*Catholic Education in America: A Documentary History,* ed. McCluskey,
p. 149; full letter, pp. 141–50. Ireland pointed out that one of his most
extreme opponents, Bishop Katzer of Green Bay—later Archbishop of
Milwaukee—"took publicly the position" that the state had no right to
pass school laws or to build schools while the parent had the right, if
he chose, "to bring up his child in ignorance, total ignorance." P. 144.

[55]*Education: To Whom Does It Belong?* November, 1891; see Reilly,
The School Controversy, 1891–1893, for full detail.

[56]Ireland letter to Gibbons, *Catholic Education in America: A Documentary History,* ed. McCluskey, p. 149.

[57]This letter is quoted in Ellis, *The Life of James Cardinal Gibbons,*
I, 664f.

controversy this apparently middle-of-the-road statement only encouraged each side to claim victory. Archbishop Corrigan of New York, Ireland's strongest opponent in high places, promptly announced that the Faribault system had been generally condemned by His Holiness while only the one special case had been excepted from condemnation.[58] Ireland, on the other hand, claimed victory for his system, and his suffragan, Bishop McGolrick of Duluth, optimistically predicted that the plan was "destined to be adopted in all the United States."[59] Finally, to clear up his position and to quiet controversy that was sharply dividing the American hierarchy and that also furnished good copy for avid editors of the secular press, the Pope sent a personal legate, Archbishop Francis Satolli, to meet with the American hierarchy.

Archbishop Satolli brought with him a set of propositions which reiterated Baltimore on the necessity for erecting Catholic schools and on the permissibility of attendance at public schools under circumstances deemed necessary by the ordinaries. These propositions then went on, in clear opposition if not open rebuke to the conservatives, to assert an obviously positive attitude toward public schools and to insist that the church must be most solicitous for the welfare of Catholic children attending those schools. Anyone, "whether bishop or priest," was strictly forbidden, "either by act or by threat," from excluding from the sacraments, "as unworthy, parents who chose to send their children to the public schools." And those in authority in the church were urged to work out with public school authorities, if possible, a suitable scheme for the religious instruction of those attending public schools. Preference was expressed for the sort of plan later to be labeled "released time." Finally, teachers in Catholic schools were encouraged to submit themselves for examination by the civil as well as the Church authorities.[60]

[58]See *Catholic Education in America: A Documentary History*, ed. McCluskey, p. 151.

[59]Cross, *Liberal Catholicism*, p. 142.

[60]"Archbishop Sattoli's Fourteen Propositions for the Settling of the School Question," *Catholic Education in America: A Documentary History*, ed. McCluskey, pp. 151–60.

While the tone and much of the content of these propositions seemed quite opposed to the position of the conservatives, they were not easily moved. Within a month of Archbishop Sattoli's presentation Bishop McQuaid wrote to Rome reiterating the old charges against the public schools—"indifferentism," promiscuous "association with all classes, Protestants, Jews, and infidels . . ." which threatened "contamination" of the faithful, and a "liberalism that borders on infidelity . . ." Using language similar to that which Hughes had used a half-century earlier, McQuaid asserted his conviction "that in this country the Catholic school was as necessary for the children as the Church was for them and their parents."[61]

The storms of controversy with regard to the public schools were far from past in Catholic circles. While Rome—especially in the person of Leo XIII—did appear to be quite sympathetic to American needs and conditions, as understood by the liberals, two pronouncements were subsequently made from that city which blunted the liberal thrust and had the effect of encouraging the continued development of a Catholic educational system and culture separate from the American mainstream. Leo's letter on "Americanism," addressed to Cardinal Gibbons in 1899, raised, by implication, serious doubts about the extent of possible rapprochement between the church and the public school system of America. The condemnation of "modernism" by Pius X in 1907 stifled free and open inquiry of the type which the liberals had supported. Together these two encyclicals had the effect of encouraging timidity and protectiveness in the intellectual life.

The Catholic liberals of the late nineteenth century were optimistic, confident, and outgoing in their outlook. In their experience, the "public spirit" of America was "fundamentally religious," not radically secularistic like that of some European countries, as Cardinal Gibbons told Rome.[62] Hence they identified with that spirit, with the best in American life and culture. They rejoiced in intellectual advance, wherever it

[61]Ibid., pp. 161–65. McQuaid letter to Pope Leo XIII, Rochester, December 13, 1892.
[62]Quoted at the opening of this chapter; see note 3, above.

occurred—whether in parochial or public schools. And they were confident that the faith itself would flourish in such an atmosphere. But the prevailing post-modernist mood came to be one of caution, of withdrawal into the relative safety of tried and tested ideas and practices. And the prevailing attitude toward the public schools, as toward much of American popular culture, tended to assume the shape of a kind of fortress or beleaguered mentality.[63]

It was clear by century's end that church religion had generally been denied a primary role in the common school, as Brown pointed out in his discussion of secularization. At the same time, however, it was also clear that Americans generally neither sought nor desired a public school atmosphere devoid of all religious influence. Neither radical atheism nor radical secularism flourished in the American body-politic. The common good appeared to require common commitments and involve common aspirations which were conditioned but not dominated by church religion. In their commonness they went beyond—or beneath—church religion, somewhat after the fashion of the "natural religion" of the eighteenth century or like that later "common faith" understood by some to emerge from the community itself as men live in vital relationship with each other. Hence the public piety sought and declared in and for the public school was neither church-religious nor anti-religious. But was it *un*-religious? Did it require the removal of all religion from the school? In the name of "a common faith," Dewey said "no" to "religion" and "yes" to "religious." We turn now to his resolution of the dilemmas posed in these past two chapters.

[63]On the post-modernist mood in Roman Catholicism see Thomas F. O'Dea, *The Catholic Crisis* (Boston: Beacon Press, 1968), pp. 68–87, and Alex R. Viller, *The Modernist Movement in the Roman Catholic Church* (Cambridge, England: Cambridge University Press, 1934).

V

Common School, Common Faith?

Issues and Trends in the Early Twentieth Century

"Ours is the responsibility of conserving, transmitting, rectifying and expanding the heritage of values we have received that those who come after us may receive it more solid and secure, more widely accessible and more generously shared than we have received it. Here are all the elements for a religious faith that shall not be confined to sect, class, or race. Such a faith has always been implicitly the common faith of mankind."

—John Dewey, 1934[1]

". . . the American people is conscious that its schools serve best the cause of religion in serving the cause of social unification . . ."

—John Dewey, 1908[2]

"The greater the proportion of our youth who fail to attend our public schools and who receive their education elsewhere, the greater the threat to our democratic unity."

—James Bryant Conant, 1952[3]

At the turn of the century the Reverend William D. Bliss, Episcopalian social reformer, suggested that there were four ways of viewing the relationship between religion and the public schools:[4]

(1) " . . . all Socialists and . . . radicals of almost every description . . ." held that the schools should have nothing to do with religion. Religion, to them, was a personal matter

---

[1]*A Common Faith* (New Haven and London: Yale University Press, A Yale Paperbound, 1964; 1st ed., 1934), p. 87.

[2]"Religion in Our Schools," reprinted in *Characters and Events*, II, 515.

[3]*Education and Liberty; The Role of the Schools in a Modern Democracy*, p. 81.

[4]*The New Encyclopedia of Social Reform*, 3rd ed. (New York and London: Funk and Wagnalls, 1910), pp. 1056ff.

which, if taught at all, should be confined to the home and the church.

(2) " . . . many Christians" contended that "the State is lost unless it teach morality, and that morality cannot be taught unless it teach religion . . ." Thus the schools must teach religion in some recognizable form.

(3) ". . . the majority of Roman Catholics" and a few others "go still further and say that morality cannot be taught except by giving the definite religious teaching which they hold true."

These first three positions had one thing in common, Bliss pointed out. All were based on a faith-commitment, on *a priori* assumptions about man, God, etc. All three pressed their views as matters of principle which transcended in importance the realities of the particular situation.

(4) There was, however, a fourth view or "method . . . perhaps, a compromise," by which the public school did not explicitly teach religion at all. Yet by the use of various devices, such as reading the Bible "more or less as literature" and the recognition of "the spiritual as a part of the universe to be studied as truly as the material," implicitly and by indirection, there was an acknowledgment of something of a religious nature. This method neither explicitly taught nor explicitly denied religion.

From Common Experience to Common Faith and Morals

The Bliss analysis is perceptive in its sensitivity to the element of compromise in handling the question of religion in the public schools and in its sense of the increasing importance of indirection, implication, generalization, and experience. The use of the Bible "more or less as literature" suggests the kind of category into which that common practice had fallen. Bible reading was not precisely literature in the same sense that reading of Shakespeare or Emerson was. Nor was it clearly religious instruction. It was somewhere in between, in a "more or less" limbo. But by many it was regarded as essential for moral reasons, for holding up what was most precious in our heritage, and for its "spiritual" content. And "spiritual" was a good word. It had the merit of seeming to say something positive and definite without actually being precise. And it offended hardly anyone.

In calling attention to this fourth "method" Bliss put his finger on what became the prevailing mood of the early twentieth century—toward experience and away from concepts, toward generalization from experience and away from stock verbal formulation or cultic practice, toward the common which emerged from experience and could be described by such generalized designations as community, social, values, spiritual, and even religious, as opposed to such specific designations as Christianity or Judaism or Catholicism or Protestantism, or even religion. This was a mood which stressed the organic nature of things. Dialectical tensions were relaxed; polarities— such as nature-supernature—were smoothed over. Life is one; life is all. Education is life; religion is life. Life is community. The individual emerges and develops in community. Man is essentially a social being. His values emerge from and must be constantly tested by life, by communal experience. Dogmas and doctrines, conceptual formulations, tend toward abstraction, away from life. They tend to impose unnecessary and even false rigidities upon experience. Still, man is religious. He aspires toward meaningful experience for himself and for others. He is loyal to his community and wishes to help it achieve noble ends. But organized, institutionalized religion threatens this religious spirit by seeking to confine it within pre-established categories.

In keeping with this mood the school was seen as being organically related to life and to the community. Its curriculum was life-centered. Its goal was to stimulate individual awareness and to achieve individual fulfillment in a communal context. School and society were two sides of one coin. While the school did not encourage the formal teaching of religion, its curriculum, daily life, and goal could be called religious. "There is no subject in the curriculum, there is no relation in the life of the school, which is not packed with potential divinity and may not make for morality," asserted Walter L. Hervey in an article quoted by Bliss to illustrate his fourth position. "Each study and each experience has its roots in the infinite, and this basic fact may be felt, may be seen, may be lived, without formal instruction therein."[5]

The American public school came of age in the early decades of the twentieth century, and with this maturity came even greater symbolic potency. Enrollments skyrocketed at a far more rapid pace than population growth. The percentage of the population in school increased dramatically. The public high school emerged as a new and crucially important institution. It continued and capped the work of the elementary school in socializing and Americanizing the youth. The comprehensive high school, offering a wide variety of subjects and experiences to students from every class, every ethnic and religious group, became the most important symbol of the unifying and democratizing role of the public school. In the American mind the public school became the primary institution of American democracy the cradle and bulwark of its liberties. It became a prime article of American faith to "believe in" the public school.[6]

Those who held the first three of the four positions mentioned by Bliss were not silent in the face of this dramatic growth and increasing symbolic importance of the public school. Some fought anything that smacked of religion in the schools, calling for complete secularization. They achieved little marked or

[5]The article appeared in *The Outlook*, February 10, 1906.

[6]Enrollments in public high schools rose from 80,000 in 1870 to 7,000,000 in 1940, a ninetyfold increase compared with a threefold increase in total population. Figures by Robert Ulich in *Crisis and Hope in American Education* (Boston: Beacon Press, 1951), pp. 10–11. See also Edgar W. Knight, *Fifty Years of American Education* (New York: Ronald Press, 1952), chs. ii, iii. On the comprehensive public high school see the report of the NEA Commission on the Reorganization of Secondary Education, *Cardinal Principles of Secondary Education*, 1918; the NEA Educational Policies Commission statement *Education for ALL American Youth, a Further Look*, 1952, especially ch. i; Conant, *The Child, the Parent and the State* (Cambridge: Harvard University Press, 1959), ch. iv, "The Transformation of the High School"; and Conant, *Education and Liberty*, pp. 60–63.

direct success in the first half of the century. Perhaps their most obvious triumph, if it can be called that, was the succesful challenge by Mrs. Vashti McCollum of a released-time religious-education program in Champaign, Illinois, in the mid-forties.[7] Most of those in Bliss' second grouping accepted and even contributed to the public school faith. They were pleased to profit from the emotional fallout that enhanced their American-ness. But Bliss was correct in distinguishing between this group and those described in his fourth category, even though the line dividing the two was quite indefinite. An articulate and often quite powerful group of Protestants continued to insist upon a measure of specificity in the religion–public school mixture. They urged upon the schools such practices as Bible reading, prayers, hymn singing, baccalaureates, religious holiday celebrations, and religious instructions, both in the form of released-time programs and accredited courses. They differed from those who stressed the religious value of the public school in and of itself.

Those in Bliss' third category, the individuals and churches who called for primary and secondary education under church control and in an atmosphere understood to be religious in a specific sense, were faced with the difficult task of justifying their endeavors and their point of view over against the public school faith. They too, as a compromise, often participated in released-time programs. In fact, official Roman Catholic attitudes underwent an interesting development in this period from suspicion and even rejection of obvious religious-education efforts in the public schools to open advocacy of these efforts.[8]

To illustrate his fourth category Bliss quoted extensively from the "Syllabus on Ethics" which had been adopted for use in the public schools of New York City. This document stressed the centrality of "moral education" in the work of the school. Such education was accomplished "not only in

[7]*Illinois* ex. rel. *McCollum* v. *Board of Education,* 333 U.S. 203 (1948). See also Vashti McCollum, *One Woman's Fight* (Garden City, N.Y.: Doubleday & Co., 1951).

[8]Those in Bliss' second and third categories are discussed more fully in Chapter VI.

formal instruction and training" but "in the general atmosphere and spirit of the class room and of the school." It depended considerably upon the personality of the teacher. And it involved such factors as the cultivation of "a sense of reverence" which "is vital to morality" and the development of a feeling of "social membership," an attitude of "loyal membership" in the family, the community, and the nation. Properly taught, any subject could contribute to the achievement of these ends. And through the accumulation of right experience after right experience, morality and loyalty would become internalized and the child would become a mature and responsible member of society.

Bliss was a social reformer. Like his fellow social-gospelers he naturally thought of morality when he thought of religion. Hence it was not strange that he should choose a "Syllabus on Ethics" to illustrate a type of relationship between religion and the public school.

This choice also indicated the increasing importance assigned to the moral task of the public school in this period. Moral education, declared E. B. Andrews in 1901 in considerable disregard of the nineteenth century, "is one of the splendid new tasks which the school of the twentieth century is to undertake and achieve."[9] In 1907 the National Education Association created a Committee on Moral Instruction in the Schools; this committee repeatedly affirmed the importance of its subject until it was replaced by the Committee on Training for Citizenship.

All could agree on the moral responsibility of the school, but it was not entirely clear just what this responsibility was or what it involved. A few communities, like the city of New York, drew up syllabi of ethics which generally called attention to high principles and all things good. Here and there efforts were made actually to instruct students in ethics or morals. But for the most part little of a direct nature was done about moral

[9]Quoted by Sister Mary of Saint Michael Hubner in *Professional Attitudes Toward Religion in the Public Schools of the United States Since 1900* (Washington, D.C.: Catholic University of America Press, 1944), p. 7.

instruction. The task was too large or too important or too vague to assign to particular courses or units of instruction. A more inclusive approach was needed and John Dewey furnished it.

DEWEY

Bliss did not allude to Dewey in illustrating his fourth type, but he might well have done so. Dewey, with greater force than any other figure in this period, argued for what he regarded as the essentially religious task of the school. This was a task which did not involve teaching religion, as Dewey understood it. Rather it was accomplished as the school became a living community out of which there emerged common morality and a common faith.

In Dewey's view, both faith and morals emerged from experience, or should emerge from experience. He set his view over against the view which allied faith and morals with a body of revealed truth handed down from a source that transcended human experience. Faith as he understood it—what he called "faith in its newer sense"—relied instead upon "the power of experience to provide, in its own ongoing movement, the needed principles of belief and action." Hence "a new and effective" morality or system of morals could "emerge only from an exploration of the realities of human association."[10]

Dewey, the foremost social ethicist as well as philosopher of education of his time, took on relatively early in his career the question of morality in the schools. In 1893 he pointed out that the interest in teaching ethics in the school was wider than ever. But alongside this great interest there existed among the experts "a general consensus . . . against teaching it." This was true because "ethics, rightly conceived, is the statement of human relationships in action." Hence the study of ethics should involve close study of human interaction and the endeavor

[10]"Credo," *Forum*, LXXXIII (March 1930), 176–82. Reprinted in *Living Philosophies,* by Albert Einstein and others (New York: Simon and Schuster, 1931), pp. 21–35; quotations from pp. 21, 32. On Dewey's understanding of faith see also *A Common Faith.*

to draw out or recognize generic elements. This was a point of view which Dewey repeated often and developed further, and which articulated well the emerging mood in the world of education. Lessons about morals were totally inadequate, he argued early in the century. They had nothing more to do with moral behavior or character "than information about the mountains of Asia." The notion that morals could be inculcated by direct instruction was a hangover from a closely knit authoritarian society in which a single view prevailed and in which a single group dominated. It also assumed too narrow and moralistic a view of morals. Dewey preferred a broader and, by his lights, more profound view which recognized that "in the last analysis," the moral and social "are identical with each other." Virtue is "to be fully and adequately what one is capable of becoming through association with others . . ." This was not so much taught through instruction as it was learned in the doing of it. The implication for the school was obvious: it must encourage the interaction of human beings and the development of self-consciousness about that interaction. Education which occurred in such an atmosphere was not a mere means to the moral life; it was such a life. "All education which develops power to share effectively in social life is moral."[11]

Long before William Whyte discovered what he called "the social ethic"[12] or David Riesman came upon "other-directedness,"[13] the school was being urged to socialize, to help people relate to each other and to the larger community, to develop a spirit of service which, in the words of the formulators of the "Cardinal Principles of Secondary Education," published in 1918, should "permeate the whole school,"[14] or, in the words of Dewey again, to provide those conditions which would "make

[11]"Teaching Ethics in High School," *Educational Review*, VI (November 1893), 313–21; "Theories of Morals" in *Democracy and Education: An Introduction to the Philosophy of Education* (New York: Macmillan, 1916), pp. 411–18; *Human Nature and Conduct* (New York: H. Holt and Company, 1922), pp. 295–96; and *Experience and Education* (New York: Macmillan 1938), p. 321.

[12]*The Organization Man*, 1956.

[13]*The Lonely Crowd*, 1953.

[14]P. 15. Cited in note 38, Chap. II, p. 61.

possible a permeating social spirit . . ." A school was to be judged by this test, Dewey urged: The "measure of the worth of the administration, curriculum, and methods of instruction" was the extent to which they were "animated by a social spirit." And, conversely, the absence of this atmosphere was "the great enemy of effective moral training."[15]

This is not to suggest that either Dewey or the formulators of the "'Cardinal Principles" maintained that one discerned right from wrong by observing what others did. They both had a sense of a larger community—the democratic community and, in the final analysis, the human community—to which the smaller community of the school was related. But one's fulfillment was understood to come through relationship to and service of these various communities. Democracy was equated with service by the NEA committee which formulated the "Cardinal Principles." And, as Professor Cremin has pointed out, Dewey saw democracy as "the persistent quest for the 'more perfect union,' a kind of social process of *e pluribus unum.*"[16]

Dewey set the stage for this twentieth-century emphasis on the socializing role of the school in his "pedagogic creed" in 1897 and in three lectures on "The School and Society" which he delivered to parents and patrons at the laboratory school of the University of Chicago two years later. "The school is primarily a social institution." It should become "an embryonic community" in which the teacher engages "not simply in the training of individuals, but in the formation of the proper social life . . ." and the child becomes consciously involved in the social process. This view of the school rested on Dewey's even more fundamental understanding of education generally as proceeding from "participation in the social consciousness of the race . . ." Hence "the only true education comes through the stimulation of the child's powers by the demands of the social situation . . ." He is stimulated to act "as a member of a unity," to emerge from narrow self-concern, "and to conceive

---

[15]Dewey, *Democracy and Education*, p. 415.
[16]Lawrence A. Cremin's summary of Dewey's *Democracy and Education* in *The Transformation of the School: Progressivism in American Education, 1876–1957* (New York: Alfred A. Knopf, 1961), p. 121.

of himself from the standpoint of the welfare of the group . . ."[17]
American educational history was viewed by Dewey as moving from individualism to an emphasis upon the social process and social aims, though in his judgment, it had not gone far enough in this direction. Thus he felt moved to advocacy, to "preach a gospel," as it were, and strong language often followed. In fact, he sometimes used the language of religion to reinforce his case. The teacher who was engaged in the socializing process was "always the prophet of the true God and the usherer in of the kingdom of God," he affirmed in his "Pedagogic Creed." The schools performed "an infinitely significant religious work" in bringing together children of "different nationalities, traditions, and creeds" and "assimilating them together upon the basis of what is common and public . . ." In doing this they promoted "the social unity out of which in the end genuine religious unity must grow." By serving "the cause of social unification," by developing an essential "state consciousness," the schools served best "the cause of religion." Indeed, under these conditions the schools were "more religious in substance and in promise" without any of the paraphernalia of traditional religion than they would have been with these.[18]

Such language might sound a discordant note in an ear sensitized by developments in Europe in the 1930's and 1940's to some of the implications of "state consciousness." But one must recall that this language emerged from a period when the unification motif seemed much in order in America considering the prevalence of sharp sectional, nationality, racial, and religious differences. Dewey wrote these words when the Civil War was still a common memory, when hundreds of thousands of immigrants poured into New York each year, when Jim Crow was becoming a pervasive and rigid reality, when Jews and

[17]*My Pedagogic Creed,* first published in 1897, reprinted by the Progressive Education Association (Washington, D.C., 1929), pp. 1, 3, 6, 17; *The School and Society* (Chicago: University of Chicago Press, 1899), first lecture, and especially p. 40.
[18]*The Educational Frontier* (New York and London: Century Co., 1933), pp. 32–35; *My Pedagogic Creed,* p. 17; "Religion and Our Schools," p. 515; and "Education as Religion," *The New Republic,* XXXII (September 1922), 64–65.

Irish "need not apply," and when even Norwegians and Swedes wrangled in Minnesota. Furthermore, Dewey was not exalting either the state or some sort of master race. (Some others were, as we shall see.) What he sought was "the great community."[19] As Christopher Dawson has pointed out, Dewey's great community was essentially a "spiritual community" based on "'the participation of every human being in the formation of social values.'"[20] Dewey held that "all positive values . . . emerged" from "human associations."[21] Hence "the great community" was one in which each individual could play a role. Democracy was understood as "participatory," to use a designation popularized many years later. It was not so much a form of government or even a system of values as it was a movement, a social process, a community, even a kind of church, in which all could be caught up and fulfilled. And the stress was on movement. Dewey's concept was dynamic; the community progressed. It progressed as men self-consciously contributed to its development, to its improvement, and to its reform.

Education became for Dewey, then, "the fundamental method of social progress and reform."[22] Its object was not to develop loyalty to predetermined forms and principles or commitment to a static system. Through it a youngster developed both community-consciousness and a dedication to community progress. By this means he helped achieve the greatest good of the greatest number as well as his own greatest good. The formulators of the "Cardinal Principles of Secondary Education" followed Dewey when they proclaimed that it was "the ideal of democracy that the individual and society may find fulfillment each in the other."[23]

Dewey's views of education, community, and democracy were, even by his own admission, religious. He likened his understanding of knowledge to what "the forefathers of some of us

[19]See Dewey's essay "The Search for the Great Community" in *The Public and Its Problems* (New York: Henry Holt & Co., 1927), pp. 143–84.

[20]"Education and the State," *The Commonweal*, LXV (January 25, 1957), 424. Dawson's analysis of Dewey's conception of education is very perceptive.

[21]*A Common Faith*, p. 74.

[22]*My Pedagogic Creed*, p. 15.

[23]P. 9. See note 32, Chapter II, p. 59.

called 'getting religion.' "[24] The youngster went through a kind of conversion process and henceforth devoted himself to the well-being and improvement of his community. And, in Dewey's view, the desired community was an almost mystical reality in which the individual would be caught up and made whole.

Dewey found something like this mystic community in his visit to the Soviet Union in the 1920's. He had associated Soviet communism too much with "intellectual theology, the body of Marxian dogmas, and too little with moving human aspiration and devotion," he reported in *The New Republic* in 1928. But during his visit he felt "as if for the first time" he might have "some inkling of what may have been the moving spirit and force of primitive Christianity." He found, perhaps with some envy and certainly with naïveté, that even the "intellectuals," who in most communities had a task which was "chiefly critical," in the Soviet Union had a role which was "total and constructive." They were "organic members of an organic ongoing movement."[25]

Dewey had a compelling vision of a wholeness which stretched from nature's smallest atom to the most distant galaxy. There were no radical disjunctures in this universe. Man was part of nature; men were one with each other; the individual found fulfillment in society; and the life of the community was a whole. What intrigued Dewey about the Soviet Union was that life there appeared to embody this unity. There was no sharp break between the sacred and the profane, no debilitating division between individual or groups of individuals and the community as a whole. Here apparently was a social movement which was "intrinsically religious" in its achievement of a life-enriching wholeness.[26]

Dewey was as determined in his pursuit of his vision as any

[24]"Religion and Our Schools," p. 511. Dewey's conception of education, Dawson pointed out, "was almost purely religious." Cited in note 20.
[25]"The Great Experiment," *The New Republic*, December 19, 1928, reprinted in *Characters and Events*, I, 422–31; quotations on pp. 426–27.
[26]Dewey described the social movement in these terms. Ibid., p. 426. On the sacred-profane distinction and its erasure see *A Common Faith*, p. 66. On Dewey's vision of wholeness see Frederic Lilge, "The Vain Quest for Unity: John Dewey's Social and Educational Thought in Retrospect," in *Dewey on Education: Appraisals*, ed. Reginald D. Archambault (New York: Random House, 1966), pp. 52–71.

prophet bent upon realizing the kingdom of God. In his determination he tended to cast aside all that impeded the achievement of wholeness. Dialectical tension was dropped from his method. Human life was without radical disjunctures, unmanageable burdens, or seemingly absurd necessities. Apparently insurmountable differences among men were glossed over.

The religious nature of Dewey's vision becomes especially evident in his treatment of traditional religion. He had little patience with the efforts of organized religious groups to influence the public school. In his article "Religion and Our Schools," published in 1908, Dewey warned that any effort to teach religion (i.e., church religion) in the common school constituted an importation of that which was both unnatural to vital human experience and divisive in its effects upon the community. As such, one might even say that it was un- or ir- "religious" because it would divert the school from the truly "religious" task of humanizing and communalizing Americans. What was needed in America was "a fuller religious consciousness" which would not be based on the supernaturalistic teachings of traditional or church religion but closely associated with "the state, the new science, and the new democracy."

The American tradition of the separation of church and state had a twofold object, Dewey maintained: (1) it put the denominations on their own, giving none an unfair advantage over others; and, even more importantly, (2) it was necessary in assuring "the integrity of the state against all divisive ecclesiastical divisions." The United States, fortunately, had become "a nation late enough in the history of the world to profit by the growth of that modern . . . thing—state consciousness." For its own well-being it could not allow institutional religion to detract unduly from this consciousness. Hence educators "rightly objected" to "sectarianism in the schools" because it "sapped . . . state consciousness . . . by the growth of factions."[27] Some thirty-five years after having written these words Dewey offered similar objections to the institution of a released-time religious-education program in New York City:

[27]*Characters and Events,* pp. 508ff.

This "introduction of religious differences into American life would undermine the democratic foundations of this country."[28] In his stress on communal values Dewey seemed to lend support to the prevailing nationalistic mood of his day. In fact, the logic of his position appears at times to point toward compulsory public school attendance. But it was foreign to Dewey's views to assume that the desired "state consciousness" could be achieved through legalistic devices. Furthermore, as is well known, he often found himself at odds with the super-patriots who sought to use the public schools as conduits for their particular notions and standards of "Americanism."[29]

Actually Dewey's notion of community did not necessitate the suppression of all group differences, and his "great community" was more than national in concept. At a time of great pressure toward a form of Americanization that sought to make all alike, Dewey expressly disavowed "the concept of uniformity and unanimity in culture" and "the theory of the Melting Pot." There was value in diversity, he held. "Hyphenism"—i.e., such designations as Irish-American and Jewish-American—should be welcomed insofar as it meant "extracting from each people its special good." In an article written in 1917 in support of Zionism, he argued that there "must be a recognition of the cultural rights and privileges of each nationality." He was using "nationality" in a broad sense to include language, literature, cultural ideals, moral and spiritual outlook, and religion. The cultivation of each group's "distinctive nationality" was definitely to be encouraged so long as this did "not become dangerous to the welfare of other peoples and groups."[30]

Dewey did not specify that point at which ethnic loyalty

[28]Quoted by Benjamin Fine in "Religion and the Public Schools," *The Menorah Journal*, XXXII (April 1944), 94.

[29]For Dewey's adverse comment on the Oregon compulsory public school act see "The School as a Means of Developing a Social Consciousness and Social Ideas in Children, *Journal of Social Forces*, I (Septemebr 1923), 515.

[30]"The Principle of Nationality," *The Menorah Journal*, III (October 1917), 203–08, and "Nationalizing Education," NEA *Addresses and Proceedings*, LIV (1916), 183–89, specifically p. 185.

might become divisive, but it is clear that he envisioned a happy symbiosis in which the individual would achieve fulfillment in the group, while maintaining distinctive individuality, and smaller groups would be functioning members of the larger society without being required to subordinate all elements of group identity. That element which was to hold the process together, aside from a common, elemental humanity, was a common faith which emerged from common experience and was expressed in common life together. This common faith transcended individual, ethnic, religious, and nationality lines. In the final analysis, it was a faith which had "always been implicitly the common faith of mankind."[31]

Few Americans matched Dewey in giving such eloquent and passionate expression to an evolving mood with regard to the nature of the public school and its role in the emerging "great community." He put into persuasive words and figures the inchoate feelings of masses of people. Many Americans longed for that "great community" of which he spoke. They felt a sense of urgency and challenge about the high calling of nationhood and democracy. And the public school easily became a target for their aspirations and a means for their programs.

In his understanding of community Dewey caught up a prevailing trend of his day. Professor Merle Curti has noted "a marked shift in emphasis" in American self-understanding after the Civil War. There was a movement "away from the older legalistic concept of the union to the organic theory of the nation." Citizenship came to be understood not only in a contractual sense but as becoming one with a living organism, taken up in and by a super person. The individual now realized his own identity and moral freedom through the nation.[32]

At its best this sense of identity with a community beyond oneself implied a living and affirmative relation with men all over the world. Here again, in his universalism Dewey high-

---

[31]*A Common Faith*, p. 87. Also *The Public and Its Problems*, pp. 154–55, and Merle Curti, *The Roots of American Loyalty* (New York: Columbia University Press, 1946), pp. 217–18
[32]Ibid., pp. 174–75.

lighted an existing element in the common American understanding of democracy as that form of life best suited for all mankind. However, this common understanding was often linked
with an American sense of world mission such as that so
eloquently articulated by such political leaders as Woodrow
Wilson. This sense of mission easily flattered the American
ego: we have a priceless possession which we magnanimously
share with others. Dewey resisted this kind of self-righteous
nationalism, but in so doing he did not represent a popular
position.

Dewey stood firmly on American soil. He was nurtured on
American confidence in education and he detected and aided
in the apotheosis of the public school. He was deeply rooted
in the "American democratic faith" and he described it with
eloquence. But he was not at ease in Zion. Rather he was a
prophet in this American Israel seeking to effect a truly
democratic community. He was a keen critic of much in
American educational theory and practice. He struck severely
at a common tendency to understand learning as a process of
pouring information into the mind like water into a glass. He
also sought to goad Americans out of their narrower provincial-
isms. But while he was not without honor in his own country,
many did not have ears to hear his critique.

Americanization and the Common School

With the movement toward what Curti called the "organic
theory of the nation" all of the skills and resources of the public
schools were called into use to accomplish a process of identification of the individual with American nationhood and democracy.
The school assumed a role comparable to that of the initiatory
rites of a primitive tribe.[33] In their zeal for the Americanizing
role of the school, and in keeping with a basic American belief
that nearly everything can be taught, state legislature after

[33] See Charles Edward Merriam, *The Making of Citizens* (Chicago:
University of Chicago Press, 1931), p. 17.

state legislature passed laws requiring that subjects thought to be especially fitted to inculcating patriotism, such as American history and civics, be taught in the public schools.[34] Patriotic organizations urged a variety of practices and literature upon the schools. Textbooks were written with an eye to Americanization.[35] Social studies emerged as a means for the "conscious and constant . . . cultivation of good citizenship . . ."[36]

The importance of the school's task was doubly underscored by the flood tide of immigrants in the early years of the twentieth century. In 1909 the U.S. Immigration Commission discovered that 57.8 percent of the children in the schools of thirty-seven of the nation's largest cities were of foreign-born parentage.[37] Under these circumstances, America looked "with anxious hope to the school as the chief instrument of Americanization."[38]

Writing at the time of this onrush of immigrants, Ellwood P. Cubberley, historian and philosopher of education, observed that these immigrants tended "to settle in groups or settlements and to set up their own national manners, customs, and observances." The task of American educators, he advocated, was "to break up these groups and settlements, [and] to assimilate or amalgamate these people as part of our American race . . ." Cubberley was more specific than Dewey. While the latter called for "state consciousness" and social unity, the Stanford professor understood assimilation in terms of "the Anglo-Saxon

[34]Most states had enacted compulsory school attendance laws already, in the nineteenth century. Mississippi in 1918 was the last state to enact such a law.

[35]Bessie L. Pierce found that from 1900 to 1917 "thirty-two states approved laws incorporating history and other social studies in the curriculum of the public schools." *Public Opinion and the Teaching of History in the United States,* p. 45. She also discusses the institution of such practices as flag-day observances and the pledge of allegiance.

[36]"The Social Studies in Secondary Education," *Report of the Committee on Social Studies of the Commission on the Reorganization of Secondary Education of the National Education Association,* U.S. Office of Education Bulletin No. 28, 1916, p. 1.

[37]Cremin, *The Transformation of the School,* p. 72.

[38]Frank V. Thompson, *The Schooling of the Immigrant* (New York: Harper & Bros., 1920), p. 1.

conception of righteousness, law and order, and popular government . . ."[39]

Others who understood Americanization in Anglo-Saxon and generally Protestant terms agitated for legislation designed to force all children into conformity with their image of what was American. In 1889 the legislature of Wisconsin passed the Bennett Law, which required every child between the ages of seven and fourteen to attend a school in his district for not less than twelve weeks. Under this law no school was acceptable unless it taught reading, writing, arithmetic, and U.S. history in the English language. This English-language provision drew strong protests from Lutherans and Catholics of German extraction, and as a result of pressures from them the law was repealed three years later.

In the aftermath of World War I similar statutes were enacted in several other Midwestern states. By 1919 several states prohibited the use of any language other than English as the language of instruction in the public schools. These statutes were directed chiefly at German. A Nebraska statute which applied to instruction in all schools made it a criminal offense to teach a foreign language to a child who had not completed the eighth grade or to teach in any language other than English. Under this act several teachers in Lutheran and Reformed parochial schools were convicted of teaching children the German language by the use of a collection of Bible stories. This conviction was reversed and the Nebraska law found unconstitutional by the Supreme Court of the United States.[40]

In the Pacific Northwest, often the destination of migrants from the Midwest, a similar anti-German sentiment developed during the war and then fed into a generally anti-foreign and specifically anti-Catholic mood in the early 1920's. In the state of Oregon, Scottish Rite Masons circulated in June 1922 an initative petition calling for submission to the voters of a compulsory education bill which would require all children between the ages of eight and sixteen to attend public schools. With

[39]*Changing Conceptions of Education*, pp. 15–16.
[40]*Meyer v. Nebraska*, 262 U.S. 390 (1923).

strong support from the Ku Klux Klan more than enough signatures were gathered to secure the popular vote in November
of that year.[41]

Advocates of the Oregon compulsory-public-school measure
argued that the assimilation of foreign-born and other elements
of dubious Americanness could best be secured in the public
schools. Foreigners must be stopped from setting up their own
schools and "thereby bringing up their children in an environment often antagonistic to the principles of our government."
Children of foreigners should be mixed with the native-born "in
the public school melting pot . . . while their minds are plas-
tic . . ." so that the "finished product" would emerge "a true
American." In fact, attendance of all children at the public
school was essential to the "perpetuation and preservation" of
American nationhood. "A divided school" could "no more succeed
than a divided nation."[42]

The Compulsory Education Bill became a central issue in the
Oregon gubernatorial campaign of 1922. Walter M. Pierce, the
Democratic candidate, strongly supported the bill. "I believe," he
declared during his campaign, that "we could have a better
generation of Americans, free from snobbery and bigotry if all
the children . . . were educated in the free public schools . . ."
As a consequence, Pierce received the support of those who
favored the bill.[43]

Private and parochial school interests strongly opposed the
measure, chiefly on the grounds that it interfered with their
property rights and with parental and religious liberty. A group

[41]David B. Tyack, "The Perils of Pluralism: The Background of the
Pierce Case," *American Historical Review*, LXXIV (October 1968), 74–98;
and Donald Lewis Zelman, *Oregon's Compulsory Education Bill of 1922*,
unpublished M.A. thesis, University of Oregon, 1964. Tyack maintains
that "there is much evidence that the KKK was using the Scottish Rite
as a front." P. 77.

[42]*Official Voters Pamphlet, Proposed Constitutional Amendments and
Measures . . . Submitted to Voters of Oregon at General Election*, Tuesday,
November 7, 1922, p. 23. These arguments were advanced chiefly by
Scottish Rite Masons. For arguments put forward by members of the
Klan see Tyack, "The Perils of Pluralism," pp. 79ff.

[43]The Medford *Clarion*, September 15, 1922. See Zelman, *Oregon's
Compulsory Education Bill of 1922*, pp. 127–28, and Tyack, "The Perils
of Pluralism," p. 91, n. 76.

of prominent citizens compared the bill with the "Prussian System" and the "Method of Bolshevist Russia" and maintained that it would "injure rather than aid the cause of education" and that it was "destructive of true Americanism." Objections were submitted for the official voters' pamphlet by various religious groups, including the Oregon and Washington District of the Evangelical Lutheran Synod of Missouri, Ohio, and other states, the Seventh Day Adventists of Oregon, the Catholic Civic Rights Association of Oregon, and twenty-five Presbyterian clergymen who felt called to speak out because "much of the propaganda" for the bill had "been conducted in the name of Protestantism . . ." According to one student of these developments, the Baptists were divided on the issue and the Methodists tried to remain neutral. Various Protestant groups formed an organization called the "Non-Sectarian and Protestant Schools Committee for Freedom in Education" to fight the measure.[44]

On November 7, 1922, the voters of Oregon elected Democrat Pierce, and they also approved the compulsory-school initiative by a vote of 115,506 to 103,685. The school measure played an important role in the election of Pierce in this heavily Republican state. The vote on the school measure itself represented a victory for those who wished to standardize Americanization through the public school. It is true that this was a relatively slim victory and, as we shall see, one that was soon to be denied by the courts. Nevertheless, it was a victory of some symbolic importance. As Professor David B. Tyack has pointed out, "Like prohibition, antievolution laws, and compulsory Bible-reading laws, the school monopoly bill . . . legitimized the values of a group through state action."[45] The Oregon measure also indicated the limits to which the Americanizing role of the public school could be taken when joined with or distorted by nativism and superpatriotism.

The Oregon Compulsory School Bill was slated to go into effect in 1926. In the meantime, however, the constitutionality of the measure was challenged. The Society of the Sisters of the Holy

[44]*Voter's Pamphlet,* pp. 25, 30; and Zelman, *Oregon's Compulsory Education Bill of 1922.*
[45]"The Perils of Pluralism," p. 91. See also pp. 75, 84.

Names of Jesus and Mary and the Hill Military Academy both initiated court action against it. Attorneys in the case used various species of the Americanization argument, the state attorneys defending the law on the ground that full Americanization required the mingling of all in the public school and the attorneys for the challengers urging that the denial of parental right of choice was not in keeping with American common law. Attorneys for opponents of the measure argued that logically the law must mean that children should either not be taught any religion or "should be trained in only one religion prescribed by the state and dictated from time to time by a majority of 'the voters of Oregon.' "[46]

The Supreme Court of the United States found the Oregon statute unconstitutional on the ground that it abridged the right of parents to direct the education of their children. The Court held that

> the fundamental theory of liberty upon which all govern-
> ments of this Union rest excludes any general power of
> the State to standardize its children by forcing them to
> accept instruction from public teachers only.

While the Court thus affirmed that the child is not "the mere creature of the state," it did not question

> the power of the state reasonably to regulate all schools,
> to inspect, supervise and examine them, their teachers and
> pupils; to require that all children of proper age attend
> some school, that teachers shall be of good moral character
> and patriotic disposition, that certain studies plainly essen-
> tial to good citizenship must be taught, and that nothing
> be taught which is manifestly inimical to the public
> welfare.[47]

Hence the rights of the state were clearly defined and delimited. Americanization might involve many things, but it must not require that all children attend the public schools.

[46]*Oregon School Cases: Complete Record* (Baltimore: Belvedere Press, Inc., 1925), pp. 239ff.
[47]*Pierce* v. *Society of Sisters*, 268 U.S. 510, 534, 535 (1924).

The Supreme Court decision in the Oregon case put a constitutional check on that kind of nativist drive which would have required that all children be initiated through the public school community. Nevertheless, the public school continued to be a primary target for self-appointed guardians of American purity. In this same period following World War I several states, under pressure from the KKK and other radical forces of Protestant fundamentalism, passed laws forbidding the teaching of evolution in the public schools. Such an obvious challenge to the "old-time religion" as that presented by Darwin was seen as a clear threat to the "American faith."

The Court decision in the Oregon case already reinforced the legal right of private and parochial schools to educate American youngsters. Still, in the eyes of a majority of the American people, American identity and purpose continued to be closely tied with the public schools. The comprehensive public high school in particular underwent a revolutionary development during this period. It now assumed in the public mind the kind of crucial role which had previously been assigned almost exclusively to the elementary school. During World War I public leaders soon recognized that "the shortest line to the people lay through the schools . . ."[48] Following the war, in thousands of communities all over the land, the public high school assumed increasing importance not only for socializing and Americanizing the youth but as a focal point of community identity and loyalty. The Commission on Reorganization of Secondary Education, in recognizing this function, pointed out that in America "The school is the one agency that may be controlled definitely and consciously . . . for the purpose of unifying our people." The high school most able to accomplish this purpose was the "comprehensive" or "composite" or "cosmopolitan" school which embraced "all curriculums in one unified organization" and accepted all qualified students regardless of race, religion, economic condition, or national background. This school, the commission argued, "should remain the standard type of secon-

[48]Edward H. Reisner, *Nationalism and Education Since 1789* (New York: Macmillan, 1929), p. 491.

dary school in the United States." It was "the prototype of a democracy" in which diversity existed within a larger unity.[49]

Summary: Unity and Multiplicity

The decisive formula of the early twentieth century was: the common school brings common experience which precipitates a common faith which is essential to the common welfare. The formula was not self-contained or self-evident in its detail. Common experience might be achieved through other means than the common school, although that institution appeared to be most conveniently available. Composed of various elements of patriotism and general idealism, the common faith appeared at times to be a bit vague and imprecise. Possibly that was of value because it encouraged breadth and inclusiveness.

In its more abstract form the formula appealed to both the nativist patriots and the professional educators. But they differed sharply over detail. To the patriot, "common faith" meant primarily "American faith"—i.e., loyalty to the nation, whereas the educators were more inclined to stress a humanistic and democratic idealism. Civic creeds and ceremonials played a large role in the patriot's understanding of the nature of the desired common experience in the common school, whereas the educators called more for "democracy in action" in the school. But both agreed on the importance of the common school.

Standing at the edge of the twentieth century, Henry Adams detected a movement, over the past seven hundred years, "from unity to multiplicity . . ." It was a rapidly accelerating movement in the ever-expanding universe discerned by science. So great were its implications for human life and values that if it were "prolonged one generation longer, it would require a new social mind."[50]

[49]"Cardinal Principles of Secondary Education," 1918, pp. 22, 26. See note 38, Chapter II, p. 61, for source. See Conant, *The Child, the Parent, and the State*, ch. iv.

[50]*The Education of Henry Adams: An Autobiography* (Boston and New York: Houghton Mifflin, 1918), p. 498.

Americans reacted variously to this onrushing multiplicity of the twentieth century. It posed a frightening threat to some, and they sought to seal themselves off from it within the fortresses of fundamentalist religion and narrow nationalism. While a few religious groups erected their own schools with such protective measures in mind, most Americans of this defensive mentality looked to the common, public school as the crucial structure within the fortress.

Some more venturesome Americans accepted the multiplicity as a reality to be faced soberly or an opportunity to be seized eagerly. The Harvard philosopher William James rejected the monistic philosophical systems of the past in favor of a "radical pluralism" which appeared to accord more with the realities of the age.[51] John Dewey also rejected past certainties to grapple with present realities. And he faced the twentieth century with the confidence that through vital experience the "new social mind" of which Adams spoke would be forthcoming. In fact, he devoted his life to developing that mind. Dewey differed from James, however. He saw beyond pluralism to a universe, the universe of "a common faith." He confidently discovered a new unity emerging from human experience. This was a grand vision, but it lacked the openness of James' "radical pluralism," an openness which the multiplicity of the twentieth century appeared to require.

Dewey and his followers in the progressive-education movement, while valuing human differences, did not evidence great ingenuity in dealing with hard-core value differences. Supernaturalism, for example, was dismissed as outmoded. In a sense, of course, they were right. The multiplicity of the twentieth century apparently foreclosed the possibility that any supernaturalistic system could adequately encompass the whole. But the progressives assumed that a naturalistic system could do what a supernaturalistic one could not. Hence there was no room for the supernaturalist within their universe. In school terms this meant that there was no place within the school for a clear acknowledgment of a supernaturalist position.

[51] *A Pluralistic Universe*, Hibbert Lectures at Manchester College on the Present Situation in Philosophy (New York: Longmans, Green, and Co., 1909).

There was another reason for excluding supernaturalism from
the common school: it was a divisive factor. The common school
must stress what was common and exclude that which divided.
This was essential to its very existence and to the general welfare.
Furthermore, the progressives tended to see a divisive influence
in private and parochial school systems. Twenty-five years after
the Supreme Court decision in the Oregon case, Professor John
L. Childs, a follower and Columbia University colleague of
John Dewey, criticized that decision for its implied encouragement of these school systems that, he claimed, standardized and
segregated "our children." The welfare of "the American community" required that all children "share in all experiences that
are essential to their becoming well adjusted and loyal members"
of it. And this meant that in "their formative years" American
children should spend "at least one-half of the compulsory
school period" in public schools.[52]

As the progressive education movement developed in the
early decades of the century, the leaders of that movement put
much emphasis upon experimentation in education. Often this
experimentation was carried on in private schools. Quite naturally, however, the experimenters wished to share both their
findings and their theories. And they developed a grand vision
of a common school system attended by all of the children of
the Republic. It was a vision that also followed logically from
the progressives' understanding of "common faith" emerging
from common experience. The implementation of the vision
required much of the public school and especially of the shapers
of the common experience. Was it possible to elicit "a common
faith" that was not monolithic in its value assumptions and
demands? As the progressive education movement declined in
vitality and influence, its leaders tended to become more and
more defensive about their value assumptions and about the
public school. By mid-century the vision of some of them was

[52]Address, "American Democracy and the Common School System,"
delivered before the Joint Conference on Jewish Education, May 29, 1949,
and printed in *Jewish Education*, XXI (1949), 32–37. See also Childs,
Education and Morals: An Experimentalist Philosophy of Education (New
York: Appleton-Century-Crofts, 1950), pp. 244–54.

directed increasingly toward a monolithic public (and secular) school image,[53] which accorded less and less with the realities of American life.

If the progressives sought to avoid supernaturalism, the protectionists hoped to nationalize it. Their "common faith" was a nativistically conceived and religiously buttressed nationalism. Since large elements of the population were excluded from this "common faith," it was, in reality, considerably less than common. Furthermore, the religious views of the protectionists looked increasingly anachronistic in a rapidly expanding universe, and their fanatical nationalism seemed increasingly dangerous in a rapidly shrinking world.

In actuality, then, although the progressives were indeed progressive in method and often in outlook, neither they nor the protectionists dealt adequately with the multiplicity of the twentieth century.

[53]See reference to John L. Childs above; John S. Brubacher, ed., *The Public Schools and Spiritual Values*, pp. 6, 83–84; Patricia Albjerg Graham, *Progressive Education: From Arcady to Academe; A History of the Progressive Education Association, 1919–1955* (New York: Teachers College Press, Columbia University, 1967); and "The Issue of Sectarianism," *Progressive Education*, XXVI (February 1949), the whole issue.

VI

Faiths and the Common Faith

Church Religion and the Public School to Mid-Century

"Religious education . . . is misconceived when it is regarded
as a branch of education. . . . It is rather education itself."
—Hugh Hartshorne, Yale religious educator,
1931[1]

Emphasis upon our "common religious faith" might "lead to a
new sect—a public school sect—which would take its place alongside the existing faiths and compete with them."
—American Council on Education statement,
1947[2]

"Mr. Darrow — Did you ever discover where Cain got his
wife? Mr. Bryan — No, sir; I leave the agnostics to hunt for her."
—*Tennessee* v. *Scopes*, 1925

Faiths in Transition: Trends in Protestant Thought

For a brief moment in 1925, American attention was riveted
on the little community of Dayton, Tennessee, where one John
Scopes, a high school biology teacher, was on trial for violating
the Tennessee anti-evolution law. In effect, the law itself was on
trial, as were also Darwin, Biblical literalism, and even the whole
American *Weltanschauung*. For more than half a century Americans had wrestled with evolution. Now in one last dramatic

[1]"The Relation of Religious to General Education," in *Studies in Education*, ed. P. Henry Lotz and L. W. Crawford (Nashville, 1931), as quoted
by John S. Brubacher, ed., *Eclectic Philosophy of Education: A Book
of Readings*, 2d ed. (Englewood Cliffs, New Jersey: Prentice-Hall, 1962),
p. 514.
[2]*The Relation of Religion to Public Education: The Basic Principles*,
Committee on Religion and Education (Washington, D.C., 1947), p. 15.

encounter between "old-time religion" and modernism, William Jennings Bryan, defender of Biblical faith, and the freethinking Clarence Darrow were locked in a seemingly gladiatorial contest. The trial brought into focus two apparently irreconcilable ways of looking at man and his universe. Darwinism—or a popular version of it—was the divide from which these views flowed their separate ways.

Darwin's *Origin of the Species,* first published in 1859, dealt a severe blow to religion in America. The notion of natural selection challenged the doctrines of creation and design. "Survival of the fittest" passed like an enormous shadow over the sunny landscape of divine goodness. The "descent of man" found Adam with animal forebears. While these ideas threatened some of the limbs of orthodoxy, it soon became evident to more perceptive observers that the very trunk itself was in danger. The whole Darwinian hypothesis subjected the Bible itself to serious questioning. And for Protestantism especially, the Bible was the source of truth.

Princeton's Charles Hodge, perhaps the ablest defender of Protestant orthodoxy in nineteenth-century America, recognized the danger signals immediately. Reading Darwin with care, he consigned natural selection "to the baggage of atheism," and sought to rally the forces of Christianity against it. The discerning scope by which Hodge scrutinized Darwinism and found it wanting was his own massive theological system which encompassed God and his creation as, according to Hodge's faith, disclosed by God in his book. Special creation, design, the uniqueness of man—all those truths controverted by Darwin— were found there. And at the foundation was Hodge's special form of Biblicism, his supreme confidence that the original manuscripts of the Bible were literally, word for word, true, inerrant, and infallible in every respect.[3]

[3]For Hodge on Darwin see *What Is Darwinism?* (New York: Scribner, Armstrong, 1874). For a summary of Hodge on Darwin see Stow Persons, *Evolutionary Thought in America* (New Haven: Yale University Press, 1950), p. 426. For Hodge's theology see Sidney Ahlstrom, "Theology in America: An Historical Survey," in *The Shaping of American Religion,* ed. James Ward Smith and A. Leland Jamison (Princeton: Princeton Uni-

Hodge's system became a rallying point for a form of conservative Protestantism which was prepared to do battle with anyone who challenged Biblical accounts. By the early years of the twentieth century this fundamentalist Protestantism, as it is often designated, was involved in mortal combat with Darwinism on every front, including—especially—the public school front. As the century advanced it picked up other enemies, including modernism, progressive education, and communism. In all of its expressions Biblical fundamentalism maintained that the Bible was essential to any education, and in its most extreme forms it held that book to be *all* that was necessary to a sound education. The Bible was, as the Great Commoner declared, all that one needed "to live by and die by."[4]

Hodge's anti-Darwinism by no means carried the day among Protestants. Many, animated by what B. J. Lowenberg called "the zeal of compromise," sought ways of bringing Darwin and Christianity together.[5] In the process God was brought down from the heavens to walk on earth with man, who now became his co-worker. Experience replaced revelation or became the primary mode of revelation as against the communication of propositional truths through a book. While the book itself was valued for its presumed high moral sentiments, its literary metaphors, and its accounts of the life and teaching of Jesus, it was no longer regarded as the sole source of religious truth. And the value of Scripture was to be determined by what it could do to enhance this life.

Professor Stow Persons has pointed out that evolutionism was most significant in its impact on American thought in shifting

versity Press, 1961), pp. 262–66; and *Theology in America: The Major Protestant Voices from Puritanism to Neo-orthodoxy,* ed. Sidney E. Ahlstrom (Indianapolis: Bobbs-Merrill, 1967), pp. 251–92.

[4]Bryan on the witness stand in the Scopes trial. For an able treatment of Biblical fundamentalism, Darwinism, and the public schools in a pivotal state see Williams B. Gatewood, Jr., *Preachers, Pedagogues and Politicians: The Evolutionary Controversy in North Carolina, 1920–1927* (Chapel Hill: University of North Carolina Press, 1966).

[5]"Darwinism Comes to America, 1859–1900," *The Mississippi Valley Historical Review,* XXVIII (December 1941), 356.

the focus of consciousness from origin and destiny to the present, and consequently in "shaping a world view as seen from the perspective of the present."[6] Those Protestants who attempted to adjust Christian thought to evolution and its consequences swung the scope around from God to man, heaven to earth, past to present. In the language of a later generation, *this* world was "where the action is." The present became the arena of Christian contest. The evils of existing society must be attacked and overcome. The past was to be judged by the present; the present marked the culminating point of the past. Modern ideals represented the fulfillment of past strivings. The kingdom of God became the kingdom of man; Christian ideals became democratic ideals. What Jesus was man was now becoming.[7]

The contrast between these two views which emerged within Protestantism in reaction to Darwinism can be clearly seen by putting Charles Hodge's *Systematic Theology* beside William Newton Clarke's *Outline of Christian Theology*. Clarke was a Baptist who occupied the chair of theology at Colgate Seminary (New York) for some years around the turn of the century. There in 1894 he first published his *Outline*. By 1914 this work had already passed through twenty editions and had become virtually the standard work in theology among liberal Protestants in America. Accepting and defending critical Biblical scholarship, Clarke turned to additional and, in his mind, equally important sources for his theology. These included science, other religions, and, above all, human history and experience. To know man was in a sense to know God since man is "a spiritual being," created in the image of God. This knowledge involved looking to man's past, present, and future. By so doing one discovered that "the great movement" of the evolutionary process "has steadily advanced" toward man and that this move-

[6]"Religion and Modernity," in *The Shaping of American Religion*, ed. Smith and Jamison, p. 378. This new point of view is commonly called "modernity."

[7]See Lyman Abbott, *Theology of an Evolutionist* (Boston and New York: Houghton Mifflin, 1897, p. 73. For a brief summary of this new mood see T. T. Munger, *The Freedom of Faith* (New York: Houghton, Mifflin, 1883), ch. i.

ment continues as man goes on toward the fullness of his
spiritual nature, i.e. as he becomes even more godlike.[8]

Clarke's style of Protestantism, sometimes called liberal, fitted
much more easily with the prevailing mood among leading
educational theorists of the early twentieth century than did that
of Hodge and his fundamentalist followers. Both the educators
and the liberal Protestant leaders agreed on the primacy of experience, the importance of group identity to individual fulfillment, and the urgency of social reform. For both, religion tended
to become generalized.

The coalescing of the sentiments of professional educators
and liberal Protestant leaders was evident institutionally in the
Religious Education Association. This association was founded
in 1903 on an interfaith basis, but in its early decades it was
dominated by Protestants. Among these was an impressive group
of college and university presidents—including Angell of Michigan, King of Oberlin, Rhees of Rochester, Harper of Chicago,
and Butler of Columbia—who played an important role in
getting the organization underway.

Speakers at the first convention of the Religious Education
Association included John Dewey, who must have thrilled the
participants with his statement that "the moral and religious"
were "the most fundamental of all educational questions . . ."
The members of the association and their like-minded colleagues
responded to Dewey in kind by wholeheartedly accepting
his view of education as being "experience centered." Subject
matter and facts about the Bible were to be replaced by "social
experience." Religious education came to be understood not as a
branch of education in either function or subject matter but
rather as "education itself." And "education itself" was understood as "participation" in "life itself." When the work of the
public schools was "well done," Walter L. Harvey, examiner for
the board of education of New York City, told this convention,

[8]William Newton Clarke, *An Outline of Christian Theology* (Cambridge:
John Wilson & Son, 1894), pp. 10–49 on the "Sources of Christian
Theology," and pp. 105f., 119f. on evolution as "the method of the
universe." See also Ahlstrom, "Theology in America: An Historical Survey,"
pp. 290–94.

it was "essentially and deeply religious . . ." Improving the work of the public schools, he concluded, brought "a forward step in religious education." Five years later at the fifth annual convention, Henry F. Cope, general secretary of the association, defined religion as "the life of ideals" and urged that far more could be accomplished religiously "through the organization and life of the school" than through efforts to present "religion as a subject itself." At that same convention Professor Clyde W. Votaw of the University of Chicago maintained that the aim of the public schools was religious because they sought to promote the same "ideal of life" which was the essence of religion. Religion meant not primarily holy book, ecclesiastical organization, creed, ritual, and emotionalism, but "reverence, trust, obedience, faith-fulness, industry, sincerity, honesty, truthfulness, righteousness, justice, purity, honor, kindness, sympathy, helpfulness, health, and happiness." Obviously these qualities were central to the task of the public school.

The psychologist of religion E. D. Starbuck, who was very active in the Religious Education Association and whose works were widely influential among religious educators, expressed the immanentist or naturalistic view in perhaps its most complete form when he argued that if the law should forbid the teaching in the schools of nearly everything that was conventionally regarded as "religion," the religious life of the children would not suffer. In fact, "it might even prove a blessing" in bringing about the realization that "the entire life of the school" could "contribute to the religious life" of the child.[9]

Most religious educators continued to use the conventional language of religion. But for many this language was little more than a convenient vehicle for conveying their newly discovered ideas. They were fond of distinguishing between two kinds of religion—the old and the new, dogma and life, truth from the

[9]*Proceedings* of the First Annual Convention of the Religious Education Association, 1903, pp. 16, 59, 67–68; *Education and the National Character, Proceedings* of the Fifth Annual Convention of REA, 1908, pp. 167–70, 220–30; Starbuck, "Moral and Religious Education—the Sociological Aspect," *Religious Education,* III (February 1909), 205; Hugh Hartshorne, "The Relation of Religious to General Education," in Brubacher, *Ecletic Philosophy of Education,* pp. 514–15.

outside vs. truth "realized in an inner experience," the "performance of rites and ceremonies" opposed by a "discovery of kinship with the eternal," God as transcendent to the world over against "the immanent God, whose authority is internal and identical with the laws of self-realization."[10] God remained —in the smiling countenance of human happiness. Jesus lingered —as the best of men. Apart from that thin thread of language that tied them tenuously to the historic Christian heritage, these men expressed a view of religion which was almost identical with that of John Dewey. Vital experience was what mattered most. Education must aim at that, enabling the young to sense their oneness with each other and to aspire toward the fullness of humanity.

The formula went something like this: religion equals life; authentic education equals education in life; hence religious education equals education in life or general education. One might refine it further by adding that education in life means education in community and, specifically, in democratic community. When pushed to be more specific than life in general, the liberal religious educators tended to gravitate more toward common than church religion. Democracy, maintained one of the ablest of the theorists, Professor George A. Coe, is the mark of the special character of American religion. "We are striving after a democratic God. . . . We Americans are asking whether a revelation of God cannot be found in the ordinary things of the common day of the common man; whether the authority of Almighty God cannot be expressed in terms of the . . . common good . . ." Speaking to the fifth annual convention of the Religious Education Association in 1908, Coe heralded that organization as "an expression of the moral and religious aspirations of democracy."[11]

---

[10]These phrases are quoted from George A. Coe, who was one of the leading figures in the religious-education movement. They are typical of the phraseology and concepts used by those who were a part of that movement. See Coe, *Education in Religion and Morals* (Chicago: Fleming H. Revell, 1911), pp. 389–90.

[11]*Education and the National Character, Proceedings* of the Fifth Annual Convention of the REA, 1908, pp. 91–92. Cf. Coe's *Social Theory of Religious Education,* which was published in 1917, just one year after

A generation later, in 1940, when the war clouds loomed large in Europe and cast a distant shadow in America, the thirty-seventh annual convention of the Religious Education Association devoted its discussions to the interrelationship between religion and democracy. It was seriously debated whether or not the two were identical. Many held that they were and that the religion which should be taught in the public schools was "the religion of democracy."[12]

But church religion was not easily abandoned, even by liberal Protestants. William Newton Clarke outlined what he regarded as *Christian* theology. As the century advanced it became more common to speak of the religions of democracy (Judaism, Catholicism, and Protestantism) rather than the religion of democracy. While some Protestant religious educators enthusiastically embraced Dewey, the majority of Protestants wanted something more exact than experience, more precise than education in general, and more marketable than life. And while most Protestants accepted the public schools as their own, they were jealous for a more recognizable religious influence than that which seemed to emerge from Dewey's vitalism. They eagerly cultivated such devices as Bible reading, released-time religious education, and accredited courses in religion to achieve this influence.

Bible Reading in the Schools

For many, regular Bible reading remained as the most significant hard-core evidence of religion in the public school. It had been common practice in the nineteenth century to open the school day by reading a few verses from the Bible. This was often accompanied by prayer and the singing of a hymn.

Dewey's *Democracy and Education,* and which did for the religious-education movement what Dewey's work did for the progressive-education movement.

[12]As reported in Hubner, *Professional Attitudes Toward Religion in the Public Schools of the United States Since 1900,* pp. 117–18.

The Protestant church historian Philip Schaff observed in the mid-1880's that "at least four-fifths of the public schools in the United States" observed this custom.[13] Surveys of major cities by the U.S. Commissioner of Education in 1896 and 1903 found that in approximately 75 percent of the school districts responding the Bible was read regularly.[14]

Bible reading in the public schools received even more formal public attention in the twentieth century than it had in the nineteenth. While the practice continued apace—often still accompanied by prayer and, less frequently perhaps, by hymn singing—legalization of it also increased markedly. At the beginning of the century only one state *required* Bible reading in its public schools; in the two decades following 1913 legislation making Bible reading mandatory was passed in twelve additional states. By mid-century thirty-seven states required, permitted, or condoned Bible reading in the schools. (It was formally not permitted in only seven states.) One indication of the incidence of formal community attention to Bible reading can be found in the fact that when Dean Alvin W. Johnson of the University of Minnesota did his study of church-state relations in the early 1930's, he devoted more than one-third of his 330-page volume to this question. While the Supreme Court of the United States did not adjudicate a case directly involving Bible reading in the public schools until 1963, when it declared this practice unconstitutional in the *Schempp* case, the courts of twenty-one states had ruled on the question earlier. Most of them had accepted the practice as being constitutional. In a survey made in 1946 only eight state superintendents of schools answered in the negative when asked whether Bible reading was permitted in their states. One student found in the late 1950's that Bible reading was conducted regularly in 42 percent of the school districts of the United States.[15] On the basis of this and

[13]*Church and State in the United States*, p. 75, quoting E. E. White, superintendent of schools in Cincinnati.
[14]"Bible Reading and Religious Exercises in the Public Schools," *Report of the Commissioner of Education* (U.S. Office of Education, 1903), II, 2445.
[15]Alvin W. Johnson and Frank H. Yost, *Separation of Church and State in the United States* (Minneapolis: University of Minnesota Press, 1948),

other evidence the Jewish legal scholar Leo Pfeffer concluded that at the time of the *Schempp* decision in 1963 probably between "a third and a half of the public schools in the nation opened their daily sessions with reading without comment from the Bible."[16] While this is a much lower percentage than Schaff's estimate of four-fifths seventy-five years earlier, considering the enormous increase in schools and enrollments it is still an impressive figure.

Bible reading has probably received more general support among Protestants than any other device designed to bring religion into the schools. It has appealed to individuals and groups across the entire theological spectrum and to both layman and clergyman, denominational executive and man in the pew. Protestant spokesmen from William Jennings Bryan to Harry Emerson Fosdick could agree on the value of Bible reading even though they were completely at odds in interpreting what they found in the book.[17] The Bible has had high symbolic intensity for most Protestants and thus has elicited considerable emotional fervor. It is "the Good Book"; few could, with impunity, raise strong objections to reading it.

Opposition to Bible reading in the public schools has come chiefly from Roman Catholics, Jews, agnostics, and atheists. Roman Catholic opposition was strong well into the twentieth century. It was based chiefly on the fact that the King James version of the Bible was the one most commonly used where the practice prevailed. Between 1890 and 1929, Catholics were

---

p. 33; Donald E. Boles, *The Bible, Religion, and the Public Schools,* 3rd ed. (Ames: Iowa State University Press, 1965), pp. 53, 58; Johnson, *The Legal Status of Church-State Relationships in the United States* (Minneapolis: University of Minnesota Press, 1934); National Education Association, *The State and Sectarian Education,* pp. 26–27, as cited by Leo Pfeffer, *Church, State, and Freedom* (Boston: Beacon Press, 1953), p. 382; R. H. Dierenfield, *Religion in American Public Schools* (Washington, D.C.: Public Affairs Press, 1962), p. 51.

[16]*Church and State in the United States* by Anson Phelps Stokes and Leo Pfeffer (New York: Harper & Row, 1964), p. 372.

[17]Fosdick, "Shall American School Children Be Religiously Illiterate?" *School and Society,* LXVI (November 29, 1947), 401–06. See Johnson, *Legal Status of Church-State Relationships,* pp. 110–13, for a discussion of organized efforts to get Bible reading into the schools.

the plaintiffs in four major court cases in which use of the King James version in the public schools was judged to be unconstitutional.[18] By mid-century, however, a distinctive change had occurred in the position of the Roman Catholic hierarchy on this and other religious practices in the public schools. And during the past twenty-five years Roman Catholics have ceased to be as active in opposition to Bible reading in the schools as they once were. (See Chapter VIII.)

"Released-Time" Religious Education

While Bible reading attracted more widespread support than did any other device for getting religion into the public schools, many within the organized faiths felt that it did not go far enough. The daily reading of a few verses without comment— even if followed by prayer—did not seem to contribute much to the child's religious education. More was needed to preserve the religious heritage and to keep the nation from succumbing to secularism. The institutional forces of church religion—and especially those of Protestantism—were mobilized to meet this need.

Organized denominational and interdenominational pressures for a share of public school time began early in the twentieth century. Recognizing that the one hour of Sunday-school time per week was not adequate for achieving a proper religious education even for those who attended, church spokesmen turned to weekdays and to the public school for additional time. Arguments used to justify this move ranged from the claim that the churches had an "inherited and inherent right" to a share of the student's time equal to that of the state to the affirmation of the necessary role of religious education in assuring the well-

[18]*Weiss* v. *District Bd.*, 76 *Wis.* 77, 44 *N. W.* 967 (1890); *People* ex rel. *Ring* v. *Bd. of Educ.*, 245 *Ill.* 334 (1910); *Herold* v. *Parish Bd. of School Directors*, 136 *La.* 1034, 60 *So.* 116 (1915); and *State* ex rel. *Linger* v. *Weedman* et al., 226 *N. W.* 1348 (1929). For a brief discussion of these cases see Robert F. Drinan, S.J., *Religion, the Courts and Public Policy* (New York: McGraw Hill, 1963), p. 92.

being of the community. Even the terminology reflected the variable tenor of the arguments. "Cooperative weekday religious education" seemed the most neutral form of description. However, the shorthand form that caught on—"released time"—is a designation which implies priority for the state's claim to the time of the young and beneficence on the part of the state in granting a portion of that time to the churches. This, of course, is an accurate description of the prevailing mood of both the public and most Protestant church leaders. (I use "released time" to refer to any program which involves the use of a certain portion of the normal school day for denominationally or inter-denominationally sponsored programs in religious education, conducted either on or off school premises, and attended by children upon parental request while nonparticipating children remain in "regular" or secular school activities.)

In 1905 the Inter-Church Conference on Federation, which brought together representatives of thirty Protestant denominations with a combined total membership of seventeen million, called upon "the public school authorities of the country . . . to allow the children to absent themselves without detriment from the public schools on Wednesday, or on some other afternoon of the school week, for the purpose of attending religious instruction in their own churches . . ."

An allotment of 8 percent of the school time was regarded as "not an immoderate allowance." Three years later this proposal was carried by its chief architect, the Reverend George U. Wenner, to the constituting assembly of what was to become the most significant Protestant interdenominational organization of the first half of the twentieth century, the Federal Council of Churches. After toning down all suggestion of the rights of churches over against those of the public schools and eliminating specific references to a percentage of time, the delegates moved to invite the National Education Association and the Religious Education Association to join them in investigating "ways and means to promote weekday religious instruction."

While this proposal to support a cooperative arrangement with the public school for purposes of religious education won the overwhelming support of the assembled representatives of various

Protestant bodies, there were some delegates who objected to it. They argued that the proposal infringed upon the separation of church and state, that, if effected, it would introduce a divisive element into the public schools which were "the greatest unifying force among us," and that the majority was actually imitating the Roman Catholic Church in claiming "the right to interfere with the public schools and public school funds . . ."[19]

These developments reveal the peculiar dilemmas confronting Protestantism in dealing with the young. While generally discarding full-time religious schools, Protestantism had advanced on several educational fronts in the nineteenth century: support of the common school and common Prostestantism or "common religion" therein; development of voluntary, nondenominational organizations such as the Sunday School Union and the International Sunday School Association; and establishment of denominational machinery for religious education. Now none of these fronts could report the kind of success that many Protestants desired or that the American situation seemed to require. Common Protestantism could not escape the impact of an increasing pluralism; what remained in the public school was often quite nebulous and ran counter to denominational self-interest. While the nondenominational Sunday-school movement had enjoyed periods of success, it was now declining in vigor. Because of this decline, and because this movement also sometimes thwarted the denominational urge, the denominations had developed their own educational organizations.[20] But the work of these organizations was insignificant when compared with the massive accomplishments of the public schools. And aside from a few culturally monolithic areas such as the South, no Protestant denomination had sufficient influence to succeed in gear-

[19]Elias B. Sanford, ed., *Report of the First Meeting of the Federal Council of the Churches of Christ in America held in Philadelphia, 1908* (New York: Revell Press, 1909), pp. 115–19, 278, 286–87. See Wenner, *Religious Education and Public Schools* (New York: Bonnell, Silver & Co., 1907), for an elaboration of the proposals and a discussion of objections to them.

[20]On the Sunday-school movement and denominational organization see W. S. Hudson, *American Protestantism* (Chicago: University of Chicago Press, 1961), pp. 118–19 and 162–63.

ing its own religious-education program into public school machinery.

Federation or interdenominational cooperation seemed, then, to offer greater strength in approaching the public school. Admittedly, it would reduce denominational distinctiveness, but it could enhance a kind of generalized Protestant stance. At the same time, it seemed a more plausible way than a strictly denominational approach of carrying out declared responsibility for the welfare of the total community. This is illustrated in one of the chief stated objectives of the Federal Council of Churches: "to secure larger combined influence for the churches of Christ in all matters affecting the moral and social condition of the people, so as to promote the application of the law of Christ in every relation to human life . . ."[21] Cooperation in weekday religious instruction was one way of carrying out this purpose.

A significant further step was taken in the mobilization of Protestant educational forces with the organization in 1922 of the International Council of Religious Education. This organization brought together various denominational boards of religious education, the International Sunday School Association, and some of the remaining regional associations and councils of the Sunday-school movement. It became the chief national body for mobilizing Protestant efforts to develop religious instruction in cooperation with the public schools. The appointment of a field secretary of the National Education Association as the first general secretary of the International Council served to highlight this interest. In his acceptance address to the founding convention, Hugh S. Magill stressed "the joint responsibility of the church and the public school in the preparation of citizens for a democracy . . ."[22]

Concern for weekday religious education was given further focus by the International Council in 1942 with the establish-

---

[21]Ibid., p. 164.

[22]On the International Council of Religious Education see William Clayton Bower and Percy Roy Harward, *Protestantism Faces Its Educational Task Together* (Appleton, Wisc.: Nelson Publishing, 1949), p. 20 (Magill quotation); H. Paul Douglass and Edmund deS. Brunner, *The Protestant Church as a Social Institution* (New York: Harper & Bros., 1935), pp. 267–68; and the *Records of Zorach v. Clauson*, 343 U.S. 306 (1951).

ment of a separate department for that work. Dr. Erwin Shaver, first director of the department, articulated well the historical concerns of Protestantism. Weekday religious education was one of the best devices for getting "religion into life." The "released-time" approach had "both psychologically and in its teaching program identified religious ideals and knowledge with the week-day as well as Sunday." Religious education was now regarded by students "as a 'subject' of importance and worth." The plan also had achieved remarkable success in "reaching the un-reached." Dr. Shaver rang the changes on this missionary theme again and again. Finally, weekday religious instruction had en-hanced the students' sense of spiritual values and moral respon-sibility and thus had tended generally to raise the tone of the whole community.[23]

Credit for instituting the first formal "released-time" program in a local community is usually accorded to Gary, Indiana, where, as a result of ministerial initiative leading to consultation with school superintendent William Wirt, a program was started in the 1914–15 school year. Under this program 619 pupils left the public schools to attend church schools—seven Protestant and two Jewish—on public school time one hour each week. Chil-dren who did not attend church schools remained at the public schools for a play period. The public school machinery was not utilized for the program beyond releasing at the stated time the children whose parents had agreed to their participation, and keeping some attendance records.

Superintendent Wirt's rationale for suggesting and supporting this type of program grew out of his much publicized and widely acknowledged "Gary Plan," under which an effort was made to involve as many segments of the community as possible in the process of education and to relate the schools to all aspects of community life. Under this plan, as John Dewey observed, children were "learning citizenship by being good

[23]As quoted by Pfeffer, *Church, State and Freedom,* pp. 327–28. See also Shaver, "The Movement for Weekday Religious Education," *Religious Education,* XCI (January–February 1946), 6–15. The International Council was one of the Protestant interdenominational agencies that was merged into the National Council of Churches in 1950.

citizens." It seemed logical, then, that in the process they might learn something about their churches by participating in the life of those institutions.[24]

Once started, this type of program apparently caught on quite rapidly. The *Christian Century* reported in 1926 that while only five cities provided for released-time programs in 1919, this number had increased to eighty by 1922 and to "at least 1,000" by 1925. This estimate seems grossly exaggerated, perhaps being based more on Protestant enthusiasm for the released-time approach than on careful analysis of what was actually going on. A more reliable figure is that reported by Mary Dabney Davis in a study conducted under the auspices of the Office of Education in the early 1930's. Miss Davis found that out of 2,043 cities answering an inquiry only 218 had released-time plans of some sort, and 82 percent of those reporting had never had plans. A follow-up survey conducted by the same investigator in 1940 revealed considerable increase in the number of programs adopted during the 1930's.[25] By the time a case dealing with a released-time program in Champaign, Illinois, had reached the Supreme Court of the United States in 1947, the number of released-time programs had reached quite impressive proportions, although still involving a relatively small minority of the nation's schools. In his concurring opinion in the *Mc-Collum* case Associate Justice Frankfurter accepted figures reported in the 1947 Yearbook of the International Council of Religious Education as being "responsible." The editors of the

[24]It was after ministerial complaint that the "Gary Plan" usurped too much of the time of school children that the released-time program was instituted. See William M. Wirt, "The Gary Public Schools and the Churches," *Religious Education*, XI (1916), 221–26. Also Arlo A. Brown, "The Week-Day Church Schools of Gary, Indiana," *Religious Education*, XI (1916), 5–19. For Dewey, see *Schools of Tomorrow* (New York: E. P. Dutton and Co., 1915), p. 200. The "Gary Plan" was started in 1907. Dewey did not mention the released-time aspect of the program. One of the best available discussions of released time, with bibliographical suggestions, is that found in Justice Frankfurter's concurring opinion in *McCollum* v. *Board of Education*, 333 U.S. 203, 223ff. (1947).

[25]*Christian Century*, XCIII (January 28, 1926), 123; Mary Dabney Davis, *Week-Day Religious Instruction*, U.S. Dept of Interior, Office of Education, Pamphlet No. 36, 1932; *Week-Day Classes in Religious Education*, U.S. Office of Education, Bull. No. 3, 1941.

Yearbook found almost 2,000,000 youngsters in some 2,200 communities participating in released-time programs.[26] Analyzing the
International Council of Religious Education figures along with
others, Leo Pfeffer concluded in the early 1950's that the former
were inflated. He estimated that approximately 5 percent of the
children in the nation's public schools (around 1,200,000) were
involved in released-time programs in 1947.[27]

Through much of the early part of the twentieth century
support for released-time religious education came primarily
from Protestants—as individuals, in denominations, and in association with "ecumenical" or interdenominational organizations.
Protestant promoters of released time were always enthusiastic
and sometimes extravagant in their claims for it. Floyd S. Gove
asserted in the mid-1920's that the "use of public school time"
for religious education was "making for greater unity in national life. . . . Absolute separation of church and state" was
"giving place to a new spirit of cooperation." Fifteen years later
Erwin Shaver of the International Council of Religious Education stated that released-time programs had "succeeded in reaching on the average one third of the neglected half of our children
and youth . . ." This was indeed "a remarkable evangelistic
record . . ." The Protestant theological scholar William Adams
Brown found in the early 1930's that all Protestant communions
"except the Unitarian-Universalist group" thought that "school
credit should be given for religious instruction, that it should
be given on school time, and the use of school buildings for the
purpose should be permitted . . ." Protestants banded together
to institute or support programs in released-time religious
education through local councils of religious education, ministerial groups, and ad hoc committees, as well as through the
International Council on Religious Education.[28] While details

[26]333 U.S. 203, 224.
[27]*Church, State and Freedom*, p. 320.
[28]Gove, *Religious Education on Public School Time* (Cambridge: Harvard University Press, 1926), pp. xv, 111, 118; Pfeffer, *Church, State and
Freedom*, pp. 328, 635, quoting Shaver; Brown, *Church and State in
Contemporary America* (New York: Charles Scribner's Sons, 1936), p. 162.
Douglass and Brunner found in a survey of "representative cities" in 1930
that cooperative Protestant work almost always included a committee for
weekday religious education: *The Protestant Church as a Social Institution*,
pp. 164–65.

varied, the usual pattern was one in which a local committee or council of Protestants, often with help from the International Council, endeavored to secure the support of as many religious leaders in the community as possible and hence to approach school officials with something like a united front. In fact, school officials frequently required this evidence of consensus before they would participate in a cooperative arrangement. Religious leaders who had serious reservations about these released-time efforts were sometimes subjected to pressures—subtle or open. An attempt was made to build up a kind of bandwagon psychology. Released-time was portrayed as something which could benefit each and all; it advanced group self-interest and it contributed to the welfare of the children and the whole community.

Despite efforts to secure cooperative support of released-time programs across faith lines, clear-cut interfaith sponsorship apparently was not commonly achieved.[29] Protestant denominations at both ends of the theological spectrum—such as the liberal Unitarians and the conservative Missouri Synod Lutherans—rarely joined in cooperative sponsorship of released-time programs. Jewish groups either refused to participate or, at most, gave reluctant support. And the attitude of the hierarchy of the Roman Catholic Church changed from stand-offish in the early part of the century to wholehearted participation by mid-century.

Jews had ample reason out of their own historical experience for being suspicious of Christian education associated with state schools. Hence they tended to stress complete separation of church and state in education while eagerly embracing the secular public school. At the same time, however, the survival of Judaism and of the Jews as a distinctive people appeared to require education of the young in Jewish religion and culture. In part because of this necessity and also in response to pressures from the majority religious community, rabbis sometimes agreed to participate in released-time programs. It is interesting, for

[29]Among the 194 sponsoring agencies described in one study only five were interfaith committees. Lois V. McClure, "Weekday Religious Education at the High School Level," *Religious Education*, XCVI (November–December 1951), 348.

example, that Jews participated in two of the most often mentioned released-time programs—the one at Gary in 1914–15 and
the one in Champaign in the early 1940's. Nevertheless, Jewish
pronouncements on the subject tended to stress that released-
time programs should be conducted off school premises and
should involve no use of public school machinery beyond the
dismissal of the designated students at the specified hour. The
Jewish community, asserted Ben Rosen in 1947, is "definitely
opposed to specific religious instruction as part of the public
school curriculum."[30]

Educational concerns of the officials of the Roman Catholic
Church were focused almost entirely upon the church's own
school system in the early years of the century. There the
child's education was understood to be permeated by religious
influence and directed by religious teaching. At the same time,
church authorities held that the public schools should not engage
in religious instruction because, as the fathers of the Third
Plenary Council of Baltimore had put it in 1884, "it does not
lie within the province of the State to teach religion."[31] In
keeping with this point of view Catholic churchmen had often
been involved in efforts to remove sectarian (Protestant) practices from the public schools. However, these attitudes changed
as it became apparent that at least half of the children and
youth of the church were attending public schools. In a pastoral

[30]Jewish participation in the Champaign program seems to have been
minimal. See Vashti McCollum, *One Woman's Fight;* and the testimony
of Rabbi Goldin, *Transcript of Record,* Supreme Court of the U.S.,
October Term, 1947, No. 90, 333 U.S. 203. For statements by Jewish
groups see the yearbooks of the Central Conference of American Rabbis,
the volumes of the *American Jewish Yearbook,* and Arthur Gilbert, *A Jew
in Christian America* (New York: Sheed & Ward, Inc., 1966), pp. 94–98.
The United Synagogue of America declared in 1925 that "the curriculum
of the public schools shall in no wise be made to include the element of
religious education" and that "the public school day shall be so arranged
as to leave time for weekday religious instruction after school hours in
places other than the public schools, and without any public school
supervision whatsoever." Quoted by Bell, *The Church, the State, and
Education in Virginia,* pp. 509–10. Rosen in the *American Jewish Yearbook,*
XCVI (1947), 107.

[31]*Catholic Education in America, a Documentary History,* ed. Mc-
Cluskey, p. 92.

letter of 1919 the hierarchy urged that it was not politically wise "to exclude from . . . public instruction, the teaching of the Gospel and of the Church."[32] The released-time approach appeared to be one way in which this teaching might become tied to public instruction. Here was a program through which the church, with the cooperation of the public school, could reach Catholic children in that institution. And by mid-century the Roman Catholic hierarchy had reached the point of advocacy, maintaining that "the State should look with favor on released-time programs" for the religious instruction of the child not receiving a church school education.[33]

Protestants tended to be ambivalent in their attitude toward the involvement of the Roman Catholic Church in released-time religious education. On the one hand, Protestant advocates sometimes looked to released-time as a significant means for maintaining Protestant strength in the face of a growing and presumably monolithic Catholicism. On the other hand, in communities with substantial Catholic populations, Protestants were forced to work with Catholic officials in presenting a united front to the school system. Ironically enough, while organized Protestantism was initially the prime mover in instituting released-time programs, it seems quite probable that by mid-century the Roman Catholic Church was benefiting more from this type of arrangement than were the Protestant denominations.[34]

Studies of released-time religious-education programs have usually concentrated on the various structures of such programs

[32]James Cardinal Gibbons, "The Pastoral Letter of 1919," *The National Pastorals of the American Hierarchy* (1792–1919), ed. Peter Guilday (Washington, D.C.: National Catholic Welfare Council, 1923), p. 308. See Frederick E. Ellis, "Aspects of the Relation of the Roman Catholic Church to American Public Education," *Educational Forum*, XIX (November 1954), 65–74.

[33]"The Child: Citizen of Two Worlds," 1950 statement, printed in *Our Bishops Speak* (Milwaukee: Bruce Publishing, 1952), p. 164.

[34]Pfeffer and Stokes, *Church and State in the United States*, pp. 334, 370. Pfeffer reports that in the 1940's as many as 80 percent of the children released from the New York City public schools for religious instruction were Roman Catholic. The percentage was also high in other metropolitan areas.

or the legal aspects of the subject. There appears to be little evidence available concerning the actual impact of such programs on students, teachers, and school systems.[35] Stokes describes a program which was instituted in Elgin, Illinois, in 1938 and which involved the cooperation of seventeen Protestant denominations. The classrooms of the schools were used for the instruction, which took place one day a week on regular school time. Classes were preceded by a devotional service involving hymn singing and led by one of the students. Instruction was given "in the fundamental teachings of the Bible, especially the outstanding characters of the New Testament, the later leaders of the Church, and the truths of Christianity." The avowed objective of the classes was "'to release the dynamic of the Christian religion' (that which has been revealed, not discovered) in the lives of the boys and girls. . . . It was believed by those connected with the movement," Stokes reports, "that it did much to encourage high ideals and standards of conduct."[36] This program was discontinued following the decision of the U.S. Supreme Court in the *McCollum* case.[37]

The plan for religious instruction instituted in Champaign, Illinois, in 1940 is one of the most widely known of such plans because of its involvement in extensive litigation which finally resulted in the Supreme Court's decision in the *McCollum* case. This plan involved the direct cooperation of religious groups with public school officials in the offering of classes half an hour per week on regular school time and in school classrooms. Participating groups included several Protestant denominations organized into a special committee for this purpose, the Missouri Synod of the Lutheran Church, the Roman Catholic Church, and, on a limited basis, a Jewish group. The courses were

---

[35]Such as William K. Muir, Jr.'s study of the impact of the Court prayer decisions on a community: *Prayer in the Public Schools: Law and Attitude Change* (Chicago: University of Chicago Press, 1967).

[36]*Church and State in the United States*, II, 507–08. Stokes found similar plans in operation in other parts of the country, "especially in communities with a relatively homogeneous Protestant population."

[37]On the general effects of the *McCollum* case see Gordon Patric, "The Impact of a Court Decision: Aftermath of the McCollum Case," *Journal of Public Law*, VI (1957), 455–63.

obviously of a religious and catechetical nature, designed to increase the student's knowledge of his own faith and to strengthen his allegiance to that faith. One of the teachers in the combined Protestant program was a retired missionary whose approach to the Bible tended to be literalistic and whose outlook on life in general was somewhat short of liberal. One ten-year-old boy, James Terry McCollum, enrolled in this course for a time—apparently with the consent of his parents—and then, under prompting from his mother, withdrew from it. It was Mrs. Vashti McCollum who initiated the legal suit, claiming that the program was unconstitutional and that it tended to isolate and ostracize her son.[38]

The *McCollum* case, then, gives us a fair amount of information about the impact of a released-time program in one community. It illustrates the kind of controversy that sometimes occurred over such a program. In fact, several communities had been divided over similar programs prior to the *McCollum* case. For example, released time had been the subject of sporadic controversies in New York City from early in the century until the institution of a program in the early 1940's. Even that program was strenuously opposed by some in the community, including Columbia University professor John Dewey. That program also later became the occasion for the second released-time case to reach the Supreme Court of the United States, *Zorach v. Clauson*.[39]

Bible and Religion Courses Accredited by Public Schools

In the early decades of the century public school machinery was sometimes used for accrediting courses in Bible and religion offered outside the regular school curriculum. In a few

[38]See Mrs. McCollum's lively account of the case in *One Woman's Fight*. For other details in the case see the relevant court decisions and the *Transcript of Record*.

[39]343 U.S. 306 (1952). On the controversies in New York see Pfeffer, *Church, State and Education*, p. 316, and Benjamin Fine, "Religion and the Public Schools," *The Menorah Journal*, XXXII (April 1944), 93–101.

instances such courses were even designed and taught by public school personnel. This type of practice is of interest as another approach to the difficult problem of religion in the public school and because it involved close cooperation between church and state officials. While few of the courses would have satisfied the recently suggested standards implied in such Supreme Court phrases as "teaching about religion" and "the objective study of" religion and the Bible, they did grow out of a concern to increase religious literacy.

The state of North Dakota instituted one of the earliest programs of this type in 1912. Under this program a student could "take Bible study in the Sunday school, parochial classes, or in separately organized classes, and secure one unit of credit toward graduation." The state department of public instruction set the standards, conducted examinations, and issued the credits. The North Dakota Council of Religious Education printed the outlines—which consisted chiefly of brief outlines of the Old and New Testaments—handled the books, and helped organize the classes. Local clergymen were encouraged to contact school authorities if they wished to institute the course. No state or public school buildings were to be used for the course nor were public school teachers to teach it during regular school hours.[40]

This type of plan caught on in a number of other states over the next couple of decades. Stokes reports that by 1927 authorized syllabi for Bible study were in common use in twelve states and a total of twenty-five states—including New York and Illinois—"permitted credit to high-school students who were reported by responsible groups to have completed satisfactory courses of Bible study."[41]

In 1916 the state board of education of Virginia authorized accredited Bible courses for high school pupils and empowered a commission to prepare the content, standards, and methods of operation for these courses. The resulting plan incorporated many of the features of the North Dakota plan but added a

[40]Johnson, *The Legal Status of Church-State Relationships,* pp. 141–42.
[41]*Church and State in the United States,* II, 504, citing Davis, *Week-Day Religious Education,* p. 22.

distinctive interfaith note. The commission membership included a Protestant minister, a Catholic priest, and a Jewish layman, as well as representatives of the educational interests of the state. The commission issued the *Official Syllabus of Bible Study for High School Pupils,* which it endorsed unanimously, and which contained course outlines in Old and New Testament literature and history and detailed directions for the operation and accreditation of these courses. Biblical references were based on the use of three versions: King James, Douay, and Lesser.[42]

In West Virginia the Council of Religious Education prepared a plan for accredited Bible study which received the endorsement of the State Sunday School Association and the State Education Association and was approved by the state board of education in 1919. A Commission on Accredited Bible Study was created by the plan. Membership included the general superintendent of the West Virginia Sunday School Association, the state supervisor of high schools, and three additional members elected separately by the state board of education, the West Virginia Council of Religious Education, and the West Virginia Education Association. Under this plan one unit of high school credit in Bible study could be substituted for any elective course. Standards required that the teacher meet the professional requirements of the high school in which the credit was sought, the use of certain minimal equipment, a recitation period of forty-five minutes, and examinations at least twice a year at the end of the regular semesters. The course could be offered either in or outside the high school involved. Students were permitted to use the King James, American Revised, Douay, or Lesser versions of the Bible.[43]

One of the most detailed syllabi for courses of this type was that prepared for use in Michigan and also adopted in Montana. This 172-page work combined outlines and notes for courses in such topics as "Great Old Testament Characters," "The Bible

[42]Johnson, *The Legal Status of Church-State Relationships,* p. 141; Stokes, *Church and State in the United States,* II, 501–03.

[43]Johnson, *The Legal Status of Church-State Relationships,* pp. 139–41.

and Literature," "The Life of Christ," "The First Century of
the Christian Church," and "The Bible as an Interpreter of the
Interrelations of Social Institutions and a Guide to Right Living."
Dean Johnson comments that this syllabus dealt with "such
controversial questions as the creation; the Garden of Eden; the
temptation of Eve and sin; Noah, the ark, and the flood; the
Ten Commandments; the Divinity of Christ and His miracles;
and many others."[44] After examining a variety of courses of
this type Johnson concluded that they differed "little from
courses of Bible study taught in church and denominational
schools."[45]

An ambitious program of this nature was initiated by the
public school officials of Chicago in 1941. This plan allowed a
maximum of two high school credits, out of a total of the fifteen
or sixteen required for graduation, for courses offered under
denominational auspices (teaching, housing, etc.), either on
Saturdays or Sundays or during released time on school days.
Public school officials reserved the right to pass upon the
competence of the teachers and the acceptability of the course
materials.[46]

About a decade earlier the proposed introduction of a similar
plan in New York City met with considerable opposition from
such quarters as the teachers' union and the American Association for the Advancement of Atheism. The teachers' union
objected to substituting courses in religion for secular courses
while the atheists torpedoed the plan by seeking the opportunity
to offer their own course for credit.[47]

The constitutionality of allowing credit for courses offered
under church auspices was challenged in the state of Washington
in 1918. The Washington state board of education had indicated
its approval of allowing credit for Bible courses and had urged
that the state department of education issue a syllabus and

[44]How, he asked, "are such subjects going to be taught in the public
schools?" Ibid., pp. 143–44.

[45]Ibid.

[46]There is a description of the institution of this program in the *Christian Century*, CVIII (March 19, 1941), 384–85. I have found no account
of its subsequent success or failure.

[47]Johnson, *The Legal Status of Church-State Relationships*, pp. 97–98.

devise appropriate rules and regulations. By unanimous decision the Washington Supreme Court held that such a procedure constituted an expenditure of public funds for "religious worship, exercise, or instruction," or for the support of a "religious establishment," and hence violated the state's constitution. This decision was reaffirmed in 1930.[48]

Interreligious Relations and the Public Schools

The major American traditions of church religion seldom achieved a united front in their approach to the public schools in this period. Their fundamental operative relationship remained one of competition and conflict.[49] Protestant church pronouncements, for example, bristled with direct or implied criticism of the Roman Catholic Church for its maintenance of a parochial school system, for coveting public support for that system, and for an approach to the public school which appeared to range from lukewarm to openly critical. On the other side, it often seemed to Catholic authorities and scholars that the major Protestant denominations had ceded far too much educational responsibility to the public schools and in the process had done a major disservice to the cause of Christian education. While keeping its attention focused on the Roman Catholic adversary, Protestantism, it seemed to these critics, had fallen captive to the secularist camp.

[48]State ex rel. *Deale* v. *Frazier* (1918) and State ex rel. *Clithero* v. *Showalter* (1930). See Johnson, *The Legal Status of Church-State Relationships*, pp. 136–38, and Boles, *The Bible, Religion and the Public Schools*, pp. 128–29. *Clithero*, in which the Washington Supreme Court refused to direct the state superintendent of schools to institute Bible reading in the public schools, was appealed to the United States Supreme Court, where it was dismissed for lack of a substantial issue: 284 U.S. 573 (1931); Pfeffer, *Church, State and Freedom*, p. 386.

[49]In 1928 George S. Counts concluded his review of the relationships between religious groups and the schools of Chicago with this pessimistic statement: "So long have Jew, Catholic, and Protestant quarreled and fought in the western world . . . that a rational ordering of relationships among them would seem to wear the garb of Utopia." *School and Society in Chicago* (New York: Harcourt, Brace & Co., 1928), pp. 245–46.

The most important single fact for the Jewish community was the continuing presence in the public schools of Christian influences and practices. For example, daily use of the Lord's prayer and school sponsorship of Christmas ceremonies were obvious and galling reminders of this presence. This tended to weld the Jewish minority together in opposition to all religious influences in the public schools. In the interest of political peace, or perhaps even out of some element of self-interest, Jews might occasionally make common cause with Protestants and/or Catholics in some public school program such as released time, but they tended to prefer a policy of no religion at all in the public schools.

Fundamental differences between the faiths in approach to religious education, and consequently to the public school, severely limited the possibility of putting up a united front. Protestantism tended to be more dependent upon the public sector for aid in religious education than either Judaism or Roman Catholicism. The liberal Protestant followers of John Dewey saw in his methods and philosophy the best approach to religious education. Hence they supported progressive education in the schools. For some Protestant conservatives, on the other hand, Dewey became one of the major symbols of the evils of modernism and communism. Progressive education—attributed to Dewey, whose ideas were often garbled by his zealous detractors—became the major divide which separated the faithful from the heretics. In the name of righteousness and the Christian gospel, Dewey and his followers were fought wherever the conservatives could engage in battle. The public schools must be made secure for God and for country.

A few Protestant groups, such as the Lutheran Church, Missouri Synod, continued to maintain their own school system. All Protestant groups, of course, maintained Sunday schools for religious education. But the groups that did not maintain their own day school system could hardly confine their educational efforts to one hour on a Sunday morning.

Catholic authorities continued to affirm the stance of the Third Plenary Council of Baltimore: a school connected with every parish. In this country, the church "is obliged, for the sake of principle, to maintain a system of education distinct and separate from other systems," declared the hierarchy in its pastoral letter of 1919. In education, as in life, first place must be given to knowledge of God and of his law. This priority could be accorded only in a school system operated by the church itself. The fathers found support for their insistence upon a Christian education in Christian schools both in fundamental principle and in the conditions of the age. They foresaw a "great coming combat between truth and error, between Faith and Agnosticism" in which the survival of Christian culture would depend to a large degree upon the laity.

This foreboding sense of cataclysmic and inevitable conflict between the forces of Christianity and those of atheism or secularism colored many Catholic discussions of education and conditioned the church's approach to the public school. The pastoral letter of 1884 had contained a "timely warning" concerning the imminence of this battle as well as the seriousness of the stakes involved. According to the pastoral letter of 1919 this had been "verified." The predicted combat had "swept around all the sources of thought," and had "centered upon the school." There, "especially, the interests of morality and religion" were at stake; and there, "more than anywhere else," the future of the nation was determined.[50] But would the *public* school be capable of facing the magnitude of this task? Obviously not if it was dominated by secularism. If there could be some place in the schools for proper acknowledgment of God, however, then perhaps there was some hope for them. Here, then, was a slight opening toward the public schools. But this opening was definitely not encouraged by the papacy.[51]

Despite these differences between religious groups, or perhaps because of them, efforts were made, both locally and nationally,

[50]In *Our Bishops Speak*, pp. 14–15.
[51]Statements by both Pius XI and Pius XII—*Divini Illius Magistri*, 1930, and *Sertum Laetitiae*, 1939. For Pius XI on education see *On Christian Education of Youth* (Washington, D.C.: National Catholic Welfare Conference, 1936). On the encyclical of Pius XII see *Progress and Problems of the American Church* (New York: The America Press, 1939), p. 13. See also Paul L. Blakely, S.J., *May an American Oppose the Public Schools?* (New York: America Press, 1937), pp. 5, 8.

to achieve a measure of interreligious cooperation vis-à-vis the public school. The Religious Education Association, for example, was interreligious in membership from its beginnings in 1903, and it was obviously concerned about religious education in the public schools. However, the large majority of that membership over the first forty years of the REA's existence was Protestant. Very few Roman Catholics were affiliated with it. In fact, its approach to religious education was sometimes subjected to criticism by Roman Catholic authorities for being too liberal.[52]

The National Conference of Christians and Jews, founded in 1927, urged the creation of materials for high school use which would be designed to cultivate appreciation of the various religious and racial groups represented in the United States. This organization also devised a format for interreligious conversation, involving a Protestant minister, a Catholic priest, and a rabbi, which was quite commonly used in high schools in the 1930's and 1940's.

"Common-Core" Religion

A few attempts were made to develop some sort of "common core" of religious faith on which all major American religious groups could agree. Some hoped to precipitate the essence of American religion in some palatable form for dispensing to public school students. Early in the century, for example, the National Education Association sponsored a contest for producing acceptable plans for introducing "religious teaching into the public schools." Under the rules, religion was to be defined so as "not to run counter to the creeds of Protestant, Roman Catholic, or Jew." The "essential points" to be observed were "A Heavenly Father who holds nature and man alike in the hollow of his hand; the commandment of Hillel and Jesus . . ."

[52]See Claris Edwin Silcox and Galen M. Fisher, *Catholics, Jews and Protestants: A Study of Relationships in the United States and Canada* (New York: Harper & Bros., 1934), p. 316.

and "the high ethical teachings and spirit of service and sacrifice indicated in the Sermon on the Mount." Five prize-winning essays and summations of others were published in 1916 under the title "The Essential Place of Religion in Education."[53] There is no evidence, however, that this book was used to any appreciable extent in the public schools.

The "common-core" approach was sometimes advocated in response to a public crisis which drew religious leaders together. American involvement in World War II elicited the issuance in 1942 of a "Declaration of Common Beliefs" by a group of Protestant, Catholic, and Jewish leaders. These common beliefs included: God as "Creator and Sustainer of the Universe"; man created in God's image; the rejection of all attempts "to explain man in merely material terms"; the rejection of any claims to a divinely instituted racial superiority; divine sanction of human rights and a system of morality; and the affirmation that the republican form of government was best "for our nation and for countries of similarly democratic traditions . . ."[54]

The "common-core" approach probably received more support from liberal Protestants than from Americans of other religious persuasions. Personnel associated with the Federal Council of Churches took the initiative in securing the World War II statement referred to above. Dean Luther A. Weigle of the Yale Divinity School argued in this same period that the "three great religious groups" of America shared "a common religious faith." Even though a few Americans did not share this faith, Dean Weigle argued that there was no reason why it could not "rightfully be assumed and find appropriate expression in the life and work of the public schools." The Yale dean's "common religious faith" included "one God, Creator of all things and Father of men," who was "revealed in the life and literature of the Hebrew people as recorded in the Bible" and who was discernible in nature and the human conscience. Adherents of "the three great religious groups" also affirmed in common certain basic ethical teachings, they could "sing hymns and

[53]Ann Arbor: University of Michigan Press, 1916.
[54]Federal Council of Churches *Bulletin,* March 1942, as cited by Stokes, *Church and State in the United States,* II, 505–06.

psalms" that transcended "differences of creed" and they could "all unite in the Lord's prayer . . ."[55] Weigle's Protestant presuppositions, and presumptions, were especially evident in his assumption that the Lord's prayer could unite Protestants, Catholics, *and* Jews.

Dean Weigle's summary of our "common religious faith" was published by the American Council on Education, a prestigious body representative of a broad spectrum of American education. It is interesting to note that the council's own Committee on Religion and Education rejected the "common-core" approach in a significant statement on religion and public education. This statement was issued in 1947 following a series of conferences and consultations involving representatives of the major faiths and public school personnel, and carried out in cooperation with the National Conference of Christians and Jews. The committee found the "common-core" approach unacceptable to the majority of religious leaders and public educators. And the committee warned about the possibility that emphasis upon our "common religious faith" might "lead to a new sect— a public school sect—which would take its place alongside the existing faiths and compete with them."[56]

The difficulties in the "common-core" approach are symptomatic of the complexities which characterize the relationship between religion and public education in America. Even the casual observer can see something of America's religious diversity, although the "common-core" advocates have sometimes seemed quite insensitive to this fact. A more careful look will soon reveal the inadequacy of any attempt to encompass American religious expression within "the three great religious groups"—Jewish, Catholic, and Protestant. There are also the various Orthodox groups, the Mormons, the Jehovah's Witnesses, the Christian Scientists, the members of the Ethical Culture

[55]"The American Tradition and the Relation between Religion and Education," *Religion and Public Education,* American Council on Education Studies, IX, No. 22 (Washington, D.C., 1945), 34–35. Cf. Conrad A. Hauser, *Teaching Religion in the Public School* (New York: Round Table Press, 1942). Hauser recommended "theistic humanism" as the belief which "unites rather than separates us."

[56]See note 2 above.

Society, and a host of others who do not easily fit into that interfaith troika. Furthermore, even the designation "Protestant" encompasses great variety of belief and practice, as is suggested at the beginning of this chapter. Finally, the "common-core" method has sometimes suffered from a failure to appreciate the intensity with which specifics of religious belief are often held. "One man's piety is another's idolatry," observed Professor Paul A. Freund[57] in a phrase that suggests not only the difficulties confronting a "common-core" approach but also captures something of both the variety and intensity that characterizes faith in America.

Given these complexities, one can well understand why John Dewey and some other educators preferred a "common faith" which bypassed all formal religion. But it was either overly optimistic or naïve to assume that church religion would disappear entirely from the public school landscape. In fact, during the period of Dewey's greatest influence the major religious denominations made stronger efforts than ever to encourage religious practices and instruction in the public schools. The very success of these efforts, however, was a contributing factor in bringing the religion–public school relationship before the Supreme Court of the United States, where America's ultimate tribunal took a turn at dealing with its complexities.

[57]*Religion and the Public Schools, the Legal Issue* (Cambridge: Harvard University Press, 1965), p. 14.

VII

A "Wall of Separation"

Religion, the Supreme Court, and the Public School

"Congress shall make no law respecting an establishment of religion or prohibiting the free exercise thereof . . ."
— First Amendment, U.S. Constitution

"In the words of Jefferson, the clause against establishment of religion by law was intended to erect 'a wall of separation between church and State.' "[1]

"Separation means separation, not something less."[2]

" 'When I use a word,' Humpty Dumpty said, in a rather scornful tone, 'it means just what I choose it to mean—neither more nor less.' "
" 'The question is,' said Alice, 'whether you *can* make words mean so many different things.' "
— Lewis Carroll, *Through the Looking Glass*

Alexis de Tocqueville remarked with characteristic insight that "there is hardly a political question in the United States that does not sooner or later turn into a judicial one."[3] The courts are required to pronounce on some of the most fundamental issues of public policy. Hence, in the past two decades most discussions of religion and public education have, figuratively, begun or ended in Washington in the court of last appeal. The Supreme Court of the United States has declared unconstitutional public school practices—prayer and Bible reading especially—which dated from the beginnings of the common school. The Court has also dealt with such complex problems as released time and aid to parochial schools. Throughout these

[1] *Everson* v. *Board of Education*, 330 U.S. 1, 16 (1947).
[2] Justice Frankfurter in *Illinois* ex rel. *McCollum* v. *Board of Education*, 333 U.S. 203, 231 (1948).
[3] *Democracy in America*, ed. Mayer and Lerner, p. 248.

cases the Justices have affirmed positions now clear and lucid and now confusing and apparently even contradictory. While it is obviously not within the competence of a layman in the law to handle these issues in their more technical aspects, no one can do justice to the continuing relationships between religion and public education without giving some attention to the relevant decisions of the Court.

Over the past forty-five years the Court has (1) affirmed the right of parents to send their youngsters to private and religious schools (*Pierce*);[4] (2) found that pupils in private and religious schools might legitimately receive certain tax-supported services, such as textbooks and bus transportation (*Cochran, Everson, Allen*); (3) struck down a statute requiring public school pupils to salute the flag and pledge allegiance to it (*Barnette*), reversing an earlier decision (*Gobitis*); (4) ruled as unconstitutional under the establishment clause of the First Amendment a released-time religious-education program within the public school (*McCollum*); (5) refused, five years later, to find unconstitutional a similar program which took place off school premises (*Zorach*); (6) struck down as an instance of "an establishment of religion" the Prayer composed by the New York Board of Regents which was used at the opening of the school day in many New York schools (*Engel*); and (7) ruled out, under the same rubric, practices of Bible reading without comment and repetition of the Lord's Prayer at the opening of school (*Schempp*).[5]

---

[4]For citations and summaries of these cases see table on p. 194. I use the short designations—Pierce, Cochran, etc.—in referring to them in the text.

[5]While all of these cases relate in some way to religion in the public schools, the earlier ones (*Pierce, Cochran, Gobitis,* and *Barnette*) were not adjudicated under the religion clauses of the First Amendment. A useful summary of these and other relevant cases is found in Sam Duker, *The Public Schools and Religion: The Legal Context* (New York: Harper & Row, 1966). All of these cases through *Zorach* (1952), plus additional church-state cases, can be found in Joseph Tussman, ed., *The Supreme Court on Church and State* (New York: Oxford University Press, 1962). The *Schempp* case is available in its entirety, together with excerpts from court records, in Arthur Frommer, ed., *The Bible and the Public Schools* (New York: Frommer/Pasmantier Publishing, 1963).

Significant Court Cases Related to Religion and the Public School

SHORT DESIGNATION	NAME OF CASE	DATE	CENTRAL ISSUE	DISPOSITION
Pierce	*Pierce v. Society of Sisters* 268 U.S. 510	1925	Oregon's mandatory public school attendance statute.	Unconstitutional (unanimous)
Cochran	*Cochran v. Louisiana* 281 U.S. 370	1930	Statute providing use of tax money for books for children attending public *and other* schools.	Upheld (unanimous)
Everson	*Everson v. Board of Education* 330 U.S. 1	1947	Tax subsidy for bus transportation for children attending Catholic schools (N.J.).	Upheld (5-4)
Allen	*Board of Education v. Allen* 392 U.S. 236	1968	N.Y. statute requiring tax-subsidized textbooks for parochial and private school students.	Upheld (6-3)
Gobitis	*Minersville v. Gobitis* 310 U.S. 586	1940	Required daily flag salute in public school (Minersville, Pa.).	Upheld (8-1)
Barnette	*West Virginia v. Barnette* 319 U.S. 624	1943	State Board of Education ruling requiring flag salute in public schools.	Unconstitutional (6-3)
McCollum	*McCollum v. Board of Education* 333 U.S. 203	1948	Released-time program on school premises (Champaign, Ill.).	Unconstitutional (8-1)
Zorach	*Zorach v. Clauson* 343 U.S. 306	1952	Released-time program off school premises (N.Y.C.).	Upheld (6-3)
Engel	*Engel v. Vitale* 370 U.S. 421	1962	New York State Board of Regents composed and school-sponsored prayer.	Unconstitutional (6-1)
Schempp	*School District v. Schempp* *Murray v. Curlett* 374 U.S. 203	1963	School-sponsored prayer (Lord's Prayer) and devotional Bible reading (Pa. and Baltimore).	Unconstitutional (8-1)

Separation

The major recent trend of Court opinion or "doctrine" in the church-state and public education area was established in the 1940's. In 1940 the Court extended the provisions of the religion clause of the First Amendment to the states by way of the Fourteenth Amendment.[6] The full implications of this action were spelled out by Justice Black seven years later in language which has since become the classic statement of separation:

The "establishment of religion" clause of the First Amendment means at least this: Neither a state nor the Federal Government can set up a church. Neither can pass laws which aid one religion, aid all religions, or prefer one religion over another. . . . No tax . . . can be levied to support any religious activities or institutions, whatever they may be called, or whatever form they may adopt to teach or practice religion. . . . In the words of Jefferson, the clause against establishment of religion by law was intended to erect "a wall of separation between church and State."[7]

Less than one year later the Court, by an 8-to-1 decision, followed the apparent logic of this position in striking down as an instance of an "establishment of religion" the released-time religious-education program of Champaign, Illinois.[8] This case, McCollum, was significant in its application of the religion clause of the First Amendment to a public school practice and in the stringency of the separationist principle followed by the Court.

It will be recalled that McCollum dealt with a released-time program which involved the cooperation of the Champaign

[6]*Cantwell* v. *Connecticut*, 310 U.S. 296, 303 (1940).
[7]*Everson*, 330 U.S. 1, 15, 16.
[8]*McCollum*, 333 U.S. 203.

Council on Religious Education and the Champaign board of
education in the offering of classes during school time and on
school premises. Legal action seeking *mandamus* against the
Champaign board of education for operating this program was
brought by Vashti McCollum, who maintained that her son,
James Terry, had been exposed to harassment for not participating in the program. The Court found that the program
was "beyond all question a utilization of the tax-established
and tax-supported public school system to aid religious groups
to spread their faith" and hence fell "squarely under the ban
of the First Amendment" as the Court had interpreted that
Amendment in *Everson*.[9]

To understand the full "doctrinal" impact of the *McCollum*
decision it is necessary to look more closely at the preceding
(and precedent) case, *Everson*. That case involved the payment
of tax money to parents for the transportation by bus of their
children to Catholic parochial schools under the provisions of
a New Jersey statute. The Court, by a 5-to-4 decision, upheld
the constitutionality of this practice. However, the language of
both the majority and the minority was the fullest and most
stringent yet uttered by the Court in a church-state case.
Justice Black, for the majority, re-erected Jefferson's "wall of
separation."[10] Justice Rutledge, for the minority, wrote a lengthy
opinion in which he spelled out in the language of sharp
separation the historical background and meaning of the First
Amendment. He maintained that, because of the decision of
the majority, Jefferson's wall was no longer "so high nor so
impregnable" as it had been or as it ought to be. The "wall"
separates or should separate completely *religion* and state,
Rutledge argued.[11]

"Two great drives," Rutledge wrote, were "constantly in
motion to abridge, in the name of education, the complete
division of religion and civil authority . . ." One was the

[9]Ibid., 210.

[10]This metaphor was used by Jefferson in a letter to the Danbury
(Connecticut) Baptists, dated January 1, 1802, elaborating on the meaning
of the First Amendment.

[11]330 U.S. 1, 59, 60.

effort "to obtain public funds for the aid and support of various private schools," such as the case under review involved. The other drive, Rutledge asserted in prophetic anticipation of *McCollum* and other later cases, was "to introduce religious education and observances into the public schools." Both of these "avenues were closed by the Constitution." This was a matter not of "quantity" but of "principle."[12]

It was this "principle" of separation, stated succinctly in the metaphor of the "wall," to which the Court clearly appealed in *McCollum:* "The majority in the Everson case, and the minority," Justice Black pointed out in writing the Court's decision, "agreed that the First Amendment's language, properly interpreted, had erected a wall of separation between Church and State." This wall "must be kept high and impregnable."[13] This "principle" was further elaborated in *McCollum* by Justice Frankfurter, who described the "relevant Constitutional principle" first formulated in *Everson* and now directed against Champaign's released-time program in the most stringent language as one of "complete," "absolute," and "eternal" separation. "Separation means separation," he emphasized; a wall is a wall, "not . . . a fine line easily overstepped."[14]

The metaphor of the "wall" has been loudly praised and scorned by both legal scholars and laymen in the law. The Justices themselves have engaged in many variations—both harmonic and discordant—on the separation theme.[15] Justice Jackson, reminding his colleagues in *McCollum* of the many ways in which religion is relevant to education, suggested that the "wall of separation" might become "as winding as the famous serpentine wall designed by Mr. Jefferson for the University he founded" if they were to adjudicate every case brought by someone dissatisfied with the way the schools were dealing with the subject of religion. While accepting the principle of separation, he flatly pointed out that not one word could be

[12]Ibid., 63.
[13]333 U.S. 203, 211, 212.
[14]Ibid., 231.
[15]Professor Philip B. Kurland has described these variations under the heading "Authorities in Search of a Doctrine" in his book *Religion and the Law: Of Church and State and the Supreme Court.*

found in the Constitution "to help us as judges to decide where the secular ends and the sectarian begins in education." Hence on this question they could find "no law but our own prepossessions."[16]

To the layman's untrained eye the aptness of this Jacksonian *caveat* was borne out in the Court's decision and language in *Zorach*. This case involved a program in New York City which permitted the public schools to release students during the school day so that they could leave the school premises in order to attend courses in religious instruction. Such a release required the permission of parents. Churches reported attendance to the Writing for the Court in *Zorach*, Justice Douglas argued that the "First Amendment . . . does not say that in every and all Court sustained this program. the program were required to stay in the public schools. The school authorities and those students who did not participate in respects there shall be a separation of Church and State." Speaking more for "the common sense of the matter" than for an absolute principle, Justice Douglas suggested that while the classrooms and "the force of the public school" might not be used for religious instruction (as in *McCollum*), the schools might still "accommodate their schedules to a program of outside religious instruction." The Constitution did not require the "government to be hostile to religion and to throw its weight against efforts to widen the effective scope of religious influence." This was no more than an acknowledgment of the fact that "We are a religious people whose institutions presuppose a Supreme Being."[17]

The word "accommodate," used by the Court in *Zorach*, has been grasped by one legal scholar as symbolic of the Court's departure from strict separation.[18] Apparently the three dissenters in *Zorach* (Black, Frankfurter, and Jackson) were not pleased with this turn toward "accommodation." Each wrote a separate dissenting opinion and each reaffirmed the separationist principle as stated in *Everson* and *McCollum*. In his usual sharp

[16]330 U.S. 203, 235–36.
[17]343 U.S. 306, 312–15.
[18]Paul G. Kauper, *Religion and the Constitution* (Baton Rouge: Louisiana State University Press, 1964), pp. 67ff.

manner, Jackson suggested that the "wall" had become "even more warped and twisted" than he had expected. The judgment in *Zorach* would be, he concluded, "more interesting to students of psychology and of the judicial processes than to students of constitutional law."[19]

The "wall" did not appear literally in either *Engel* or *Schempp*, the most significant religion-public school cases following *Zorach*. Possibly the metaphor had lost some of its usefulness, though separationist doctrine is evident in both cases. In a most unusual fashion, Justice Black, in writing the opinion of the Court in *Engel*, did not appeal to a single Court case as precedent setting. The opinion consists largely of historical references to such things as actions involving the Book of Common Prayer. The Justice apparently assumed that the separationist history of *Everson* and *McCollum* was self-evident.

Perhaps the most significant aspect of *Engel* with regard to the separationist principle was Justice Douglas' concurring opinion in which he repudiated his earlier vote with the majority in *Everson*. "Mr. Justice Rutledge stated in dissent," he confessed, "what I think is durable First Amendment philosophy." Governmental financing of a religious exercise was, he concluded, "an unconstitutional undertaking whatever form it takes." To illustrate his point he listed a variety of governmental "aids to religion" which did not accord with the separationist principle. These included, for example, the word "God" in the pledge of allegiance, "Bible-reading in the schools of the District of Columbia," and the availability "to students in private as well as public schools" of "the benefits of the National School Lunch Act."[20] It seems that Douglas here was also repudiating his accommodating approach in *Zorach*. Apparently now he would, in the words of one commentator, "root out . . . every vestige, direct and indirect, of religion in public affairs."[21]

[19]343 U.S. 306, 325.
[20]370 U.S. 421, 443, 437, note 1, 437.
[21]David W. Louisell, "The Man and the Mountain: Douglas on Religious Freedom," *Yale Law Journal*, LXXIII (1964), 991. Both Black and Douglas reaffirmed strict separation in dissent in *Allen*, a case requiring public school officials to lend textbooks to students in private and parochial schools. 392 U.S. 236 (1968).

The relentless logic of separation turns, like a vortex, ever in upon itself. It is an attractive logic—neat, sharp, decisive, pure. It is also a fateful logic which can only lead in its conclusion to the complete separation of religion from public life. The merits of such a result are arguable; the possibility of its achievement in the United States remote. Much as the mind of logic might wish to articulate a clear-cut principle for encompassing relationships between religion and the state, American community experience will not be so easily encompassed. As Justice Holmes pointed out in another connection, "a page of history is worth a volume of logic."[22] More of this later, but first an analysis of another principle which has emerged from recent decisions.

Neutrality

The Court appealed to the separationist principle again in *Schempp*. The Court drew heavily upon statements in *Everson*, including Rutledge's "complete and permanent separation of the spheres of religious activity and civil authority . . ."[23] However, Justice Clark, writing for the Court, chose to couch the balance of his opinion in terms of the notion of neutrality rather than separation. The neutrality principle was formulated in the following test: ". . . to withstand the strictures of the Establishment Clause there must be a secular legislative purpose and a primary effect that neither advances nor inhibits religion."[24]

Possibly neutrality was a more plausible shorthand summary of the Religion Clause than separation; and perhaps Clark's test was a usable one. In fact, neutrality had appeared even before *Schempp*. In justifying a decision which seemed to fall short of stringent separation the majority in *Everson* had appealed to something similar to Clark's test. The First Amendment, the Court said in upholding tax subsidy for transportation to parochial schools, "requires the state to be a neutral in its

[22]*New York Trust Co.* v. *Eisner*, 256 U.S. 345, 349 (1921).
[23]374 U.S. 203, 217.
[24]Ibid., 222.

relations with groups of religious believers and non-believers; it does not require the state to be their adversary. State power is no more to be used so as to handicap religions, than it is to favor them."[25]

Like any formulation, neutrality must be interpreted. The range of possible constructions is evident both in the modifiers used and in the implications drawn. Justice Jackson argued in *Everson* that the First Amendment required that the state "maintain a strict and lofty neutrality as to religion."[26] But Justice Clark chose in *Schempp* to summarize previous Court decisions in terms of a "wholesome 'neutrality.' "[27] And one astute constitutional expert has pointed out that on the same day in which the *Schempp* decision was announced the Court handed down its decision in another case in which it departed from the "strict neutrality idea" and moved at least to "the concept of benevolent neutrality . . ."[28] Clearly, as Justice Brennan suggested in his concurring opinion in *Schempp*, "the line which enforces the Amendment's injunction of strict neutrality, while manifesting no official hostility toward religion," is an "elusive" one;[29] and, as Justice White pointed out in *Allen*, that other line "between state neutrality to religion and state support of religion is not easy to locate."[30]

Just how variously the concept of neutrality can be interpreted is suggested by the use of this very idea by the lone dissenter in *Schempp*, Justice Stewart. Neutrality, Stewart argued, should

---

[25]330 U.S. 1, 18. Many have noted the apparent discrepancy between the stringent language of the majority in *Everson* and their actual decision. Twitting his colleagues on this point, Justice Jackson suggested that the "most fitting precedent" for this discrepancy was the case "of Julia who, according to Byron's reports, 'whispering "I will ne'er consent,"—consented.' " Ibid., 19.

[26]Ibid., 24.

[27]374 U.S. 203, 222.

[28]Paul G. Kauper, "Schempp and Sherbert: Studies in Neutrality and Accommodation," in *Religion and the Public Order, 1963*, ed. Donald A. Giannella (Chicago: University of Chicago Press, 1964), p. 29. The Court held in *Sherbert* that the religious freedom of a Seventh Day Adventist had been abridged by a denial of unemployment compensation to her because of her refusal to take a job which required Saturday work.

[29]374 U.S. 203, 245.

[30]392 U.S. 236, 242.

permit religious exercises in the schools for those who wanted them. A refusal to do so constituted not "the realization of state neutrality, but rather . . . the establishment of a religion of secularism . . ." or at least government support for those who regarded religion as being strictly private. What "governmental neutrality" actually involved was "the extension of even-handed treatment to all who believe, doubt, or disbelieve—a refusal on the part of the State to weight the scales of private choice."[31]

It is clear, then, that while Justice Clark's test formula affords a certain usability, it also involves real difficulties. The most obvious of these has to do with decisions about "purpose," "primary effect," "advancement," and "inhibition." Over these there hovers a problem which may prove to be the most formidable of all: distinguishing between the religious and the secular. That question we shall leave for later exploration. At this point it might be well to summarize where we have arrived.

The Court appears to have moved in two directions beginning with *Everson*: (1) toward fuller elaboration of what has sometimes been called the "child-benefit" theory under which some forms of public aid to private and parochial school students are regarded as legitimate by virtue of an argument couched in terms of public function and welfare and using the rubric "secular" rather than "religious"; and (2) toward discontinuance of religious observances and sectarian instruction in the public school, especially where these practices involve direct sponsorship by the school or close cooperation with religious groups. In the first instance it appears that the Court has followed more the neutrality notion than strict separation, as suggested by its decision in *Everson* in 1947. This same tendency was reinforced in the Court's decision in *Allen* twenty years later. In this case the Court upheld the constitutionality of a New York statute requiring public school authorities to lend textbooks free of charge to all students, including those in private and parochial schools.[32] This line of reasoning would appear to move something like this: The First Amendment was not meant

[31]374 U.S. 203, 313, 317.
[32]As pointed out above, Justices Black and Douglas appealed to the separationist principle in their dissent in *Allen*.

to penalize belief (or unbelief). Hence public aid granted school youngsters for secular purposes might also legitimately be granted to youngsters in parochial schools for the same purposes.[33]

In the second instance it would appear that the Court has followed both the separationist and the neutrality principles. The operation of the former seems obvious. But a layman might find some difficulty in understanding how the discontinuance of an historical practice, such as Bible reading, which has presumably been supported by a majority of the American people, constitutes neutrality—even "wholesome" neutrality. Of course, constitutionality is not determined by majority sentiment. Furthermore it is clear that the *Schempp* decision rested on the assumption that Bible reading in a devotional context is a religious act and hence that by sponsoring that act the public school system was aiding religion—that is, not being neutral. Neutrality equalizes majority with minority and even non-believers with believers.

The Court as "a National School Board"?

In considering implications of the Court's decisions for the public school it is relevant to note that the Court has been especially protective in its approach to that institution. The Court has wished to maintain the traditional Americanizing and unifying function of the public school. This concern has been most dramatically evident to the public eye in the Court's most famous and significant decision in recent times, *Brown* v. *Board of Education,* dealing with desegregation of the public schools.[34] It has also been a persistent theme in the Court's religion–public school decisions. "The public school is at once the symbol of our

[33]See Wilber G. Katz, *Religion and American Constitutions* (Evanston, Ill.: Northwestern University Press, 1964); and Kurland, *Religion and the Law.* Both of these legal scholars argue on the basis of something akin to the neutrality principle that aid to parochial schools might not be unconstitutional.

[34]347 U.S. 483, especially 493.

democracy and the most pervasive means for promoting our common destiny," Justice Frankfurter pointed out in *Mc-Collum*.[35] Fifteen years later Justice Brennan stressed the "uniquely *public* function" of the public schools. By this he meant "the training of American citizens in an atmosphere free of parochial, divisive, or separatist influences of any sort—an atmosphere in which children may assimilate a heritage common to all American groups and religions."[36] The introduction of a religious factor, whether in a released-time program, a publicly supported prayer, or reading from the Bible, was judged to have a divisive effect and hence to mitigate against the central task of the school.

This Court concern for the unifying and nationalizing role of the public school led one constitutional scholar to suggest that the Court has acted as a "national school board."[37] By ruling out certain types of religious observances in the public schools under the Establishment Clause rather than the Free Exercise Clause of the First Amendment the Court has given a formalized and universal character to its prohibitions. Declaration of unconstitutionality under the Free Exercise Clause requires demonstration that a practice involves governmental coercion or undue interference with religious liberty. Such is not the case under the Establishment Clause. Under this clause there are certain things which the government—e.g., the public school—cannot do regardless of whether someone's rights are directly abridged. The schools cannot do these things because they constitute "an establishment of religion."[38] It appears, then, that the Establishment Clause is given a status once removed from human encounter such as the Free Exercise Clause does not enjoy.[39] It has also been given a universal applicability

[35]333 U.S. 203, 231.

[36]374 U.S. 203, 241–42.

[37]Edward S. Corwin, "The Supreme Court as National School Board," *Law and Contemporary Problems*, XIV (Winter 1949), 3–22. Professor Corwin directs sharp criticism at the Court's decision in *McCollum*.

[38]For the Court's distinction between the effects of the Establishment Clause and the Free Exercise Clause see *Engel*, 370 U.S. 421, 430, and *Schempp*, 374 U.S. 203, 223.

[39]This interpretation of the Establishment Clause was apparently given further force in *Flast* v. *Cohen*, 392 U.S. 83 (1968). This case dealt with

which does not require proof of injury in each local instance. Hence the type of practices ruled out under the Establishment Clause in Champaign, New Hyde Park, Abington Township, and Baltimore were apparently prohibited also in Dallas, Gary, and Los Angeles.

It is not my intention to deny or denigrate this national role of the Court. Obviously the Court plays a significant role in protecting the rights of minorities and in helping to clear the fogs of provincialism. This is essential constitutionally and to the national welfare. However, both the Constitution and national welfare also require a delicate balance between national and local interests and between unity and diversity. Stress on the unifying role of the schools within the framework of a rigid separationism and a broad interpretation of "establishment" might possibly contribute to an excessive nationalism and secularism.

Some of the justices have been especially sensitive to these complexities. Justice Jackson observed in McCollum that since "neighborhoods differ in racial, religious and cultural composition . . . it must be expected that they will adopt different customs which will give emphasis to different values and will induce different experiments. . . . We must leave some flexibility," he urged his colleagues, "to meet local conditions, some chance to progress by trial and error."[40] Justice Stewart went considerably farther in Schempp when he flatly stated that "religious exercises are not constitutionally invalid if they simply reflect differences which exist in the society from which the school draws its pupils."[41] But he argued as sole dissenter.

One can argue for experimentation, flexibility, and variety over against standardization (whether in inclusion or exclusion) in such areas as values and religion. America has not been monolithic in religion (or irreligion); and a meaningful realization

---

the question of standing to sue. Reversing a precedent which disallowed certain taxpayer's suits against the federal government, the Court, in *Flast*, permitted suits relative to federal subsidy of programs in private and parochial schools. The Court relied primarily upon the Establishment Clause in making this decision.

[40]333 U.S. 203, 237.
[41]374 U.S. 203, 317–18.

of values would appear to require some experimentation, as John Dewey so often urged. Such an argument would not justify the use of the school's machinery to forward the cause of any religion. When experimentation becomes an "experiment on our liberties" (Madison) it has reached the point of dubious constitutionality, and dubious pedagogy. But a rigid exclusion of religion can lead to the same danger of enforced uniformity as can the use of devices cited by the Court as instances of "an establishment of religion."

There are indications that the Court has become sensitized to the dangers inherent in a rigid exclusion of religion from the public school. Some Justices have taken considerable pains to deny the charge that the Court's decisions have, in effect, established secularism. But what is perhaps more significant than these direct denials is the question of what the Court, by direct decision or by implication, has left to the public schools that has any relation to religion.

Court Guidelines for Religion in the Public Schools

On-premises released-time religious education, ceremonial Bible reading, and school-sponsored group prayer are excluded under *McCollum, Engel,* and *Schempp.* But at least three things are left to the school following these decisions: (1) accommodations of the type permitted in *Zorach;* (2) ceremonies of a civic, patriotic, or secular nature in which religious terminology and allusions appear; and (3) the "objective study of" or "teaching about" religion. Number one has the force of law; two and three are suggestive dicta. Let us have a look at each.

RELEASED TIME—OFF SCHOOL PREMISES

Even though some have regarded *Zorach* as a sport,[42] it is the most recent case in which the Court ruled on a released-time

[42]Pfeffer, *Church, State and Freedom,* pp. 156–59.

religious-education program and that permissive ruling still stands. Arrangements involving limited cooperation between public schools and church officials for religious-education classes off school grounds are constitutionally permissible. Educators and churchmen might debate whether arrangements of this type are sound educationally—or even religiously. Such a debate would not be merely academic. The Court has not foreclosed all released time activity.[43]

Beyond the central issue at stake in *Zorach* one can conclude that indirectly this decision encourages experimentation in religious education in relation to the public school. It represents the Court in an accommodating mood. Professor Kauper cites *Zorach* as the most persuasive demonstration of what he calls "the accommodation theory" as contrasted with "the separation theory" and "the neutrality theory."[44] He uses such words as "pragmatism" and "pragmatic" to describe the Court's decision in *Zorach,* as contrasted with the "conceptualism" evidenced in such decisions as *Everson, McCollum, Engel,* and *Schempp.* Following Professor Kauper's lead the layman can conclude that the door that might be closed by "separation" and "neutrality" may be opened slightly by "accommodation."

PATRIOTIC EXERCISES—WITH "GOD"

Direct Court discussion of the relationship between the religious and the patriotic occurs in a footnote in *Engel.* It will be recalled that in that decision the Court struck down the use of the New York Board of Regents prayer. Two things were crucial to the decision: (a) the identification of the prayer as religious, and (b) the conclusion that its use constituted "an establishment of religion." There was little difficulty in the first task. The regents' prayer, with its invocation of God's blessings, was,

---

[43]State supreme courts in Washington and Oregon have ruled released time programs constitutional since *Zorach.* For citations and a brief discussion of the Oregon case see LeRoy J. Peterson, *et al., The Law and Public School Operation* (New York: Harper & Row, 1969), p. 395.

[44]*Religion and the Constitution,* ch. iii, and especially pp. 67–70.

without doubt, "a religious activity."[45] This was concluded from the beginning, and the remainder of the argument was given over to proving that the use of the prayer constituted "establishment." In the course of this argument the Court took note of the charge that its decision implied "hostility toward religion or toward prayer." Nothing could be farther from the truth, the Court responded. Indeed, the Court acknowledged the power of prayer; and one could argue that its decision might even have the effect of strengthening rather than weakening religion. What the Court was concerned to do was to get government "out of the business of writing or sanctioning official prayers and leave that purely religious function to the people themselves and to those the people choose to look to for religious guidance."[46] It was at this point in the argument that the Court attached the footnote in which it maintained that there was nothing in the *Engel* decision

> that is inconsistent with the fact that school children and others are officially encouraged to express love for our country by reciting historical documents such as the Declaration of Independence which contain references to the Deity or by singing officially espoused anthems which include the composer's professions of faith in a Supreme Being, or with the fact that there are many manifestations in our public life of belief in God. Such patriotic or ceremonial occasions bear no true resemblance to the unquestioned religious exercise . . .

struck down in the Court's decision.[47]

Given this footnote, we might paraphrase Justice Black's argument as proceeding something like this: Schools cannot sponsor religious exercises. Schools can sponsor patriotic exercises. But Americans inevitably mix their religion with their patriotism—as, for example, in the affirmation "In God is our

---

[45]370 U.S. 421, 424. The Regents' Prayer went as follows: "Almighty God, we acknowledge our dependence upon Thee, and we beg Thy blessings upon us, our parents, our teachers and our Country." Ibid., 422.
[46]Ibid., 434–35.
[47]Ibid., 435, note 21.

Trust" in the last stanza of the National Anthem. To deal with this undeniable fact only so much religion can be accepted in school ritual as can be accommodated under the patriotic umbrella. What we have, then, is a patriotic and not a religious ceremony.

This line of reasoning would appear to leave the schoolman with something like a guideline: Students can continue to recite the Declaration of Independence and to sing the *Star Spangled Banner*. (Of course, few ever manage to get to the last stanza.) And, although the Court did not include the pledge of allegiance in its footnote, one can probably also assume the legitimacy of that rite—even with the recently added "under God."[48] This is probably a sufficient guideline for the practical ordering of daily affairs, and we might leave the question here. Still the pledge of allegiance does raise some questions which are worth exploring, even though they divert us momentarily from our immediate concern with guidelines.

Once the Court assumed the task of applying the Establishment Clause to public school practices it took on a bundle of lively issues. To decide whether or not a particular practice constitutes an "establishment of religion" one must decide whether or not that practice is religious. On this question the Constitution offers no help.[49] Here the Court must appeal to precedent, common usage, and its own powers of ratiocination.

On this question of definition let us look first at the words "under God" in the pledge. Do they make the pledge a *religious* rite? When used in a public school ceremony does this relatively new form of the pledge constitute "an establishment of religion"? The point of the Court's footnote in *Engel* was that "God" and synonyms did not, in and of themselves, make an exercise religious. But it is worth noting that in another *Engel* footnote Justice Douglas, in his concurring opinion, included among questionable governmental "aids" to religion this addition of

[48]In 1954 Congress amended the pledge of allegiance to insert "under God." *U.S. Code*, Title 36, Chap. X, Sec. 172.

[49]"There is in the Constitution no definition of 'religion' or 'religious.'" Milton R. Konvitz, *Religious Liberty and Conscience: A Constitutional Inquiry* (New York: Viking Press, 1968), p. 31. Konvitz discusses the question of definition in chs. ii, iii.

"God to the pledge of allegiance."[50] Furthermore, the constitutionality of this addition has been challenged in the courts by those who obviously do see it as converting the pledge from a secular into a religious exercise.[51]

Most everyone assumes that "God" has something to do with religion. And until recently the Court itself apparently regarded "God" or some variation thereof—such as "Creator" or "Supreme Being"—as one of the chief distinguishing factors in defining or describing religion.[52] But this does not necessarily mean that the Court would find the pledge unconstitutional because of the added words. If such deliberations were undertaken, obviously other factors in addition to phraseology would be of importance. These would include the setting and the purpose of the exercise under consideration. The word "God" alone would not determine whether or not the rite was religious.

To illustrate this point about context and purpose let us come at the question of definition from a different angle. The Jehovah's Witnesses objected to the flag ceremony even before the words "under God" were added to the pledge of allegiance. And they objected on the grounds that the flag salute was a religious rite. They argued that "the saluting of the flag of any earthly government by a person who has covenanted to do the will of God is a form of religion and constitutes idolatry."[53] The Court decided the flag salute cases on other grounds than the religion clauses of the First Amendment. Hence the Court did not become involved directly in ascertaining whether the

[50]370 U.S. 421, 437, note 1.
[51]*Lewis* v. *Allen*, 159 N.Y. Supp. 2d 807 (1957) and Application of Lewis, 207 N. Y. Supp. 2d 862 (1960). Also *Holden* v. *Board of Education*, 216 A. N.J. 2d 387 (1966). For a brief discussion of these cases see Peterson, *et al.*, *The Law and Public School Operation*, p. 423.
[52]"The term 'religion' has reference to one's views of his relations to his Creator . . ." *Davis* v. *Beason*, 133 U.S. 333, 342 (1890). Justice Hughes cited this definition in *U.S.* v. *MacIntosh* in support of his own argument that "the essence of religion is belief in a relation to God involving duties superior to those arising from any human relation." 283 U.S. 605, 633–34 (1931). On the Court's definitions of religion see Kauper, *Religion and the Constitution*, pp. 24–34; and Konvitz, *Religious Liberty and Conscience*, ch. ii.
[53]Argument for Respondents, *Minersville School District* v. *Gobitis*, 310 U.S. 586, 590 (1940).

flag salute was a religious act or even whether the Jehovah's Witnesses were sincere in their religious views. Nevertheless, the Court did acknowledge in *Barnette* that the West Virginia compulsory flag salute did require students publicly to profess a belief or recite a "patriotic creed."[54] Such language implies that under some circumstances the pledge might be seen as a religious act—or, at least, a religionlike act.

Further light on the question of definition can be gained from two relatively recent Court decisions. In *Torcasso v. Watkins* the Court declared unconstitutional a provision in the Maryland constitution which required a declaration of belief in the existence of God by state officeholders. The Court held that "neither a State nor the Federal Government . . . can aid those religions based on a belief in the existence of God as against those founded on different beliefs." And in a footnote the Court listed among those "religions which do not teach what would generally be considered a belief in the existence of God . . . Buddhism, Taoism, Ethical Culture, Secular Humanism and others."[55] Clearly the Court's understanding of "religion" was a broad one and one that did not turn on "God" or a "Supreme Being."

In *United States v. Seeger* the Court decided a case involving an extension of the "Supreme Being" clause of the Universal Military Training and Service Act. Under this act it was possible for Selective Service boards to grant exemption to men "who by reason of their religious training and belief are conscientiously opposed to participation in war in any form." "Religious training and belief" was described further in terms of "an individual's belief in a relation to a Supreme Being involving duties superior to those arising from any human relation . . ." The Court found that in using "Supreme Being" instead of "God" the Congress meant "to embrace all religions . . ." And the Court concluded that "under this construction, the test of belief 'in a relation to a Supreme Being' is whether a given belief that is sincere and meaningful occupies a place in the life of its posses-

[54]319 U.S. 624, 631, 633, 634.
[55]367 U.S. 488, 495 and note 11 (1961). See the Court's citation of *Torcasso* in *Schempp*, 374 U.S. 203, 220.

sor parallel to that filled by the orthodox belief in God of one who clearly qualifies for the exemption."[56] Hence in *Seeger* the Court accepted as religious a belief *analogous to* the traditional belief in God.

Under the *Seeger* decision a belief can be understood as religious if it affords a kind of Archimedian platform on which one could stand over against the military requirements of the state. The Court found that any "sincerely held belief" performing this Archimedian function might qualify the registrant for conscientious-objector status. The test might be rephrased in the Tillichian language of ultimacy. Indeed, the Court was reminded of that language and used it in the *Seeger* decision: If the word "God" does not have much meaning for you, wrote Professor Tillich, then "translate it, and speak of the depths of your life, of the source of your being, of your ultimate concern, *of what you take seriously without any reservation.*"[57]

Under *Torcasso* and *Seeger* it is clear that any belief professed from the depth of one's being might be called religious. Such a belief need not require "God" as its object. What is crucial is what we have called ultimacy. The immediate implication of this understanding for our discussion is that someone might well see the pledge of allegiance to the flag—with or without "God"—as violating that which he holds to be most precious and hence running counter to his religion.

Beyond this immediate implication we can ask whether it is possible that the pledge—when required by law or administered under the aegis of the state—might constitute "an establishment of religion"? Does an exercise become "an establishment of religion" if through it the state seeks to elicit in the youngster a belief which occupies in his life the same place that belief in God has occupied in the life of orthodox believers? Professor Tillich's discussions of the nature of religion might be helpful

[56] 380 U.S. 163, 164–66, 176 (1965). See also Justice Douglas' concurring-opinion discussion of nontheistic religions, 188–93. Also Robert L. Rabin, "When Is a Religious Belief Religious: *United States* v. *Seeger* and the Scope of Free Exercise," *Cornell Law Quarterly,* LI (Winter 1966), 231–49.

[57] 380 U.S. 163, 187, citing Tillich, *The Shaking of the Foundations* (1948), 57. Court's emphasis.

at this point also. One can, he argued, subsume under "religion those secular movements which show decisive characteristics of the religions proper . . ." Tillich called such secular movements "quasi-religions." The most significant of the decisive characteristics of religion evidenced by such movements is ultimacy. Hence in the realm of politics or civic life Tillich pointed to fascism and communism as secular movements in which nationalism was stretched to the point of ultimacy. When nationalism commands "unconditional concern" it becomes a "quasi-religion."[58]

There is a thin line which divides nationalism from religion, a patriotic rite from a religious one. The Court understandably sought in *Engel* to widen that line into a clearly marked boundary. It would appear that the Court has not made this task easier by its open-ended understanding of religion in *Torcasso* and *Seeger*. Still, I would argue for that understanding, and especially in this context I would call attention to the most obvious implication of this understanding for patriotic exercises in the school. Such exercises ought not be carried on in such a high-pressured way as to compel all to participate regardless of personal conscience or to force the acceptance of a particular point of view. And that might be another guideline.

TEACHING ABOUT RELIGION

One of the approaches to which the Court gave more than a little encouragement in *Schempp* was the "objective" study of religion. This suggestion was made in connection with the Court's response to the charge that unless prayer and Bible reading were permitted a "religion of secularism" would be "established in the schools." After denying this charge the Court went on to observe that

it might well be said that one's education is not complete without a study of comparative religion or the history of religion and its relationship to the advancement of civiliza-

58*Christianity and the Encounter of World Religions*, pp. 4–6.

tion. It certainly may be said that the Bible is worthy of study for its literary and historic qualities. Nothing we have said here indicates that such study of the Bible or of religion, when presented objectively as part of a secular program of education, may not be effected consistently with the First Amendment.[59]

This suggestion was echoed in concurring opinions by Justices Brennan[60] and Goldberg. The language of the latter was perhaps the strongest of any used by the Court:

> Government must inevitably take cognizance of the existence of religion and, indeed, under certain circumstances the First Amendment may require that it do so. And it seems clear to me from the opinions in the present and past cases that the Court would recognize the propriety of . . . the teaching *about* religion, as distinguished from the teaching *of* religion, in the public schools.[61]

Having included the *study* of religion as one of the possible areas of endeavor left to the school after the removal of such obvious religious exercises as prayer, and Bible reading, the Court, of course, could offer little further by way of guidance. Effecting a program in the study of religion ought to be entrusted "very largely to the experienced officials who superintend the Nation's public schools," Justice Brennan pointed out.[62] However, the Court did leave these officials the major caveat suggested in such words and phrases as teaching *about* as against teaching *of* and "objectively as part of a secular program of education . . ."[63] The purpose must be primarily informational and the methods must be those of secular rather than religious education.

The caveat, of course, offers only the broadest guidelines. Difficulties associated with the study of religion within those guidelines should be no more minimized than those encountered

[59]374 U.S. 203, 225.
[60]Justice Brennan pointed out that "the holding of the Court . . . plainly does not foreclose teaching about the Holy Scriptures or about the differences between religious sects in classes in literature or history." Ibid., 300.
[61]Ibid., 306.
[62]Ibid., 300.
[63]Ibid., 225.

in distinguishing between religious and patriotic exercises. Justice Jackson reminded his brethren, and others, of these difficulties in his concurring opinion in *McCollum*. The school ought to educate the student, he pointed out, in "the currents of religious thought that move the world for a part in which he is being prepared." But how a teacher could handle such a sensitive area satisfactorily was a big question indeed. It was "too much to expect that mortals" would "teach . . . with . . . detachment . . ." controversial areas which arouse the passions of their contemporaries. "When instruction turns to proselyting and imparting knowledge becomes evangelism" was, the Justice opined, "except in the crudest cases, a subtle inquiry."[64]

Because of such difficulties as Justice Jackson alluded to, the study of religion is an area which the public school administrator might be tempted to avoid. While acknowledging the forcefulness of Justice Jackson's caveat upon a caveat, it is clear, however, that the schools cannot carry out their responsibilities adequately by shunning sensitive and controversial areas, especially when such areas are directly related to human history and civilization. Religion is, perhaps, no more sensitive than such areas as politics, economics, and, still in some communities, biology. Like these other areas—and in teaching generally—the study of religion requires in the teacher a functioning combination of learning and sensitivity. Done properly this study might enhance the student's knowledge of the depth of human aspirations and the diversity of expression of those aspirations without unduly weighting the balance of his own choice.[65]

"WALL" OR "LINE"?

". . . the life of law has not been logic: it has been experience."[66]

—Justice Holmes

It might appear to the layman that, like Nehemiah's wall, the Court's "wall of separation" has demanded uncommon skill,

---

[64]333 U.S. 203, 236.
[65]This position is developed more fully in Chapter IX.
[66]Oliver Wendell Holmes, Jr., *The Common Law* (Boston: Little, Brown and Company, 1881, 1938), p. 1.

subtlety, zeal, and vigilance on the part of its builders and defenders. Indeed, the "wall of separation" does appear to this layman to be an unfortunate, albeit dramatically effective, metaphor. I conclude this on three grounds: (1) Literally, at the least, it is not constitutional. That document does not refer to a "wall of separation" nor does it refer to "church and state." (2) The metaphor does not do justice to the actual situation in America. As Professor Kauper has pointed out, "Church–State terminology comes to us from Europe and recalls a background which is quite unlike the American scene."[67] There is no monolithic church or state in the United States. There are churches—religious groups, denominations, sects, cults, societies, etc. There are also many manifestations of civil authority, ranging from county supervisors to the Court itself. And there are complex relationships between these religious groups and the various manifestations of civil authority that range from a zoning exemption granted to a local congregation by a city council to the cooperative machinery for the selection of chaplains for the military forces. Hence, as Professor Mead has suggested, James Madison's "line of separation between the rights of religion and civil authority" is much more apt in describing the actual situation in America than is Jefferson's "wall of separation between church and state."[68] (3) The metaphor of the "wall" also conveys a sense of finality that may be an attractive abstraction to some but hardly does justice to the manner in which the constitutional process operates. There is a temptation to give ontological status to a decision of the Supreme Court of the United States, especially when such sharp language is used by the Court. But each Court decision deals with all of the complexities and intricacies of a specific case, with flesh and blood in relation to constitutional principles. One decision may build on another, as *McCollum* did on *Everson*. One decision may appear to modify another, as *Zorach* appeared to modify *Mc-*

---

[67] *Religion and the Constitution*, p. 3. For elaboration on this point see Sidney E. Mead, "Neither Church nor State: Reflections on James Madison's 'Line of Separation,'" *A Journal of Church and State*, X (Autumn 1968), 349–63.

[68] Ibid., p. 349, referring to a letter written by Madison in 1832 to the Reverend Jasper Adams.

Collum. And one decision may reverse another, as *Barnette* did *Gobitis.* "A course of decisions may be principled," Professor Freund has suggested, and we have examined the principles of separation and neutrality as they have emerged in recent decisions. But, as Professor Freund also points out, such a course of decisions need not be "doctrinaire."[69] The problem is that the layman, and even some jurists, may be inclined to make a full-bodied doctrine out of the "wall of separation." But to do so is to oversimplify the actual historical and constitutional situation and to go beyond where the Court itself has gone. For while the Court has used the metaphor of the "wall" quite extensively, in its decisions it has revealed, for the most part, a real sensitivity to the complexities of the American scene. Hence the actual situation facing the public schoolman is not a firmly erected wall with the church on one side and the public school on the other but a couple of lines between released time on and off school premises and between Bible reading as devotional and as academic study. Instead of a decalogue of "thou shalt nots" which covers all the relationships between "church and state," the schoolman has one or two such prohibitions that deal with relationships between "religion" and "civil authority." These are important prohibitions that should be taken seriously, but they still leave the schoolman and the citizen with some latitude in dealing with relationships between religion and the public school.

Lest I be misunderstood, may I conclude by indicating that I am favorably disposed toward the Court's decisions in *McCollum, Engel,* and *Schempp,* even though I find the metaphor of the "wall" misleading. These decisions have put something of a brake on the powerful propensities of major religious groups to utilize public means to advance their own cause. Together with *Barnette,* and a recent decision upholding the right of student protest,[70] they also contain warnings concerning the undesir-

[69]*Religion and the Public Schools: The Legal Issue,* p. 12.
[70]*Tinker* v. *Des Moines Ind. Community School Dist.* 37 LW 4121 (1969). Three students were suspended for wearing black arm bands to school in protest against American involvement in the war in Viet Nam. The Court, by a 7 to 2 vote, found this to be in violation of the students' freedom of speech.

ability of a state enforced uniformity in practice and attitude. And I would hope that one of the long-range results of the Court's decisions might be the encouragement of experimentation and diversity in the public school's approach to religion and values.[71]

---

[71]Suggestions in the next chapter and the Positional Postscript.

VIII

The Churches, the Public, and the "Wall," 1947–

"Nothing contained in this constitution shall prohibit the . . . [public] school . . . from providing for or permitting the voluntary participation by students . . . in prayer."
—A portion of the "prayer amendment" proposed by Senator Everett McKinley Dirksen

President Kennedy "did not venture a personal opinion about the merits of the Court decision [*Engel*]. Instead, he said that the Court has spoken and that it was the duty of all Americans, whether they agreed or not, to support the Constitutional processes. He added that everyone had a remedy to a ban on prayer in the schools, namely, 'to pray ourselves' at home and in the church, and to provide religious guidance for 'our children.'"
—New York *Times*, July 1, 1962

"The public schools have an obligation to help individuals develop an intellectual understanding and appreciation of the role of religion in the life of the people of this nation. Teaching for religious commitment is the responsibility of the home and the community of faith (such as the church or synagogue) rather than the public schools."
—From a policy statement of the National Council of Churches, June 7, 1963

The High Mark of Piety

In the fifteen years following World War II Americans were more religious than ever. At least the outward signs of increasing religiosity were abundantly evident. Statistics gathered by the National Council of Churches indicated that church membership rose from 49 percent of the total population of the United States in 1940 to 63.7 percent in 1960, an all-time high in American history. According to Mr. Gallup, eight out of ten adult Americans claimed affiliation with a religious organization in 1954; over 95 percent of all adult Americans professed belief in God in that same year; church attendance reached the high point of almost 50 percent of the adult Americans interviewed in 1955; and almost 70 percent of those interviewed in 1957 believed that religion was increasing in influence upon American life. Spending on church buildings rose to new highs in this period, religious books appeared in increasing numbers on best-seller lists, and evangelists like Billy Graham reported great numerical successes. Such quantitative measures say little directly about depth of conviction. But they do clearly indicate that this was a period of increasing personal and national identification with religion as an objective entity.[1]

America's postwar piety was perfectly symbolized in Dwight David Eisenhower. He was an immensely popular figure who seemed to exemplify a typically American combination of qualities—humble origins, open personality, uncomplicated philosophy, unstinted devotion to the American cause of democracy, and a commitment to faith. Following the war an uneasy America looked increasingly to General Eisenhower for leadership and for inspiration. In his response he often utilized the language of faith. Religion—"deeply held faith"—was the most important element in "developing human character . . ." Man's "spiritual side" was "the dominant one." Moral and spiritual values were those held in highest esteem by Americans and of greatest importance to American well-being. A personal, party, or national endeavor was often best described in terms of a "crusade."[2]

[1]*Yearbook of American Churches for 1968,* ed. Whitman, pp. 228–29; A. Roy Eckhart, *The Surge of Piety in America: An Appraisal* (New York: Association Press, 1958), p. 39 and ch. i; Will Herberg, *Protestant, Catholic, Jew* (Garden City, N.Y.: Doubleday & Co., 1955), p. 85; William Lee Miller, *Piety Along the Potomac* (Boston: Houghton Mifflin, 1964), pp. 125–31.

[2]*Eisenhower Speaks,* ed. Rudolph L. Turenfels (New York: Farrar, Straus, 1948), p. 144; Eisenhower, *Peace with Justice: Selected Addresses* (New York: Columbia University Press, 1961), p. 15. See also Paul Hutchinson, "The President's Religious Faith," *Christian Century,* LXXI (March 24, 1954), 362–69; and Miller, *Piety Along the Potomac.* Charles L. Sanford reports that Kenneth Boulding once remarked that "if he could 'explain' President Eisenhower satisfactorily, he would hold the key to the meaning of human history." *The Quest for Paradise* (Urbana: University of Illinois Press, 1961), p. 1.

After his election to the Presidency by a previously unsurpassed majority Mr. Eisenhower publicly identified himself even more fully with religion. He opened his inaugural address with prayer, the only President ever to do so. He joined a church on the Sunday following his inauguration. And he continued to employ the language of faith in describing America's place in the world.

Standing slightly past the midpoint in the century, President Eisenhower looked back in his first inaugural upon a time of "tempest" and "recurring trial" for the nation and the world. While one groped in such a time in order "to know the full sense and meaning" of the age, while he sought "God's guidance" in coming to understand at what point man stood in his "long pilgrimage from darkness toward the light," it was clear, the President indicated, that this was a point in history when "we who are free must proclaim anew our faith." That faith was described variously by the new President as "the abiding creed of our fathers"; "faith in the deathless dignity of man, governed by eternal moral and natural laws"; a faith which "rules our whole way of life"; and "faith in our country and in the watchfulness of a Divine Providence." Standing against this faith were its (and America's) enemies who knew "no god but force, no devotion but its use." Their differences from America were so fundamental that they could be expressed only in antinomies: "freedom . . . pitted against slavery; lightness against the dark." Americans were locked, then, in a conflict which struck "directly at the faith" of their "fathers. . . . No principle or treasure" was safely beyond the reach of this struggle. Americans were not alone in this struggle, however, for the faith they held belonged not to them alone "but to the free of all the world," the responsibility for whose leadership "destiny" had laid upon this country.[3]

The President's words and acts of piety met with strong approval throughout the land. In a glowing editorial *Life* magazine said the inaugural address "nobly and precisely described our national situation . . ." At the same time, the President

[3]*The Presidents Speak,* pp. 257–61.

offered "a coherent and timeless view of the human situation," a view which happened also to be "peculiarly American . . ."[4]

President Eisenhower's stress on faith had some immediate obvious effects in the nation's capital. It was reported that cabinet sessions were opened with prayer and that attendance at Senate, House, and departmental prayer groups increased noticeably. The International Council of Christian Laymen's annual prayer breakfasts were attended by the President, the Vice President, and other high officials. Congress authorized the provision of a "prayer room" for its members. This room was to be maintained "for individual use rather than assemblies" and "appropriate symbols of religious unity and freedom of worship" were to be placed in it. Congress also unanimously approved a resolution to change the pledge of allegiance so as to add the words "under God." One report had it that the impetus for this resolution began with a sermon which the President heard and in which the preacher argued that the pledge lacked a basic element because it did not refer to God.[5]

While this upsurge of religious affirmation and action was especially noticeable in the early Eisenhower years, the President and the Congressmen were not really departing from tradition. From George Washington on it had been customary for Presidents to call upon the name of God in their public addresses, and especially in their inaugurals. So also divine providence and "American" faith commonly constituted the canvas of public piety upon which Presidents painted their pictures of the state of the nation and of mankind. In his inaugural address in 1949, Harry S Truman proclaimed "to the world the essential principles of the faith by which we live," a faith from which "we will not be moved." He too saw that faith vigorously opposed by the "false philosophy" of communism, discerned that the world was divided into two warring camps which differed on the most fundamental issues of life, and allied the American cause with the cause of good all over

[4]XXXIV (February 2, 1953), p. 24.
[5]Hutchinson, "The President's Religious Faith"; Miller, *Piety Along the Potomac*, p. 41; Stokes and Pfeffer, *Church and State in the United States*, pp. 570–71.

the world.[6] This sort of sanctioning of American policy, ambition, and action in religious terms was at least as old as the Declaration of Independence. My chief point in this section is that this kind of public piety fell upon especially receptive soil in the years following World War II.

Piety and the "Wall"

Public reaction to the Supreme Court's erection of the "wall of separation" can best be understood in terms of this context of religiosity. To many the Court appeared to be rending the very fabric of American life. The pastor of the First Presbyterian Church of Champaign, Illinois, bitterly commented that the Court's *McCollum* decision committed the United States "to a definite irreligious attitude" that was hardly in keeping with its history.[7] Fourteen years later, following the Court's action in striking down the New York Board of Regents prayer (*Engel*), prominent church leaders were reportedly "shocked," "scandalized," and "frightened." The decision struck "at the very heart of the Godly tradition in which American children have for so long been raised," asserted Cardinal Spellman of New York. "Another step toward secularism," prophesied Billy Graham, "a most dangerous trend."[8] A year later the Reverend Robert A. Cooke, president of the National Association of Evangelicals, proclaimed that the Court's decision in *Schempp* constituted still "another step in creating an atmosphere of hostility to religion."[9]

The extent of national concern over the *Engel* and *Schempp* decisions is evident in the alacrity and profusion with which Congressmen introduced prayer amendment resolutions, such as New York Congressman Becker's proposed amendment: "Prayers may be offered in the course of any program in any public school

[6]*The Presidents Speak*, pp. 251–55.
[7]New York *Times*, March 9, 1948.
[8]Ibid., June 27, 1962.
[9]Ibid., June 23, 1963.

. . . in the United States." More than 150 such proposed constitutional amendments to encourage prayer and the recognition of God in the public schools were introduced into the House of Representatives in the 88th Congress (1963–64).[10] Similar proposals were introduced into the Senate, including the one by the prestigious minority leader Senator Everett McKinley Dirksen, quoted in part at the beginning of this chapter. At the same time, some Congressmen openly defied the Court in the name of civic piety. The Justices, said one southern Congressman in a comment of simplistic cynicism, "put the Negroes in the schools and now they've driven God out."[11]

In the name of piety the Court's "wall" decisions (*McCollum, Engel,* and *Schempp*) were sometimes openly resisted or interpreted in the narrowest possible terms by public and church officials. Many released-time advocates assumed in the years immediately following the *McCollum* decision that it outlawed only programs conducted on school premises. In some instances apparently even on-premises programs were continued. Following *Schempp* public officials in the South especially defied the Court. Governor Wallace of Alabama announced that he himself would read the Bible in school. Until directed to do so by the United States Supreme Court the Florida Supreme Court refused to apply *Schempp* in a case contesting the constitutionality of a state statute requiring that the Bible be read in the public schools.[12] While such open resistance on the part of public officials was not as dramatically evident in other parts of the country, practices declared unconstitutional by the Court con-

[10]*School Prayers; Hearings Before the Committee of the Judiciary, House of Representatives, 88th Congress, 2nd Session* (Washington, D.C.: U.S. Government Printing Office, 1964), Part I, pp. iii-v. For a detailed analysis of the Becker amendment see John H. Laubach, *School Prayers; Congress, the Courts, and the Public* (Washington, D.C.: Public Affairs Press, 1969), Chs. III, IV.

[11]New York *Times,* July 1, 1962.

[12]Gordon Patric, "The Impact of a Court Decision: Aftermath of the McCollum Case," *Journal of Public Law,* VI (1957), 455–64; *American Jewish Yearbook,* LX (1959), 37; *Chamberlain v. Dade County Board of Public Instruction,* 143 So. 2d 21 (Fla., 1962), 374 U.S. 487 (1963), 377 U.S. 402 (1964); Muir, *Prayer in the Public Schools; Religion and the Public Order, 1964,* ed. Donald A. Giannella (Chicago: The University of Chicago Press, 1965), pp. 205–09.

tinued to be observed in many school districts. In the five years following the *Schempp* decision prayer and Bible-reading cases reached federal courts and state supreme courts in eight other states: New Jersey, Massachusetts, Delaware, Idaho, Michigan, Pennsylvania, New York, and Illinois. These cases dealt with efforts to avoid, oppose, or ignore the Court's decisions in *Engel* and *Schempp*. It was reported in 1964 by the director of the project on Religious Freedom and Public Affairs of the National Conference of Christians and Jews that studies undertaken in cooperation with that agency "reveal that the majority of the school systems, particularly in the rural parts of the United States, will continue with the regimen of religious practice, prayers, and Bible readings at the opening of their school day."[13] For many the traditions of public piety appeared to require this.

The most common complaint about the "wall" among religious leaders was that it aggravated the problem of *secularism* in the public schools. Variations on this theme ran from the blunt "anti-religious" to the picturesque "throwing God out" to the milder "secularization." Secularism was understood to mean a view of life without regard to "man's relation to God here and hereafter," as the hierarchy of the Roman Catholic Church put it,[14] or the organization of life without reference to the transcendent, as it was sometimes put in more abstract language.

"In no field of social activity," affirmed the American bishops of the Roman Catholic Church, "has secularism done more harm than in education." Secularists had deliberately set out not only to advance but to exploit the removal of religion from the common schools. It was their intention "to secularize completely the public school and then claim for it a total monopoly of education." But they must be resisted by all thoughtful Americans. In the first place, secularism represented a break "with our historical tradition." Beyond that, it was clear that the exclusion of religion from the public school was "a hasty and

[13]On the court cases see Laubach, *School Prayers*, ch. v. The quotation is from Rabbi Arthur Gilbert in *Religion and the Public Order, 1964*, ed. Giannella, p. 116. See also the summary of these studies found in the "Year in Review" section of the same volume, pp. 243–48.

[14]Statement of the Hierarchy of the United States on "Secularism," November 14, 1947; found in *Our Bishops Speak*, p. 138.

shortsighted solution of the very difficult problem that con-
fronts public authority in a nation of divided religious allegiance." The real danger, the bishops argued, was not divisiveness
due to religious difference but "the weakening of religion as a
constructive force." Religion was "a nation's most vital asset."
In a state where it was denigrated or denied the state tended
"to become an instrument of tyranny."[15]

Many Protestant leaders also expressed firm reservations about
secularization of public education and grave doubts about the
"wall." "On no account must an educational system which is
permeated by the philosophy of secularism . . . be allowed to
gain control of our public schools," proclaimed an assembly of
the most representative Protestant body in the United States,
the National Council of Churches, in 1953. In an obvious appeal
for released time the Council stated, "In some constitutional
way, provision should be made for the inculcation of the principles of religion, whether within or outside the precincts of
the school, but always within the regular schedules of a pupil's
working day." Public school "awareness of God" should also be
increased through such devices as "the reverent reading of
selections from the Bible . . ."[16]

Following the Court decision in *McCollum* a group of well-
known Protestant scholars and religious leaders issued a statement in the journal *Christianity and Crisis* declaring their basic
disagreement with the majority of the Court. Labeling the "wall
of separation" a "misleading metaphor" the group complained
that the Court's decision would "greatly accelerate the trend
toward the secularization of our culture." This statement was
signed by several substantial shapers of Protestant opinion, including Reinhold Niebuhr, the leading American figure in the
so-called Neo-Orthodox movement in theology; Henry P. Van
Dusen, president of Union Theological Seminary; Harry Emerson
Fosdick, widely known liberal Protestant preacher and interpreter

[15]Ibid., pp.138–41; New York *Times,* November 16, 1952. In 1952
the bishops reacted sharply to President Conant's argument that religion
tended to be a divisive element in public education. See Brother Edmond
G. Dronin, *The School Question* (Washington, D.C.: Catholic University
Press, 1963), pp. 227–30, for a list of titles in reaction to Conant.

[16]Quoted in Drinan, *Religion, the Courts, and Public Policy,* p. 49.

of Christianity; and two well-known bishops, McConnell of the Methodist Church and Scarlett of the Protestant Episcopal Church.[17]

Van Dusen and Niebuhr expressed similar doubts about separation following the Court's decision in *Engel*. The notion of the "wall" was not to be found in the First Amendment, Van Dusen argued. What was excluded was preferential aid to religion, not aid to religion generally. Hence there was room in the public schools for a religion which was "freed from sectarian bias and control."[18] Niebuhr wondered whether *Engel* might not "work so consistently in the direction of a secularization of the school system as to amount to the suppression of religion and to give the impression that government must be anti-religion."[19]

"Secularization" or "secularism" were relatively mild words for describing a supposed Court-encouraged trend in the public schools. This type of language was generally preferred by respectable church leaders. However, "godless" or "atheistic" were favorite epithets among those who found both the Court and the schools lacking in civil piety and who attacked both with the full force of their own theological arsenal. This type of religio-political critique was much in evidence in this period of rising criticism of the public schools.[20]

The one element that most objectors to the "wall" appeared to have in common was an understanding of public piety involving the kind of traditional religious practice that the Court's decisions ruled out. This sort of practice was seen as being important symbolically in conveying a proper sense of what was regarded as characteristic of the American heritage and in acknowledging the transcendent element in public piety. "Secu-

[17]*Christianity and Crisis,* VIII (July 5, 1948), p. 90.
[18]Ibid., XXII (October 15, 1962), 178–80. See also Van Dusen *God in Education* (New York: Scribner, 1951).
[19]*Christianity and Crisis,* XXII (July 23, 1962), pp. 125–26.
[20]In 1953 two leading historians of education listed "religion" in first place among the categories under which they treated the rising tide of criticism of the public school in the years following World War II. R. Freeman Butts and Lawrence A. Cremin, *A History of Education in American Culture* (New York: Holt, 1953), p. 539. See also Mary Anne Raywid, *The Ax-Grinders: Critics of Our Public Schools* (New York: Macmillan, 1962).

larism" was a label used to describe the removal of this factor from public piety.

The "Wall" Supported

While many religious leaders wailed or whimpered at the "wall of separation," others greeted it with good cheer. The liberal Protestant journal the *Christian Century* affirmed that in *McCollum* the Court had given "strong and we hope decisive endorsement . . ." to "the principle of separation of church and state . . ." The *Century's* Protestant myopia was amply evident in its legally dubious conclusion that the Court's decision constituted "a resounding defeat for the efforts of the Roman Catholic Church to secure tax funds to support its schools." Fourteen years later the *Century* concluded that by its decision in *Engel* the Court had "rendered a service of the greatest importance to true religion as well as to the integrity of a democratic state." This decision had "placed one more obstacle in the way of those who desire to use the power of the state to enforce conformity to religious or political ideas."[21]

Even before the Court's decision in *McCollum* an enthusiastic, dedicated, and varied group joined together to form Protestants and Other Americans United for the Separation of Church and State (POAU). The charter membership of this organization included the presidents of two Protestant seminaries, a prominent Methodist bishop, the president of the Southern Baptist Convention, the secretary of the National Association of Evangelicals, a former editor of the *Christian Century,* an associate editor of a Scottish Rite journal, and an official of the National Education Association. The group dedicated itself to resisting any further "widening of the breach" in the "wall of separation." This seemed primarily to mean blocking efforts of the Roman Catholic Church to extend its influence in American public life generally and to gain public funds for its educational system in particular.

[21]LXV (March 17, 1948), 294; LXXIX (July 4, 1962), 832–33.

In this latter connection the POAU was critical of the Supreme Court's decisions in *Cochran* and *Everson,* cases involving publicly financed textbooks and bus transportation for parochial school students. While eagerly accepting the Court's stringent language in *Everson,* the group argued that the majority of the Court had failed to act in keeping with that language. The POAU continued to regard itself as a watchdog at the "wall," sniffing out all suspicious-looking groups and practices which attempted to scale, breach, or sneak around that barrier.[22]

Perhaps the most vocal of all the "wall" defenders with an anti-Catholic bias was the lawyer, journalist, and liberal religionist Paul Blanshard. Like the organizers of the POAU he too saw the Roman Catholic Church as constituting a major threat to the separation of church and state and even to American freedom generally. His accusations in *American Freedom and Catholic Power,* published in 1949, received a wide circulation. This was the first of several Blanshard volumes dealing with this theme.[23]

The one major religious group which most consistently supported the "wall" was the Jewish. Most organizations which were representative of some aspect of Jewish opinion publicly endorsed separationist sentiments and several of the more powerful groups actually engaged in litigation in this area. The Synagogue Council of America, which represented the Orthodox, Conservative, and Reform wings of Judaism, filed *amici curiae* briefs in the United States Supreme Court in support of Mrs. McCollum, in opposition to the New York Board of Regents prayer as tested in *Engel,* and in support of the Schempps and Mrs. Murray in the two prayer and Bible-reading cases adjudicated by the Court as *Abington School District* v. *Schempp.* In addition, the American Jewish Committee took similar action

[22]Organization statement and charter membership in *The New York Times,* January 12, 1948. See also Thomas G. Sanders, *Protestant Concepts of Church and State* (New York: Holt, Rinehart and Winston, 1964), pp. 161–65.
[23]Blanshard, *American Freedom and Catholic Power* (Boston: Beacon Press, 1949); *Communism, Democracy, and Catholic Power* (Boston: Beacon Press, 1951); *The Irish and Catholic Power, an American Interpretation* (Boston: Beacon Press, 1953).

in *Engel, Schempp* and *Allen,* and both this group and the American Jewish Congress supported the Zorach suit against the New York released-time program.[24]

Changing Attitudes

In the years following the Court's *Everson* decision the stances of the various religious groups in relation to the "wall" were as follows: solid Roman Catholic opposition, mixed Protestant reactions ranging from rigid separationism to considerable protest against the "wall," solid Jewish support of the "wall," and similar support by various liberal religious spokesmen. While these positions were assumed following *Everson* and *McCollum* and quite consistently maintained through *Engel* and *Schempp,* signs of change have appeared in recent years. A few Jewish spokesmen have argued that the rigid separationism of the typical Jewish position has entailed a secularistic commitment which was foreign to historic Judaism and inappropriate for a group committed to the importance of the religious life. Signs of change appeared in the Jewish community in the late 1950's when a vocal minority of the Central Conference of American Rabbis (Reform) objected to the conference's continuing support of a sharp separationist position. Spokesmen from the various segments of the Jewish community, including Arthur Gilbert, Arthur Hertzberg, Seymour Siegel, William W. Brickman, and Will Herberg, objected to the fullness and consistency of Jewish acceptance of the "wall of separation."[25]

[24]Data on *amici curiae* briefs gathered from the respective cases as found in the relevant volumes of *U.S. Reports.* On Zorach see Pfeffer, *Church, State and Freedom,* p. 354.

[25]The New York *Times,* June 27, 1958. Rabbi Gilbert reports that he "came to believe that the rigidity . . . of the Jewish position on church–state matters was in great measure an understandably defensive posture arising from past memories of Christian church-statism rather than deriving from an intrinsic requirement of Jewish faith. Seeking a modification in the Jewish position" he wrote many articles on the subject. *A Jew in Christian America,* p. x. Also Hertzberg, "Church, State and the Jews," *Commentary,* XXXV (April 1963), 277–88; Siegel, "Church and State,"

Within the Protestant community, the influence of Protestants and Other Americans United for the Separation of Church and State declined. Some Protestants were even open to the possibility of legislation and local experimentation that might indirectly benefit Roman Catholic schools. What seemed to be needed in the face of a major educational crisis in America's cities was a will to experiment with various approaches involving federal aid and all school systems rather than the closed approach of the rigid separationist.[26]

Secularization also came to be regarded with less apprehension by some Protestants. Perhaps a secularized school was to be preferred to one which attempted to promote a vague and generalized religiosity. Such a school would put the responsibility for a vital religious life directly upon the home and the church. Reinhold Niebuhr confessed in May of 1964 that he and others had had "second thoughts" about their original negative reactions to the Court's decisions in *Engel* and *Schempp*. The varied and sometimes acrimonious testimony of representatives of religious groups in the Congressional hearings concerning the proposed prayer amendment to the Constitution had impressed upon him anew the fact of the pluralism of America's religious symbols. While it was true that a "completely secularized education" involved "the danger of a completely secularized culture," given the American situation, it was equally clear that the public school could hardly become a center for vital religion. Since such vitality seemed to be closely related to pluralism and voluntarism in America, an attempt to enforce a generalized religion in the public school would be of dubious

---

Conservative Judaism, XVII (Spring–Summer 1963), 1–12; Brickman, "Public Aid to Jewish Schools," *Tradition; A Journal of Orthodox Thought,* III (Spring 1961), 151–90; and Herberg, "Religion and Education in America" in *Religious Perspectives in American Culture,* ed. James Ward Smith and A. Leland Jamison (Princeton: Princeton University Press, 1961), pp. 11–51, especially pp. 45ff.

[26]*Newsweek,* LXIV (October 5, 1964), 102–03; *Christian Century,* LXXVII (April 12, 1961), 448–50, LXXXI (May 27, 1964), 695, LXXXIII (November 23, 1966), 1459; Sanders, *Protestant Concepts of Church and State,* pp. 216–20; *Christianity and Crisis,* XXI (May 1, 1961), 61–62, XXII (May 28, 1962), 79, XXXIII (October 28, 1963), 189–95.

value. It seemed entirely possible, Niebuhr concluded, "that noncoercive religious instruction in home and church preserves the religious substance of our culture more effectively than semi-compulsory public instruction."[27]

In this same period several Protestant spokesmen, following the lead of Harvey Cox, eagerly embraced secularization as a way of emancipation from the restrictive religious rigidities of the past. The old religious symbols had become empty in "the secular city." Hence these celebrators of that city were not about to become unduly agitated over the Court's decision to outlaw prayer and Bible reading in schools. If anything, the whole school system needed overhauling—not in the hope of introducing or maintaining a religious rite or two but in order to make it more responsive to basic human needs.[28]

Evidence of a change of attitude among Protestant officialdom can be found in the policy statement on "The Churches and the Public Schools" issued on June 7, 1963, by the general board of the National Council of Churches. The board recognized "the wisdom as well as the authority" of *Engel* and affirmed, in anticipation of *Schempp*, that "neither true religion nor good education is dependent upon the devotional use of the Bible in the public school program." Six months later, a majority of the participants in a National Council of Churches conference on church and state concluded that "Christians should welcome" the Court's decisions in *Engel* and *Schempp*. "Far from being antireligious," these decisions offered churchmen "a real opportunity to explore in a new way the relationship of religious values to the total program of the public school."[29]

Protestant denominational pronouncements also reflected this change in attitude. One of the most dramatic instances of this

[27]*Christianity and Crisis*, XXIV (May 25, 1964), 93–96.
[28]See the following by Harvey Cox: *The Secular City* (New York: Macmillan, 1965); "The Relationship between Religion and Education," *Religion and Public Education*, ed. Theodore R. Sizer (Boston: Houghton Mifflin, 1967); pp. 99-111, *Commonweal*, XC (March 21, 1969), 376; and a review of the movie "High School" in *Tempo*, I (July 1, 1969), 12.
[29]Philip Wogaman, "The National Council of Churches National Conference on Church and State," *Religion and the Public Order, 1964*, ed. Giannella, pp. 136ff.

change was that which occurred in the United Presbyterian
Church in the U.S.A. Throughout the 1950's the highest official
body of the Presbyterian Church in the U.S.A.—the general
assembly—continued to issue stock statements in opposition to
any form of public aid to parochial schools, and in defense of
"our schools" which, together with the churches—as one statement put it—"stand as a bulwark for our Protestant concept of
morality, democracy, and freedom."[30] But in a significant statement on "Relations Between Church and State in the United
States of America," adopted in 1963, the Presbyterians argued
that religious observances should not "be held in a public school
or introduced into the public school as part of its program," and
that "Bible reading and prayers as devotional acts tend toward
indoctrination or meaningless ritual and should be omitted for
both reasons . . ." Further, in another remarkable reversal of
earlier positions, the Presbyterians spoke with favor of the job
of education being done by private and parochial schools, acknowledged the severe financial needs of the Catholic parochial
school system, and, while still opposing any form of direct aid
to these schools, called for support of "welfare services to all
children . . ." Finally United Presbyterians sought "discussion
with Roman Catholics" who shared "a deep concern for maintaining a strong public school system, with a view to finding
new and creative solutions to the present public-parochial
school dilemma." Such devices as "shared time" and "tax support
of scientific and technical parts of school curricula" were suggested in this connection.[31]

A similar change of attitude is evident in one of the major
Lutheran groups, the Lutheran Church of America. The second
biennial convention of that body declared in 1964 that it did
not appear that "the church need be alarmed over" *Engel* and
Schempp. Actually these decisions might even have "a whole-

[30]Statements of the general assembly of the United Presbyterian Church,
USA, from the 1954 statement. The Presbyterian Church, USA was the
larger of two bodies which merged to form the United Presbyterian Church,
USA in 1958.

[31]Pamphlet issued by the United Presbyterian Church in the United
States of America, Office of the General Assembly, Philadelphia, Pa.,
pp. 7, 12.

some effect in clarifying the role of the public school with respect to religious matters." Traditional religious practices in the public schools needed "re-evaluation" in this pluralistic age. Furthermore, it was very questionable whether this nonreligious institution, the public school, should become involved in religious practices.

While being generally supportive toward the Court in *Engel* and *Schempp*, the Lutherans expressed caution about its "concept of neutrality." If this notion meant excluding all references to religion in the public school it could easily open "the door to the cult of secularism." However, the Lutherans noted that the Court itself had been mindful of this possible effect and, in counteracting it, had "wisely stated" that the schools might "properly present programs for the objective study of the Bible and of religion."[32]

There were also signs of change within the Roman Catholic community. Despite the unfavorable reactions of several bishops to the Court decisions in *Engel* and *Schempp*, one Catholic newspaper concluded that Catholic opinion generally had recognized the "constitutional soundness" of those rulings.[33] A combination of factors—including the symbolic significance attached to the election of a Catholic to the Presidency in 1960 and the spirit of *aggiornamento* (renewal) advanced by Pope John XXIII—prompted Catholics to seek to join with members of other religious groups in confronting the enormous educational task in America through both public and parochial schools. The pronouncements of Vatican II relative to education tended to be more irenic and positive in tone than earlier papal pronouncements on this subject. The spirit of reform also led many Catholics to turn a new critical eye on their own school system.

[32]"Prayer and Bible Reading in the Public Schools," adopted by the Second Biennial Convention of the Lutheran Church in America, July 20, 1964. See also "Church and State—A Lutheran Perspective," a report of the Commission on Church and State Relations in a Pluralistic Society, under the auspices of the Board of Social Ministries of the Lutheran Church in America, 1963; and "A Position Statement on Religion in the Public School," the Board of Parish Education of the Lutheran Church, Missouri Synod, March 19, 1968.

[33]*The Pittsburgh Catholic*, as reported in *Commonweal*, LXXX (July 3, 1964), 442. See also the statement of the Catholic Press Association quoted in the same editorial in *Commonweal*.

Such criticism was directed more toward the improvement of that system than its discontinuance. Hence old myths were challenged, old rigidities relaxed.[34]

From "Wall" to "Bridge"?

The Court's erection of the "wall of separation" appears to have had a twofold effect among religious groups: (1) On the one hand, the doctrine of separation tended to polarize religious opinion and denominations; (2) on the other hand, the "wall" decisions contributed to a developing dialogue across religious lines.

(1) Religious leaders and groups were prompted generally to take "stands" for or against separation, as we have seen. And these "stands" tended to exacerbate old animosities. The *bête noire* of Protestants and Other Americans United for Separation of Church and State was the Roman Catholic Church. Likewise the POAU became a major target for Catholic shafts. Within that amorphous entity labeled "Protestantism" much tension also existed. Those who did not join the POAU, or take a similar "stand," were seen as being woolly-headed in their understanding of constitutional principle and starry-eyed in their failure to grasp the nature and extent of the Catholic threat. On the other hand, supporters of the POAU were criticized by other Protestants for allowing strong doctrine to becloud their focus on the realities of church-state relations and religious pluralism in the United States.

Polarities within the Christian camp were sometimes overshadowed by differences between Christians and Jews on the question of religious influence and practice in the public schools.

[34]Vatican Council "Declaration on Christian Education," in *The Catholic Educational Review,* LXIV (March 1966), 145–58; Mary Perkins Ryan, *Are Parochial Schools the Answer? Catholic Education in the Light of the Council* (New York: Holt, Rinehart, and Winston, 1964); McCluskey and Sharper articles on Catholic education in *Commonweal,* LXXIX (January 31, 1964), 507–11, 533–38; Andrew M. Greeley and Peter H. Rossi, *The Education of Catholic Americans* (Chicago: Aldine Publishing, 1966).

One celebrated instance illustrates the point. Following the Court decision in *Engel,* the Jesuit magazine *America* addressed an editorial "To Our Jewish Friends." The editorial was bitterly critical of Leo Pfeffer, counsel for the American Jewish Congress, and of "a few Jewish organizations" for conducting an "all-out campaign to secularize the public school and public life from top to bottom . . ." *America* appealed to the wider Jewish community to exercise some control over these secularists and to make it known that they did not represent the Jewish position generally. It was suggested further that failure to practice restraint of this sort might increase the incidence of anti-Semitism in the country. The editorial immediately elicited a variety of reactions, including a sharp rebuke from the liberal Catholic journal *Commonweal* and a strongly worded reply from the American Jewish Committee.[35]

What was perhaps most revealing about the editorial in *America* was the fact that it failed to evidence any understanding of the basic difference between Judaism and Christianity in approaching religion in public life. The editorial writer apparently assumed that all religious groups in America shared a concern as old as Christendom that religion should permeate public life as much as possible (or as the law would allow). But, having inherited a history of more than a thousand years as a minority in Christendom, it is understandable that many within the Jewish community might prefer a secularized school to one even vaguely tinged with Christian influence.

The *America* controversy over Jewish opposition to the Board of Regents prayer attracted national attention. At the local level, animus between Jews and Christians was likely to be aroused over any type of religious observance, and especially over such issues as holiday celebrations and baccalaureate services. This type of controversy has come to be especially sharp in recent years in communities with substantial Jewish minorities. Observances in connection with Christmas, such as carol singing and pageants depicting the birth of "the Christ child," have

[35]Editorial in *America,* CVII (September 1, 1962), 665–66; replies in subsequent issues; *Commonweal* editorial, LXXVI (September 7, 1962), 483–84 and several articles on the subject in *Commonweal,* LXXVI (September 28, 1962), 5ff.

been common in American public schools. Such observances have also often been a source of embarrassment and even resentment among Jews. Some resourceful public school and community leaders have attempted to handle this source of tension between members of the two religious traditions by planning observances of both Christmas and the Jewish holiday of Hanukkah. In his analysis of this practice, Leo Pfeffer concludes, however, that "most Jewish parents" and "all major Jewish organizations are opposed in principle to joint holiday celebrations."[36]

(2) Litigation relative to religion in the public schools had the effect of dramatically increasing the amount of lay and expert examination of constitutional principles and of the relation of religion to public life. No other single factor was as responsible for the enormous volume of literature and the significant number of committees, conferences, etc. concerned with religion and public life generally and religion in the public school in particular. Some of the literature was polemical; some was ill informed. But religious leaders and spokesmen, in unprecedented numbers, became articulate about this constitutional question. And they began to discuss it across religious lines and even with secularists with some hope of developing positive approaches to the relationship between religion and public education. One articulate Catholic spokesman, Father Neil G. McCluskey, S.J., expressed the hope that dialogue between Catholics and Protestants might be "preparing for the day when cooperative ventures, like the shared-time program or a completely overhauled released-time program [would] become part of public education . . ." While in the past the question of religion in education had been "an almost constant source of Church-State tension and inter-Church friction," perhaps in the future it might "well become a bridge."[37]

"Dialogue" became the watchword for interreligious relations. Protestants had been conversing across denominational lines

---

[36]Pfeffer and Stokes, *Church and State in the United States*, p. 383 with documentation from a statement issued by the Synagogue Council and the National Community Relations Advisory Council. For an exception to Pfeffer's conclusion in the case of one large community, see Herberg, "Religion and Education in America," as cited in footnote 25 above, pp. 45–46.

[37]*Commonweal*, LXXIX (January 31, 1964), 511.

in the ecumenical movement for some time. Vatican II dramatically increased conversation between Catholics and Protestants
and gave some encouragement to friendly exchange between
Christians and Jews. With slight exaggeration, Rabbi Arthur
Gilbert reported in 1964 that "for the first time in American
history, religious and community leaders are now talking to
each other."[38] Under Rabbi Gilbert's direction, and with the
cooperation of other religious leaders and representatives, the
National Conference of Christians and Jews, through its project
on Religious Freedom and Public Affairs, organized eighty-
seven interreligious dialogue groups in fifty-nine communities
between 1961 and 1965. The question of religion in the public
school was one of the major items of concern in these discussions.[39]

This type of interreligious dialogue, like discussions involving
religionists and secularists, churchmen and educators, jurists and
school officials, etc., was characteristic of an American orientation toward problem solving. The Court had declared certain
public school religious practices unconstitutional. But this was
not generally understood as closing off all avenues of contact
between religion and the public school. Rather it served as a
stimulus to explore other avenues. And in the late 1960's
Americans—religious leaders, schoolmen and educators, public
officials—pursued this kind of exploration at local, state, and
national levels. In May of 1966, for example, a conference on
religion and public education was held in Cambridge, Massachusetts, under the sponsorship of the National Conference
of Christians and Jews, the Harvard Graduate School of Education, and the Harvard Divinity School. Participants included
representatives of religious organizations, school administrators
and teachers, and college and university professors in such
fields as law, education, sociology, philosophy, and theology.
The volume published following this conference[40] contains essays

[38]*Religion and the Public Order, 1964,* ed. Giannella, p. 118.
[39]See Claud D. Nelson, *Religion and Society; the Ecumenical Impact*
(New York: Sheed and Ward, 1966), pp. 172–73.
[40]*Religion and Public Education,* ed. Theodore R. Sizer. Cited in
note 28 above.

from a variety of religious and nonreligious perspectives addressed to such issues as "Secularism, Pluralism, and Religion in Our Society," "Theological Perspectives on Public Education," and "Teaching *About* Religion." While elements of religious defensiveness and glimpses of doctrinal "stands" occasionally appear in these essays, so also do fresh approaches to an important and complex question. There is no consensus of point of view in the essays, other than a common acknowledgement of the significance and relevance of the general question under discussion. In this the volume is a good illustration of Americans engaged together in discourse about a commonly acknowledged problem.

Positive Approaches

One of the effects of the Court's "wall" decisions has been to swing public attention toward possible constitutionally acceptable devices for dealing with religion in the public school. Two avenues have frequently been suggested for the public schools themselves: stress on commonly held moral and spiritual values, and teaching courses or units "about" religion in the regular curriculum. Two other approaches, involving some cooperation between religious groups and public school authorities, have seemed viable: some form of released time which does not entail use of public school buildings, and what has come to be called "shared time" or "dual enrollment"—that is, some meshing of public and parochial school resources. We shall examine these latter two first.

RELEASED TIME AND SHARED TIME OR DUAL ENROLLMENT

The Supreme Court's decision in *Zorach* encouraged the continuation of existing off-school-premises released-time programs and perhaps gave impetus to the inauguration of additional programs. The major religious groups—especially the

Roman Catholic Church and the Protestant churches affiliated with the National Council of Churches—have continued to pursue this course as one of the more fruitful avenues for the religious education of public school students. The general board of the National Council of Churches declared unanimously at a meeting on June 3–4, 1965, that "the contemporary situation makes more necessary than ever before reinvigorated, extended and expanded programs of Christian education through the week." Among the approaches suggested by the board for this type of education were "dual school enrollment" and "released or dismissed time" programs. Following the issuance of this statement, the Department of Educational Development of the Council prepared an attractive packet containing many materials that describe the educational "benefits" to be derived from "The New Through-the-Week Christian Education Curriculum Series" and explaining "how churches can coordinate their teaching with public education." The packet cover somewhat extravagantly affirms in large, bold type that "42,000,000 American school children can now combine their public education and their church education in a way that is practical, legal, and beneficial . . ."

The designations "shared time" and "dual enrollment" are used to refer to arrangements whereby pupils in non-public elementary or secondary schools attend public school for instruction in certain subjects—usually of a technical or scientific nature. While this practice is not entirely new, it has received national attention only in the past decade. It is a practice which has been favorably received by Catholic and Protestant religious leaders and in some educational circles. It has been seen as offering a possible solution to such problems as inadequate religious education, the financial and enrollment crises of the Catholic school system, Catholic opposition to the financing of public schools in some communities, and the legal difficulties of a federal aid program which includes parochial schools. However, some observers have regarded shared time with reservations on legal, ideological, and/or practical grounds.

Shared time or dual enrollment developed into a legislative issue in the early 1960's when a proposal was made that federal funds be used for helping to finance shared-time programs. The practice received considerable encouragement in the federal Elementary and Secondary Education Act of 1965, which provided federally supported programs for pupils in non-public as well as public schools.

The National Education Association found in 1964 that shared-time programs existed in at least 183 school districts in twenty-five states. The National Catholic Education Association reported in 1965 that 251 Catholic elementary schools and 182 Catholic high schools had shared-time programs. Within the context of America's vast educational enterprise these figures are not very impressive. But with additional encouragement from federal funds this practice might grow. It is a practice, however, which will probably come under court scrutiny as the various aspects of the Elementary and Secondary Education Act of 1965 are challenged by those who tend to follow separationist doctrine in their interpretation of the First Amendment.[41]

It does not appear likely at this point that either released time or shared time will become effective programs in a majority of the public school districts of the United States. Furthermore, neither is a direct approach to the question of religion in the public school curriculum. At most, they are for our analysis significant even though relatively small approaches which have some bearing on our subject.

[41]Two excellent brief analyses of shared time with bibliographies are: "Proposed Federal Promotion of 'Shared Time' Education: A Digest of Relevant Literature and Summary of Pro and Con Arguments," prepared by the Legislative Reference Service of the Library of Congress for the Subcommittee on Education of the Committee on Labor and Public Welfare of the United States Senate (Washington, D.C.: U.S. Government Printing Office, June 14, 1963); and "Shared-Time Programs: An Exploratory Study," (Washington, D.C.: National Education Association, 1964). The latter reports on a mail survey in 1963 of the superintendents of all school districts with enrollments of 300 or more. See also "Dual Enrollment in Public and Nonpublic Schools: Case Studies of Nine Communities" (Washington, D.C.: U.S. Department of Health, Education, and Welfare, Office of Education, 1965); *U.S. News and World Report*, LVIII (May 3, 1965), 51–54; and *Wilson Library Bulletin*, XLI (March 1967), 682–718. In *Flast* v. *Cohen* the U.S. Supreme Court permitted suits relative to federally subsidized programs involving parochial schools. 392 U.S. 83 (1968).

MORAL AND SPIRITUAL VALUES

"Moral and spiritual values" became a popular catch-combination following the Court's decision in *McCollum*. In 1951 the Educational Policies Commission of the NEA listed ten values on which "the American people are agreed":

(1) human personality—the basic value;
(2) moral responsibility;
(3) institutions as the servants of men;
(4) common consent;
(5) devotion to truth;
(6) respect for excellence;
(7) moral equality;
(8) brotherhood;
(9) the pursuit of happiness; and
(10) spiritual enrichment.

After discussing the varied and differing sanctions for these values among Americans, the commission turned to a series of "shoulds" for the public school, including that "moral and spiritual values should be stated as aims of the school"; that "the teaching of values should permeate the entire educational process"; and that "all the school's resources should be used to teach moral and spiritual values."[42]

This statement appeared to meet several needs and conditions of the times. Stress on *spiritual* values countered those critics who accused the school of giving over to secularism. It also fitted well with the prevailing mood of public piety. At the same time "spiritual" did not stir up either sectarian or constitutional hackles like "religious" might have done. It was acceptable to the Court, to most religionists, and even to many secularists—including the members of the John Dewey Society.[43] It was a commodious term, apparently well suited to express both the

[42]Summaries based largely on chs. ii and iv of "Moral and Spiritual Values in the Public Schools," first cited above in footnote 10 of Chapter I.
[43]*The Public Schools and Spiritual Values,* ed. John S. Brubacher, Seventh Yearbook of the John Dewey Society.

common loyalties of public piety and the noblest aspirations of man.

There are three relevant points to note about this subject in addition to the fact of the general acceptance of the importance of moral and spiritual values in the public schools: (1) the public schools cannot escape value formation and value questions; (2) hence, this is an area to which schoolmen and educators might well give even more serious and self-conscious attention than has been customary; (3) but this is also an area which bristles with difficulties—including the inescapable question of the relation of religion, and, more specifically, of religious pluralism to moral and spiritual values. Obviously, then, this subject has ramifications which go much beyond the question of the role of religion. There are, for example, hard questions of definition and implementation which we shall not deal with here.[44] I wish only to include a reminder of the continuing tension between unity and diversity in value affirmation, especially as this is related to religion.

The NEA Educational Policies Commission stressed the values Americans hold in common. Such an emphasis is understandable and—within limits—necessary. Centrifugal forces have often threatened national well-being. Common experience and affirmation have been needed to counteract such forces. Hence in the unity-diversity tension the public school has almost always stressed the former. From Mann to Dewey to Conant, educators have emphasized the unifying role of this common institution. But Americans have not been monolithic in their value systems. Attempts to state our common values either must force re-

[44]There is a large body of literature on this subject. For a sampling I suggest William Clayton Bower, *Moral and Spiritual Values in Education* (Lexington, Ky.: University of Kentucky Press, 1952), which describes a carefully conceived state program; Louis E. Raths, Merrill Harmin, and Sidney B. Simon, *Values and Teaching: Working with Values in the Classroom* (Columbus, Ohio: Charles E. Merrill Books, 1966); and Lawrence Kohlberg, "Moral Education, Religious Education, and the Public Schools: A Developmental View," in *Religion and Public Education*, ed. Theodore R. Sizer, pp. 164–83; and *Religious Information and Moral Development:* The Report of the Committee on Religious Education in the Public Schools of the Province of Ontario (Toronto: Ontario Department of Education, 1969), with a useful bibliography.

calcitrant elements into the unity container or so thin out the value affirmations that little is left. The commission's second value, "moral responsibility," illustrates the point. Moral responsibility to whom or what and with what sanctions and means of implementation, one might ask. And immediately we are plunged into a discussion of differences. As Professor Freund has pointed out, "a serious dialogue on problems of moral conduct will soon reach an essentially religious core."[45] "Moral responsibility" is inextricably bound up with questions of loyalty and commitment. And once again the chasm of religious difference yawns before us.

The moral and spiritual values package has been grasped in the hope that it could avoid religious differences while still stressing something more than the material or the completely secular. It is not entirely clear, however, that the package is that potent. Still, sensitive men are hopeful. Rabbi Eugene Borowitz has argued, for example, that the public schools should instill that "sense of awe" and that "sense of unity which underlies all multiplicity." At the same time, because of its divisiveness religion must have no part in this process.[46] In a similar vein, Professor Robert Ulich of Harvard has urged that the public schools should be "completely separated from the nation's religious heritage" if by "religion" is meant "allegiance to a particular creed." However, if "'religion' connotes an attitude or sentiment that expresses a person's reverential feeling concerning the cosmic powers which surround him, which nourish him and sustain him, and on which he depends in birth, life, and death . . ." then obviously the school must have something to do with it. The public school, says Professor Ulich, has not been released by the Supreme Court from "its responsibilities for the whole and wholesome development of the student's personality." And what he calls "the spiritual tradition of humanity," as contrasted with the specific historic religious traditions, is an essential element in meeting that responsibility.[47] It is not clear to this observer, however, how

[45]*Religion and the Public Schools: The Legal Issue,* p. 20.
[46]"Judaism and the Secular State," in *Religion and Public Education,* ed. Sizer, pp. 280–81.

anyone—whether in or out of public school—can deal with "the spiritual tradition of humanity" without referring to religious traditions, or how one can instill a transcendent "sense of unity" while bypassing multiplicity.

The problem is an old one. How will the public school help to achieve that unity necessary to human development and national well-being without so rounding off the edges of diversity that the finished product emerges in fabricated and standardized form? It would seem that some frank facing of differences must accompany cultivation of commonality. Possibly a sympathetic exposure to the various ways in which men understand themselves at their deepest levels of commitment might actually lead to a greater recognition of commonality. In any case, I have serious doubts concerning the wisdom of ignoring or suppressing religious diversity all the way through the public schools. Possibly the Court-encouraged interest in "teaching *about* religion" opens up one additional way of dealing with the unity-diversity tension.

TEACHING ABOUT RELIGION

The notion of teaching about religion has received significant support from educators and, as we have seen, from some members of the Court, some religious leaders, and some religious groups. The Educational Policies Commission of the NEA suggested in its statement on moral and spiritual values that the public school could "and should teach much useful information about the religious faiths . . ." The school could "teach objectively *about* religion without advocating or teaching any religious creed," the commission confidently asserted.[48] The American Council on Education issued three reports dealing with religion in public education, in 1944, 1947, and 1953. The third report summarized the recommendations of the council with the affirmation that "a factual study of religion" was "the best approach to a solution of the problem confronting public

---

[47]*Religion and the Public Schools: The Educational Issue,* pp. 45–46.
[48]*Moral and Spiritual Values in the Public Schools,* pp. 77–78.

education in dealing with religion."[49] A decade later the Commission on Religion in the Public Schools of the American Association of School Administrators held that religion, "as an integral part of man's culture . . . must be included" in the curriculum of the public schools. The commission also distinguished between "teaching *about* religion and teaching *for* religion, between examining religion as a cultural phenomenon and indoctrinating in a religion." Furthermore, the commission ruled out a kind of "neutralism" which would eliminate all reference to religion or seem to give a monopoly to "a nontheist humanism." In order to accomplish the kind of sensitive and informed teaching that is needed in this area the commission called for better preparation of teachers and the production of more accurate and useful materials.[50]

Encouraging statements of the Justices in *Schempp* gave considerable impetus to the interest in providing for the study of religion and the Bible in the public schools. Following that decision the California Board of Education issued a statement in December of 1963 advising that the "schools should have no hesitancy in teaching about religion . . ." Dr. James E. Allen, New York state commissioner of education, urged public schools to teach about religion and especially about its role in shaping America's heritage. Archibald Shaw, associate secretary of the American Association of School Administrators, summed up a point of view that was receiving increasing support among educators and religious leaders when he observed that the Supreme Court's decision might "well turn out to have done more for both education and religion than all the legislative hearings and church pressures together. Now," he concluded, "we can at last get to building a curriculum that will lead our young people to a steadily broadening understanding of the role religion plays in the affairs of mankind."[51]

Shortly after the *Schempp* decision had been handed down by

[49]*The Function of the Public Schools in Dealing with Religion* (Washington, D.C.: American Council on Education, 1953), p. 85.

[50]*Religion in the Public Schools* (Washington, D.C.: American Association of School Administrators, 1964), pp. 55ff.

[51]Reports of reactions of school personnel in *The American Jewish Yearbook*, LXV (1964), 52; and Bert S. Gerard, "Teaching About Religion:

the Court the Abington (Pennsylvania) Township school district
—the locale of the *Schempp* suit—issued a policy statement
which included the assertion that the "study of religions of the
world is an essential part of the curriculum of the schools," but
the teachers must maintain a climate of "neutrality." The Pennsylvania state department of justice advised schoolmen that while
Schempp outlawed "group Bible reading and prayer," a variety
of "nonreligious" practices could still be sponsored by the
school. These included "the objective study about religion as a
cultural force; objective study of comparative religion or the
history of religion; and Bible study for literary and historic
qualities as part of a secular program of education." Late in
1965 the Pennsylvania legislature adopted an act calling for
"a secondary course in the study of religious literature."
Specifically, the legislature mentioned "courses in the literature
of the Bible and other religious writings" which it permitted
to be "introduced and studied as regular courses in the literature
branch of education by all pupils in the secondary public
schools." It was specified that such courses should be "elective
only and not required of any student." In order to give the
statute more than the force of sentiment the legislature provided for implementation by directing that such courses
should be prepared and adopted "by the Department of Public Instruction with the advice and counsel of the Council of
Basic Education and the approval of the State Board of
Education."[52]

Reactions to the proposed study of religion and religious
literature have not been universally favorable, however. While
major Protestant groups and Protestant educators have generally
supported the notion,[53] some Jewish leaders have expressed
keen reservations about it. Rabbi Eugene B. Borowitz has argued

When and Where to Begin," *Religious Education*, LXIII (May-June 1968),
215–18; Shaw as quoted in *The Reader's Digest*, LXXXVI (February
1965), 54.

[52]*The American Jewish Yearbook*, LXV (1964), 52; and John R.
Whitney, "Introducing Religious Literature in Pennsylvania Secondary
Schools," *Religious Education*, LXIII (March-April 1968), 89–96.

[53]See, for example, Niels C. Nielsen, Jr., *God in Education: A New
Opportunity for American Schools* (New York: Sheed and Ward, 1966).

that "philosophically . . . there is no such thing as objectivity,"[54] hence countering Justice Clark's *dictum*. Rabbi Robert Gordis suspected that teaching about religion was a device by which the head of the Christian camel could be thrust under the public school tent.[55] Some educators have also expressed reservations about the study of religion in the public school. Professor Ulich argued that "a history of religion presented in a scholarly fashion" belonged "not in the public school, but on the higher academic levels." Religion is, he claimed, too difficult and controversial a subject to handle in the public school.[56] Frederick A. Olafson, professor of education and philosophy at Harvard, expressed reservations concerning such items as qualified teachers, place in an already crowded curriculum, and possible impact on the student's faith.[57]

Obviously this is an area which warrants caution. The prepositional reservation "about" is no guarantee that materials and courses introduced under this rubric will be essentially different from stock catechetical or Sunday-school fare which is designed as much to promote and reinforce a position as to inform. In fact, there is considerable evidence that such material has been commonly used in some school districts.[58] Even more important than the question of materials is that of the sensitivity, skill, and knowledge level of the teacher. A

[54]*Religion and Public Education*, ed. Sizer, pp. 278–79. But see Rabbi Arthur Gilbert's cautious support of teaching about religion, in the same volume, p. 80.

[55]*The Root and the Branch; Judaism and the Free Society* (Chicago: University of Chicago Press, 1962), pp. 110ff.

[56]*Religion and the Public Schools: The Educational Issue*, pp. 45.

[57]"Teaching *About* Religion: Some Reservations," in *Religion and Public Education*, ed. Sizer, pp. 84–95.

[58]For some examples of the use in the public schools of materials of dubious quality and intent see Arthur Gilbert, "Reactions and Resources," in *Religion and Public Education*, ed. Sizer, pp. 37–83. For an especially flagrant instance see Laubach, *School Prayers*, pp. 118–25. For some notion of the vast range of possible materials available in this area see James U. Panoch and David L. Barr, *Religion Goes to School; A Practical Handbook for Teachers* (New York: Harper & Row, 1968), chs. iv-vi. These authors have assembled an impressive amount of data. They tend to lump together, however, items which are clearly suitable for use in a secular educational context with those which are designed primarily for religious education in a religious context.

skilled teacher might produce good educational results with inadequate materials, while an unskilled teacher might be unable to do much even with the best of materials. Furthermore, an insensitive and uninformed teacher might even do more harm than good—by reinforcing prejudices and hatreds, for example, or by deliberately undermining a student's religious orientation.

While this is admittedly a difficult area, there are some encouraging signs that educationally sound work can be done where sufficient knowledge, skill, and patience are applied. One of the more carefully conceived programs is that which has been developed by Pennsylvania State University and the University of Pennsylvania in cooperation with the Pennsylvania state department of public instruction under the act of the Pennsylvania legislature referred to above. Two courses—"Religious Literature of the West" and "Religious Literature of the East"— have been developed after extensive consultation with scholars, educators, and schoolmen from a variety of religious and academic communities and after being tried in selected school districts in Pennsylvania. Teachers who do such "trial runs" have been given careful advance preparation in special short-term institutes. Following this testing procedure, the courses have been made available to all of the school districts of the state. It is noteworthy that a constant effort has been made to develop and improve these courses in accordance with high standards of scholarship and educational technique. What has been developed differs in kind from typical courses offered in released-time programs or from the various Bible courses accredited by some states earlier in the century. For example, "Religious Literature of the West" includes selections from the Talmud and the Qur'an, in addition to selections from the Hebrew Bible and the New Testament.[59]

Another project of considerable significance to the "objective study of religion" or the "teaching about religion" is the Religion–Social Studies Curriculum Project at Florida State University. The goal of this project is to enrich social-studies programs in

[59]For a fuller description of this program see John R. Whitney as cited in note 49 above, and in *The Religious Situation* (Boston: Beacon Press, 1968), ed. Donald Cutler, pp. 365–81.

secondary schools, with special reference to religion. The project is a result of the deliberations of a twelve-member interreligious and interracial "State Committee on Study About Religion in Public Schools" which was appointed by the Florida superintendent of public instruction in 1965. With the aid of a grant from the Danforth Foundation extensive work has been done at Florida State in selecting and preparing usable materials and units and in training social-studies teachers. For example, three resource volumes have been projected under the heading "The Social Studies Curriculum: Issues in Religion." These include one volume on America, one on Western civilization, and one on world cultures.[60]

Both the Pennsylvania and the Florida projects have been developed to relate to the existing structures and personnel of the public school, the former relating to the English or literature division and the latter being geared directly into the social studies program. Both have sought to do essentially two things relative to the existing situation—to produce usable materials and to increase the knowledge level in religion of literature and social-studies teachers. This appears to be a practical and fruitful approach in the existing circumstances.

In some local school districts efforts have been made to develop new and separate courses in the study of religion—for example, "History of World Religions" at Claremont High School (California) and "Religion in Culture" at North Haven High School (Connecticut).[61] Courses of this type have generally been offered as electives at the senior level. To be educationally sound, such courses obviously require a teacher who is knowledgeable in religious studies.

It is worth noting that university departments of religion

[60]Professor Edwin Scott Gaustad, Principal Investigator in Religion for The Religion–Social Studies Project, Florida State University, has described and evaluated that project in "Teaching About Religion in the Public Schools: New Ventures in Public Education," *A Journal of Church and State,* XI (Spring 1969), pp. 265–76.

[61]Joseph Forcinelli, "The History of World Religions: A Course as Taught at the Claremont, California, High School," *Journal of Secondary Education,* XLII (April 1967), 162–65; and course outline from North Haven High School.

have played significant roles in most of these recent developments to which I have referred. The Pennsylvania course "Religious Literature of the West" was developed primarily under the auspices of the department of religious studies at the Pennsylvania State University, and "Religious Literature of the East" by the department of religious thought at the University of Pennsylvania. The key figure in the Florida project has been Dr. Robert Spivey, chairman of the department of religion at Florida State University, and his department has played an important role in developing the project. The courses mentioned at North Haven and Claremont have been developed "under the wing," as it were, of religion departments at Yale and Claremont Graduate School, respectively. This fact is of significance in at least two ways. It suggests there there are university personnel and resources available for the development of materials and the education of teachers in religious studies. It also reminds us of the remarkable growth of college and university religious-studies departments and programs in recent years. This growth is especially noteworthy in state universities, as is evident in the fact that at least a dozen major state universities have established departments or other types of curricular programs in religion since World War II.[62] This steady growth in religious-studies programs at colleges and universities has already had an effect upon the public school by increasing the religious literacy of teachers who have taken religious-studies courses as part of their undergraduate preparation. Beyond this, it is clear that the growth of such programs will have the effect of increasing the amount of formal attention by schoolmen to the study of religion in the public schools. This is immediately evident in Pennsylvania and Florida. It is a common pattern that curricular developments in the colleges

[62]These include Pennsylvania State and Florida State and such other universities as North Carolina, Tennessee, Alabama, Indiana, Illinois, Southern Illinois, Western Michigan, Michigan State, Michigan, Montana, and California at Santa Barbara. Programs have also been instituted at such private institutions as Princeton, Yale, Oberlin, and Stanford. See Robert Michaelsen, *The Study of Religion in American Universities* and "The Study of Religion: A Quiet Revolution in American Universities," the *Journal of Higher Education*, XXXVII (April 1966), 181–86.

and universities invariably influence practices in the elementary and secondary schools.

The Court and Public Opinion

Supreme Court decisions perform a peculiar function in American public life. In a formal sense they deal centrally with questions of law which are often highly technical in nature and very narrow in application. However, as final arbiter of the Constitution the Court is sometimes called upon to decide issues of great import to public life. In such cases the Court performs a combined judicial, political, and moral function. This is true because the Constitution itself is both a legal document dealing with the structure and operation of government and a document containing fundamental affirmations concerning national purpose and human rights. The provision in the First Amendment that "Congress shall make no law respecting an establishment of religion or prohibiting the free exercise thereof" has implications for the self-understanding of the nation, the role of religion in relation to the civic process, and even the health of the religious life itself. Whenever the Court is called upon to decide a case under this provision these issues are likely to be aired again—by the Court and by the public in response to the Court's decision. This is especially true if the case deals with a practice in such a major institution as the public school.

Alexis de Tocqueville noted the immense power of the Court under the Constitution. But he pointed out that at the same time, this power sprang "from opinion." The justices were "all powerful" so long as the people consented "to obey the law," but they could "do nothing" when the people scorned the law. Hence the Justices must be statesmen; "they must know how to understand the spirit of the age, to confront those obstacles that can be overcome, and to steer out of the current when the tide threatens to carry them away . . ."[63] Have the justices

[63]*Democracy in America*, ed. Mayer and Lerner, p. 137.

discerned public opinion aright in the recent religion in public-education cases? Has the flow of civic life in the public-education channel been enhanced or markedly hindered by these decisions? It is clear that these decisions have stimulated an amount of discussion in this area unparalleled in American history. Some have even felt so strongly about the Court's prayer decisions that they have sought to contravene the Court through constitutional amendment. Others have sought what I would regard as more fruitful ways of dealing with the realities of the constitutional guarantees and limits and of a religiously pluralistic nation. In fact the Court's decisions have actually prepared the ground for carefully conceived experimentation. And there is some reason for being cautiously optimistic that significant academic programs in religion will be developed in the public school in the years ahead.

IX

Piety and Learning, Unity in Diversity

A Concluding Positional Postscript

"In abbreviation: religion is the substance of culture, culture is the form of religion."

—Paul Tillich[1]

"If there is any fixed star in our constitutional constellation, it is that no official, high or petty, can prescribe what shall be orthodox in politics, nationalism, religion, or other matters of opinion or force citizens to confess by word or act their faith therein."

—The Supreme Court of the United States, 1943[2]

"Education's first duty is to make possible the survival of our country."

—Dr. Max Rafferty[3]

Seldom has so much been expected from one institution as Americans expect from their public school. Is there a national crisis? Send the school to the rescue. Is our democratic faith in jeopardy? The school must instill that faith and elicit whole-hearted commitment to it. Is the very survival of the country at stake? The school must save it. Two generations ago the school was called upon to Americanize the immigrant; today it is expected to bridge the widening chasm between white and black Americans. During the 1930's the school helped ease the pains of the great depression; today it must gird our loins for the continuing global struggle with communism while coping

[1]*Theology of Culture*, p. 42.
[2]*Board of Education* v. *Barnette*, 319 U.S. 624, 642. The words are Justice Jackson's.
[3]This is the opening sentence of Dr. Rafferty's book *Suffer, Little Children* (New York: Devin-Adair Co., 1962), p. ix. Dr. Rafferty is superintendent of public instruction for the state of California.

with burgeoning numbers of teen-agers who have no other socially acceptable place to go. In American society the school has taken over many of the functions of the family, the church, and the job. It must look to the child's personal development and keep the youth occupied with meaningful tasks. It must be concerned with value commitments as well as with skills. And the magnitude of the school's task has grown with the lengthening of expected years in school and the enrollment explosion.

Given this ascending level of public expectation it is clear that any attempt to reduce the role of the school is not likely to succeed. There is no return to the primacy of the three R's—if, indeed, such a condition ever existed. It also seems unrealistic to hope that questions of values, faith, and commitment can be set aside. While religious rituals—such as the devotional utterance of the Lord's Prayer—might be discontinued in regular school practice, religious issues cannot be entirely eliminated. If this is indeed the case then what is needed is as intelligent an approach as possible to these issues.

Let us begin with the suggestion that such an approach would eschew claims to the omnicompetency of religion in solving the school's problems or correcting the nation's ills. Recently the board of education of Santa Barbara, California, voted to permit distribution of New Testaments to pupils in the fifth through twelfth grades. This action was vigorously supported as a way of providing "guidelines for youth" and dealing with "declining moral values" and the "increased use of drugs." The vice president of the board hailed the vote as "a step forward."[4] This action, and the rhetoric in which it was smothered, is a type of simplistic approach to religion and morality which has little relevance to the complex realities of individual and group behavior. Furthermore, such exaggerated claims for the possession of the New Testament—or, for that matter, for public school reading from the Bible or public school prayer—tend to hinder rather than facilitate the possibility of achieving an educationally sound and effective approach to religion in the public school.

I am not saying that if we are to dismiss the simplistic

[4]Santa Barbara *News-Press*, February 7, 1969.

approach we can come up with a more sophisticated one which *will* solve all our problems. Obviously I am persuaded that there are sounder and more viable ways of handling the subject, but I would make modest claims for them. The issue of religion in the public school must be seen in proper perspective. The public school today is in deep trouble because of its own past inadequacies and increasing social turmoil. Disaffected citizens, especially blacks, reacting in part to the grossly inadequate public school system they have known, forcefully proclaim a new declaration of independence, affirming their right and intention to assume control over their own and their children's formal education. Critics assert that the public school system has become so overly-standardized that it has gone stale. The high school course, writes one of these critics, has become "more and more tightly standardized, scheduled, and graded. . . . Rival world-views, whether folk, traditional, sectarian, or artistically and philosophically heretical, are less and less available; the exposure to one world-view is always more intense and swamping."[5] Even religious groups which have traditionally been among the strongest supporters of the public school now, in part out of disenchantment with that institution, debate the advisability of starting their own full-time day schools.[6] Given these realities, the suggestion that the introduction of religion into the school—whether as Bible reading or even study of the subject—will go a long way toward solving the school's and the nation's problems is like suggesting that a Piper Cub or even a supersonic jet will go a long way toward the moon.

[5]Paul Goodman in *The New Republic,* CXLVIII (March 16, 1963), 28. Also by Goodman, *Compulsory Mis-Education* (New York: Horizon Press, 1964). For a more systematic and documented critique along these lines, see the works of Edgar Z. Friedman, especially *Coming of Age in America* (New York: Random House, 1965). For a summary of various critiques of this sort, see Friedman's survey article, "New Value Conflicts in American Education," *School Review,* LXXIV (Spring 1966), 66–94.

[6]For example, in 1963 the vice-president and the director of education of the Union of American Hebrew Congregations publicly approved of the establishment within Reform Judaism of all-day schools. *The New York Times,* November 17, 1963. Also *Journal* of the Central Conference of American Rabbis, XII (April 1964), 3–10, and (October 1964), 3–9. See also Sklare, *Conservative Judaism,* p. 156.

Having made this disclaimer, I hasten to add that I obviously do regard the question of religion in the public school as being significant. Both our history and our present circumstances testify to this. "Common religion," as understood by such men as Horace Mann, William Ruffner, A. D. Mayo, and Josiah Strong, and as symbolized—for example—in Bible reading, seemed essential to the founding and functioning of the common school. This compound of evangelical Protestantism and Enlightenment deism continued to be a major component in the public school mix throughout the nineteenth century. That mix was complicated further, however, by the great influx of immigrants and by the addition of that volatile element called modernity. In fact, the figure of a chemical compound breaks down at this point. A great number of the immigrants were Roman Catholics. And mixing Catholic religion with "common religion" was like trying to mix oil with water. Perhaps a military figure would be more appropriate to describe what occurred. For more than a century the scene of the issue often resembled a battlefield.

This kind of religious warfare led many to conclude that the common school could survive only if all semblance of church religion were removed from it. Some were confident that something resembling the old "common religion" would survive. But the already uneasy stability of that compound was further threatened by the acids of modernity—as pointedly symbolized, for example, in the juxtaposition of Darwin and the Bible.

At this juncture, what seemed to be needed was a "common faith" which would emerge from the democratic community itself and which would have little or nothing to do with church religion or even with the supernaturalism of Enlightenment deism. Commonness would emerge from life together, not from a transcendent entity or a historical tradition or a religious institution. Epitomized in the work of John Dewey, this was a noble and influential vision. But it overlooked the continuing strength of church religion. While the vision captured the imagination of some religious leaders who were deeply influenced by modernity, many did not share it. Most churchmen wanted more of tradition and the transcendent. And there developed a running encounter between Deweyites and churchmen which detracted from the realization of the "common faith." The public school itself was often the scene of this encounter, as progressives sought to remove all elements of traditional religion from it and churchmen mobilized in support of such symbolically significant practices as Bible reading, prayer, and released time.

The Dewey vision also underestimated the ramifications of the ever-present human quest for ultimacy. In retrospect—after the horrors of the Soviet purges and the Nazi concentration camps, for example—the vision seems naive. We gained some sense of what men can do in ultimate commitment to party or race or nation. I am not suggesting that the Soviets or the Nazis exemplified Dewey's "common faith." That would be ridiculous. What I am suggesting is that a faith that emerges from the national community alone cannot be trusted to lead to the greatest human good. To cultivate such a "common faith" in the common school, while ignoring the diversity of religious commitments and any element of transcendence, is to open the possibility of religionizing the nation. This is a tempting route for the school to follow, but it is one which can lead to disaster.

The Supreme Court entered the religion–public school scene at an important juncture and in a significant way. Court decisions reduced or diverted the pressures of church religion upon the public school. At the same time, the Court made it clear that the public school must not become the nation's formally established church. These Court decisions, coupled with other factors in our present situation—including a reduction in inter-religious tension—have opened the way for a new approach to religion in the schools. Now it may be possible to approach religion in a somewhat more objective—less subjective, less perspectival, less self-interested—fashion than in the past. Such an approach might further reduce interreligious tension. It might also serve as a hedge against fanatical nationalism. And finally, it might become a viable way of conveying significant elements in the religious heritage. Let us briefly explore these possibilities.

We begin with the assumption that religion is a significant

phenomenon in human life and culture. Mircea Eliade, the historian of religion, has demonstrated that for archaic man the world of sacred time and space is the *real* world; it is the cosmos, the locus of meaning and power. The sacred center, like the sun, radiates meaning into every corner of tribal life. The sacred thread holds the fabric of life together. Hence an understanding of archaic man requires that he be seen as *Homo religiosus*, as religious man.[7] The situation in higher cultures is more complex, but religion remains as a central culture-shaping element. This is evident from ancient Babylon to modern India. Thus the study of religion is also important to an understanding of these cultures.

The process of secularization complicates our picture. Now it appears that the role of religion is sharply reduced—as in modern Europe, for example. In a very real sense this is true. But because of a human propensity toward religion or toward religionizing—because man is "grasped by an ultimate concern," to put it in Tillichian language—there appear to be but two alternatives open to secular society vis-à-vis religion: (1) either the state or some other sociopolitical entity becomes religionized and takes on the unifying and signifying role played by religion in archaic culture; or (2) the society evolves a procedure for living with religious pluralism. In the first instance the secular is absolutized, as in the exaltation of nation or party or race to a position of pre-eminence in the life of the people. In the second case, society tacitly or openly accepts an operational relativity in which the role of the state or nation is understood to be limited to facilitating human development and a free expression of religion—including religious difference—is encouraged.

The United States was founded on the second assumption. The fathers understood themselves to be launching a new secular society in which the state would play a limited role in human affairs, religion would not be used by the state to sanctify itself, and "the free exercise" of religion would be encouraged. The result is a society in which many religious positions flourish.

[7]Mircea Eliade, *The Sacred and the Profane: The Nature of Religion* (New York: Harcourt, Brace, 1959; and subsequent editions).

But the achievement of such a society is not a once-and-for-all proposition. The history of the public school illustrates this. Pressures toward religionizing the nation have been evident in the school both in the use of the traditional symbols of historic religion—such as public school prayer and Bible reading—for civil purposes and in the *required* salute and pledge of allegiance to the flag. The U.S. Supreme Court has declared both of these practices to be unconstitutional under the First Amendment.

There are implications in this history beside the obvious ones that the school not promote group prayer and devotional Bible reading or require a uniform participation in the pledge to the flag. One is that if the school is going to deal with religion it is best advised to do so in an *academic* manner. That means, again, seeing religion in its various forms and functions from archaic to secularized cultures. Within the American context in particular this means giving due attention to religious pluralism. A second implication relates to the manner of instilling loyalty to the nation. While this is not our central concern here, the question of religion in the schools does have implications for it. Hence it is worth a word before giving more direct attention to the school's treatment of religion itself.

The rigid enforcement of patriotic ceremonials or the required use of highly nationalistic textbooks tends toward a religionizing of the nation. This is especially evident when these devices are used to the exclusion of attention to various ultimate value orientations—such as the traditional Western religious assertions of the supremacy of God over all nations and the oneness of mankind. The Constitution of the United States does not require this kind of ultimate commitment.[8] In fact, as the Court argued in *Barnette,* "there is no mysticism in the American concept of the State . . ." Hence it is in the spirit of the Constitution to encourage diversity of opinion, openness in outlook, and even

---

[8]Justice Goldberg argued in *Schempp* that the Constitution "prohibited" what he called "a brooding and pervasive devotion to the secular . . ." 374 U.S. 203, 306. Such devotion, I would argue, is an instance of religionizing or absolutizing the secular.

tentativeness about the things of this world.[9] The Constitution,
wrote, Justice Holmes in an earlier case, 'is an experiment, as
all life is an experiment."[10] Patriotism, as the Court pointed
out in *Barnette*, is best inculcated in a "voluntary and spon-
taneous" way instead of by "a compulsory routine . . ."[11] Among
other things, this would involve the school in a recognition of
differences and tensions within America as well as the elements
of unity.

I hope not to be misunderstood on this matter of public piety.
The public school is obviously of central importance to national
welfare; it is the primary institution in which a sense of
common citizenship is developed. And with Chesterton,[12] I
would regard the "pure classic conception" of citizenship as the
most important single element in American public piety, and
hence it is of fundamental concern to the public school. By
this Chesterton meant "the theory of equality." Less abstractly
this means that "no man must aspire to be anything more than
a citizen"—that is, by reason of heredity, wealth, race, religion,
or some other factor, claim the right to rule over his fellow
citizens. At the same time, "no man shall endure to be anything
less" than a citizen—that is, willingly permit his rights to be
abridged or taken away. From this conception one can draw a
hundred implications about the rights, responsibilities, and
dignity of American citizenship. These range from rights of
self-determination, self-expression, and the pursuit of self-ful-
fillment to responsibilities for the health and well-being of the
civil community. They include a necessary dedication to the
conception of citizenship itself, a needed loyalty to that most
fundamental element in the nation's heritage and among its
principles. Patriotism in the school? Of course—if one means
by that love of the country for its affirmations and achieve-

[9]319 U.S. 624, 640–42 (1943). *Barnette*, it will be recalled, was the
second flag-salute case decided by the Court, a case in which the Court
ruled unconstitutional a West Virginia statute requiring all public school
pupils to participate in the salute and pledge to the flag.

[10]In dissent, *Abrams* v. *United States*, 250 U.S. 616, 630 (1919).

[11]319 U.S. 624, 641.

[12]"What I Saw in America" in *The Man Who was Chesterton*, p. 195.

ments in human dignity. But I do not think it is morally, religiously, or constitutionally right to use public school machinery for whipping up intense, zealous, and unreflective loyalty to the state. Perhaps many Americans would agree with Dr. Max Rafferty's bald affirmation that "education's first duty is to make possible the survival of our country."[13] At first blush this looks like a truism. But if called upon to speak in terms of "education's first duty" and 'survival" I would substitute "the human race" for "our country." Then I would work for a kind of education that would be conducive to the survival of both.

America's position in the world today requires of us more than blind patriotism. A young and relatively weak nation might be permitted a liberal expression of jingoism. But such an expression does not befit maturity, and it may actually be self-defeating to a nation of great power.

To return to religion itself: If we understand religion in terms of ultimacy it is by definition a subject which has obvious value implications and about which people feel strongly and often disagree sharply. As such it should be neither inculcated nor neglected in the public school, which is an instrument of the state. It should not be inculcated because this would, in effect, involve the instilling of one of the historic faiths or a public school faith or a religion of the nation. That would be contrary to our constitutional history. But because of religion's importance to human self-understanding and motivation it should not be ignored in the school. Here the Court's use of such language as "teaching about" as against "teaching of" and teaching "objectively as a part of a secular program in education"[14] is useful. What is needed is an approach which will help the student to understand something of the nature and history of religion without requiring him to abandon, change, or adopt a faith stance. It is true that understanding might affect one's faith, but this is true of almost any subject one encounters in school—from the findings of geology to the poetry of William Blake. Understanding might also broaden one's horizon to include and even accept those who differ markedly from oneself.

[13]See note 3 above.
[14]374 U.S. 203, 225, 300, 306.

And this is an especially important achievement in our pluralistic society.

The school's record in handling pluralism has not been a particularly bright one. Textbooks, for example, tend to project an image of a rising tide of national oneness of mind, ignoring the ebb of group difference. Religion is seldom dealt with at all. Where it is the picture is likely to be either a bland one which stresses agreement on what matters most or one which focuses almost exclusively upon the major religious tradition. For example, a recent study of forty-eight "leading secondary history and social studies textbooks," conducted under the sponsorship of the Anti-Defamation League of the B'nai B'rith, found that a majority of the books "present a largely white, Protestant, Anglo-Saxon view of history and the current social scene. The complex nature and problems of American minority groups," the study concludes, "are largely neglected or, in a number of cases, distorted."[15]

Americans generally have had difficulties in evolving a viable style for living with group differences. The famed melting pot, as George R. Stewart pointed out, was in actuality a "transmuting pot."[16] But some could not or would not be transmuted into the majority notion of what it meant to be an American. Religiously, there were and are many beside the white Anglo-Saxon Protestants—and even a sizable number beside the recently popularized troika of democracy, the Protestant-Catholic-Jew configuration. Racially, there remains the most obvious minority of all—the blacks. It seems to be generally assumed that to become "fully" American the black man must become in some sense white. But this implies that a more or less uniform life style is necessary to Americanness, when what is needed, on the contrary, is an American canopy which is ample enough to include a variety of styles of life and commitment. It is noteworthy, for example, that while most blacks are Protestants religiously the typical religious life style among black Protes-

---

[15]Lloyd Marcus, *The Treatment of Minorities in Secondary School Textbooks* (New York: Anti-Defamation League of the B'nai B'rith, 1961), p. 3.
[16]*American Ways of Life* (Garden City, N.Y.: Doubleday, 1954), pp. 23, 28; cf. Will Herberg, *Protestant, Catholic, Jew,* ch. ii.

tants is markedly different from prevailing white Protestant styles.[17] I am not suggesting that these differences necessarily reach to fundamental disagreements on ultimate questions, but they do exist. It is well for Americans to recognize and acknowledge these differences. And the school can do a significant job in helping to bring this about.

There are, of course, real risks in openly acknowledging religious differences among Americans. Our society has at times been held together only by the most tenuous strands of common affirmation and interest. As Father John Courtney Murray so ably put it, this pluralist society "has received its structures through wars and . . . the wars are still going on beneath a fragile surface . . ."[18] To highlight differences in such a circumstance opens the possibility of fragmenting the body politic. But given the nature and extent of the differences, they can hardly be ignored. It seems, then, that they are best exposed in an atmosphere that is conducive to conversation and learning rather than warfare.

Actually the public school has not had much experience in dealing with religious differences in a controlled classroom atmosphere conducive to learning. There are some indications, however, that such an approach can achieve positive results in increasing the desire to know and in raising the level of understanding. This has been the prevailing experience of those of us involved in the study of religion in state universities. There is little evidence from the high school level. Dr. John R. Whitney, director of the Pennsylvania State University project described in Chapter VIII, does report that divergent religious views among high school students taking a course on Western religious literature did not "polarize the participants into alienated groups." On the contrary, teachers report: "Differences in

[17]Gerhard Lenski recognized this in dividing the American community into four rather than three major religious groups—white Protestants, Negro Protestants, Roman Catholics, and Jews. *The Religious Factor: A Sociological Study of Religion's Impact on Politics, Economics, and Family Life* (New York: Doubleday, 1961).

[18]"America's Four Conspiracies," in *Religion in America*, ed. John Cogley (New York: Meridian Books, Inc., 1958), p. 32. Father Murray's "Four Conspiracies" are Protestant, Catholic, Jewish, and secularist.

religious background appear to enhance classroom discussion. The student seems to feel responsible *to* the class for clearly expressing not only his own personal and traditional understandings, but also his interest in the understandings of the other students."[19]

I do not wish to leave the impression that the study of religion in the public school should focus exclusively or even primarily upon religious differences. I have raised this subject once again because of the fact that difficulties in dealing with religious differences are often cited prominently by those who object to the study of religion in the school. But religion is a sufficiently pervasive and universal human phenomenon that its proper scholarly study involves looking abroad as well as to America itself and to history as well as to the present. Indeed, in so pushing back one's horizons differences may be seen in a larger perspective.

I am arguing for a critical and appreciative study of religion in the public school. By "critical" I mean that the primary goal of such a study is accurate knowledge and that all available tools and resources are used to that end. I add "appreciative" since Americans often understand "critical" only in the sense of adverse criticism. What is sought is genuine understanding, a sympathetic entering into the subject with the goal in mind of trying as best one can to see it as it is. The rationale and technique of this kind of approach differ sharply from those most commonly evidenced in typical public school religious practices of the past. Unlike prayer and devotional Bible reading, this approach does not require personal participation in what is in effect an act of religious worship. And unlike the released-time approach, it does not require opting for or against a particular religious position.

An academically fruitful study of religion may be compared with an educational trip to a foreign land. One needs adequate guides and guidebooks if he is to achieve some measure of understanding. Such guidance will begin where the traveler is and lead him into a depth exposure to the strange land. Without

[19]*Religious Education,* LXIII (March-April, 1968), 95–96.

this kind of help the traveler's ignorance and prejudice may only be reinforced. Without adequate preparation, for example, he might well experience a violent case of "culture shock" and be led to conclude that all the natives are crazy and his own land is the only inhabitable real estate on the face of the globe. Or—less probably—he might decide that he has now arrived in utopia. He needs to be prepared for the shock of difference and, at the same time, to be reminded that the natives share a common humanity with him. If our traveler has proper guidance he might learn much about the land and return home the better for it.

Let me illustrate my point by referring to the Qur'an. This book is central in the religion of Islam. To most Americans it is very much like a strange and foreign land. Skilled guidance is needed to begin to see it with understanding eyes. Such guidance will involve careful attention to this holy book in terms of its historical, religious, and theological setting, the ways in which Muslims commonly understand it, and even such technical questions as problems of translation. Admittedly, few American teachers are qualified to offer this sort of guidance single-handedly. But through formal classes and written materials they can repair to those who are qualified. And perhaps they can help their students in fashioning a small opening into this fascinating land. As a result the students might learn something —about Islam and Muslims, possibly about cognate and other religious traditions, and perhaps even about themselves.

In the academic study of religion one moves from where he is to look at others. With skilled help he tries to see what others see—both in themselves and in the world beyond. To this end, he attempts to hear what they say and comprehend what they have recorded. One returns from such a journey possibly prepared to put aside a shaft he might one time have sent in another's direction, possibly with new insights into himself and his fellow human beings, possibly inspired to take another trip. Through such a process one may not get to the promised land, but the journey should be worthwhile.

What Professor Ninian Smart calls "the religious experience

of mankind"[20] is a long, complex, and extraordinarily rich experience. It offers the student an almost infinite number of possibilities for exploration. Where, then, shall one begin? There are basically two criteria for selecting which aspects of the subject to study. The more obvious relates to questions of influence and importance in one's own cultural and personal experience. Hence the study of the Bible is more important for most Americans than the study of the Qur'an. The other criterion has to do with the fact that while man's religious experience evidences great variety there are also common elements in it. Hence one might profitably investigate similar phenomena from various cultural settings. For example, the study of the Bible *and* the Qur'an side by side or in tandem might elicit insights not easily gained by studying either by itself. Both criteria are relevant to public school efforts in the study of religion. The school can and should give more attention than it has to the religious aspects of the American experience, for example. It may also assist students in achieving a further realization of both the commonality and the diversity of human experience by comparing aspects of the American experience with similar phenomena in other cultures.

This approach will no doubt strike some as being difficult to effect. Aside from the problem of finding or producing skilled and knowledgeable teachers, there are real difficulties stemming from the communal context of the school itself. I do not wish to minimize the difficulties involved, but I reiterate that they seem to me to be no more insurmountable than those associated with the study of such other aspects of human experience as politics. Furthermore, the history of our subject leads me to conclude that we have reached a point where, as a result of continuing secularization and the growing acknowledgement of the realities of pluralism, we are better prepared for this kind of approach than we have ever been.

[20]*The Religious Experiences of Mankind* (New York: Charles Scribner's Sons, 1969).

Index

Adams, Jasper, 216
Adams, Francis, 109, 122
Adams, Henry, 156
Adams, John, 2, 37, 70, 78
Advance (journal), 116
Allen, Dr. James E., 246
Allen case, 193, 194, 201, 202, 230
America (magazine), 236
American Association for the Advancement of Atheism, 184
American Association of School Administrators, 246
American Board of Commissioners for Foreign Missions, 24
American Churchman (publication), 117–118
American Council on Education, 160, 190, 245–246
American Freedom and Catholic Power (Blanchard), 229
American Jewish Committee, 236
American Protective Association, 126–127
American Sunday School Union, 74, 172
Anderson, R. B., 119
Andrews, E. B., 139
Angell, James B., 164
Anti-Defamation League of the B'nai B'rith, 263
Antin, Mary, 14
Asbury, Francis, 23

Bailyn, Bernard, 47

Barnette case, 193, 194, 211, 217, 260, 261
Beecher, Henry Ward, 116–117
Beecher, Lyman, 73, 83, 105
Bible
    accredited courses, 181–185
    influence upon American culture, 32–33
    Mann on, 78
    as symbol for common religion, 78–79
Black, Hugo, 1, 3, 195, 198, 199, 202, 208
Blaine, James G., 67
Blake, William, 262
Blanshard, Paul, 229
Bliss, William B., 134–40
Borowitz, Rabbi Eugene, 244, 247–248
Bouquillon, Thomas, 130
Brennan, William J., 201, 204, 214
Brickman, William W., 230
Brogan, D. W., 19, 20, 62, 63
Brown, Samuel W., 109–110, 112, 113
Brown, William Adams, 176
Brown v. Board of Education, 203
Brown College, 51
Bryan, William Jennings, 41, 161, 169
Bryce, James, 12
Buchanan, James, 42
Bushnell, Horace, 122
Butler, Nicholas M., 164

Cabell, Joseph, 80
Campbell, Alexander, 69, 82–84, 105
Carroll, Lewis, 192
Catholic Citizen (journal), 126
Catholic Telegraph (journal), 93
Catholic University, 25
Central Conference of American Rabbis (Reform), 230
Chesterton, G. K., 40, 58
Childs, John L., 158
Christian Century (journal), 175, 228
Christian Intelligencer (publication), 118
Christianity and Crisis (journal), 226, 227
Cincinnati Board of Education, 89–98
Clark, Thomas C., 200, 202, 248
Clarke, William Newton, 163, 164, 167
Clay, Henry, 117
Cochran case, 193, 194, 229
Coe, George A., 166
Commission on Reorganization of Secondary Education, 155
Commonweal (journal), 236
Conant, James Bryant, 46, 58, 134
Congregational Home Missionary Society, 121
Cooke, Robert A., 223
Cope, Henry F., 165
Corrigan, Archbishop Michael A., 131
Cox, Harvey, 232
Cremin, Lawrence A., 61, 142
Crèvecoeur, Michel de, 39
Cross, Professor, 126
Cubberley, Ellwood P., 45, 60–61, 150–151
Curti, Merle, 129, 148, 149

Darrow, Clarence, 161
Darthmouth College, 51
Darwin, Charles, 18, 160, 161, 251

Davis, Mary Dabney, 175
Dawson, Christopher, 144
Day of Doom (Wigglesworth), 17
De Smet, Pierre-Jean, 23
Death-of-God movement, 15
Dewey, John, 6, 57, 59–63, 113, 133, 134, 157, 158, 164, 166, 167, 174–175, 181, 186, 191, 206, 257, 258
view of faith and morals, 140–149
Diman, J. L., 1, 6, 123
Dirksen, Everett McKinley, 219, 224
Dorchester, Daniel, 112
Douglas, William O., 13, 58, 64, 202, 209–210
Dwight, Timothy, 51

Eckel, Herman, 100, 102
Edwards, Jonathan, 17–18, 23, 49, 52, 96
Eisenhower, Dwight D., 39, 41, 42, 46, 220, 221–222
Elementary and Secondary Education Act of 1965, 241
Eliade, Mircea, 259
Emmons, Nathaniel, 73, 74
Engel case, 64–65, 193, 194, 199, 206–209, 213, 217, 223–225, 228, 230–234, 236
Everson case, 193, 194, 196, 199, 200–203, 207, 216, 229, 230
Evolution, 18, 30, 160–164

Federal Council of Churches, 171, 173, 189
Finney, Charles G., 23–24, 52
First Amendment, 3–4, 35, 64–65, 192, 195, 202, 210, 252
Florida State University, 249–250
Fosdick, Henry Emerson, 169, 226–227
Fourteenth Amendment, 195
Frankfurter, Felix, 175, 197, 198, 204
Franklin, Benjamin, 2, 3, 16, 20, 52, 78

Free School Society, 85
Freund, Paul A., 191, 217

Galer, Roger, 14
Gibbons, Cardinal James, 109, 123, 125, 127–129, 132
Gilbert, Rabbi Arthur, 230, 238
Gilman, Daniel Coit, 67, 106
Gobitis case, 193, 194, 217
God, concepts of, 13–20
Goldberg, Arthur, 214, 260
Gordis, Rabbi Robert, 248
Gove, Floyd S., 176
Graham, Billy, 23, 24, 52, 220, 223
Grant, Ulysses S., 112–113
Great Awakening, 48–50

Hagans, Marcellus, 32, 96, 97
Harper, William R., 164
Harris, William Torrey, 56–57, 107, 108, 113
Harrison, Benjamin, 39–40
Hartshorne, Hugh, 160
Harvey, Walter L., 164–165
Healey, Robert M., 81
Hecker, Father Isaac Thomas, 127
Hertzbert, Arthur, 230
Herald (journal), 116
Herberg, Will, 230
Heschel, Abraham Joshua, 19
Hoadly, George, 96
Hodge, Charles, 161–162, 163
Holmes, Oliver Wendell, 200, 215, 261
Hughes, Charles Evans, 8
Hughes, Archbishop John J., 54–55, 69, 86–89, 91, 132
Hutchinson, Ann, 22

International Council of Religious Education, 173–174, 176
Independent (journal), 116
Inter-Church Conference on Federation, 171
Ireland, Archbishop John, 109, 115, 125, 127–131

Jackson, Andrew, 41
Jackson, Robert H., 198–199, 201, 205, 215
James, William, 34, 154
Jefferson, Thomas, 2–3, 69, 78, 197, 216
Jenkins, Father Thomas Jefferson, 125
John XXIII, Pope, 234
John Dewey Society, 58–59, 242
Johnson, Alvin W., 168

Kaplan, Mordecai, 19
Katzer, Archbishop, 130
Kauper, Professor, 207, 216
Keane, Bishop John J., 127–128
Kennedy, John F., 41
King, Henry C., 164
King, Rufus, 93, 98
Ku Klux Klan, 17, 152, 155
Kurland, Philip, 59

Laski, Harold, 11–12
Latourette, Kenneth Scott, 24
Lee, Daniel, 23
Lee, Jason, 23
Leo XIII, Pope, 109, 123, 130, 132
Lilienthal, Rabbi Max, 31, 93, 96, 103, 104
Lincoln, Abraham, 17, 38, 39, 43–44
Lowenberg, B. J., 162
Lyon, William Penn, 112, 114

McCluskey, Father Neil G., 237
McCollum James Terry, 14–15, 181, 196
McCollum, Mrs. Vashti, 138, 181, 196
McCollum case, 175–176, 180, 193, 195–198, 199, 204, 205, 206, 207, 215–217, 223, 224, 226, 228, 230, 242
McConnell, Bishop Francis J., 227
McGolrick, Bishop, 131
McKinley, William, 41–42
McQuaid, Bishop, 132

Madison, James, 3, 43, 206, 216
Magill, Hugh S., 173
Mann, Horace, 28, 54, 55, 68, 69, 70–79, 82, 100, 257
Mann, Stephen, 73
Mather, Increase, 17
Matthews, Stanley, 96, 100, 101, 104
Mayo, Amory Dwight, 93, 95, 99–100, 107, 257
Merton, Thomas, 35
Mead, Sidney E., 45, 216
Miller, Perry, 33
Miller, Samuel A., 94, 95, 100, 102, 103, 104
Moody, Dwight L., 23, 24
Murray, Father John Courtney, 264
Murray, Mrs. M., 229

National Association of Evangelicals, 223, 228
National Catholic Education Association, 241
National Conference of Christians and Jews, 188, 190, 225, 238–239
National Council of Churches, 27, 219, 226, 232, 240
National Education Association, 46–47, 53, 128, 139, 171, 174, 228, 243, 245
National Teachers Association, 67
Natural Theology (Paley), 77–78
New Republic, The (publication), 145
New York Times, The, 219
Niebuhr, Reinhold, 226, 227, 231, 232
Niebuhr, H. Richard, 19
Northwest Ordinance, 69, 90, 91

Olafson, Frederick A., 248
Origin of the Species (Darwin), 161
Orton, Harlow South, 111
Our Country (Strong), 119–120

Outline of Christian Theology, An (Clark), 163–164

Packard, Frederick A., 74–75, 78
Paley, William, 77–78
Parsons, Stow, 162–163
Peale, Norman Vincent, 34
Penn, William, 22
Pennsylvania State University, 249, 251, 264
Pfeffer, Leo, 169, 176, 236
Pierce, Walter M., 152–153
Pierce case, 193, 194
Pierepont, Sarah, 17–18
Pius X, Pope, 132
Pledge of Allegiance, 12, 62, 210–211
Polk, James K., 39
Princeton University, 50, 51, 52
Protestantische Zeitblaetter (journal), 102
Protestants and Other Americans United for the Separation of Church and State, 228–229, 231, 235
Public school, religion and
    educational system, 45–66
    nineteenth century, 67–133
    piety in America, 1–44
    Supreme Court, 192–253
    twentieth century, 135–267
    unity and diversity, 254–267
Public School Society, 85, 86, 88
Purcell, Archbishop John B., 82–83, 91, 93, 104–105

Rafferty, Dr. Max, 254
Reconstructionist movement, 25, 31
Released-time religious education, 170–181, 239–241
    Court guidelines for, 206–207
Religion in America
    piety and, 1–44
        aspects of, 11–44
        meaning of, 1–11
    public school and

educational system, 45–66
    nineteenth century, 67–133
    Supreme Court, 192–253
    twentieth century, 134–267
    unity and diversity, 254–267
Religious Education Association,
    164–166, 171, 188
Rhees, President, 164
Riesman, David, 141
Robinson, Pastor John, 21
*Romanism versus the Public School
    System* (Dorchester), 112
Roosevelt, Franklin D., 42
Roosevelt, Theodore, 39, 40, 41
Rosen, Ben, 178
Ruffner, William H., 68, 82, 84–85,
    257
Rutledge, Wiley B., 196–197, 199

Stallo, J. B., 57, 100–101, 102, 104
Satolli, Archbishop Francis, 131, 132
Scarlett, Bishop, 227
Schaff, Philip, 109, 114, 168
Schempp case, 55, 65, 168, 193,
    194, 199, 201, 202, 203,
    205, 206, 207, 213, 224, 230,
    231, 232, 233, 234, 246,
    247, 260
Scopes, John, 160–161
Seward, William H., 87
Shaver, Dr. Erwin, 174, 176
Shaw, Archibald, 246
Siegel, Seymour, 230
Skandinaven (journal), 119
Smart, Ninian, 266–267
Smith, Gerrit, 117
Smith, Joseph, 35
Smith, Matthew Hale, 75–76
Smith, Payson, 55
Smith, Wilfred Cantwell, 9
Society of the Sisters of the Holy
    Names of Jesus and Mary,
    153–154
Spalding, Mr. and Mrs. Henry, 23
Spalding, Bishop John, 127
Spear, Samuel T., 116

Spellman, Cardinal Francis, 223
Sperry, Willard, 26
Starbuck, E. D., 165
Stewart, George R., 263
Stewart, Potter, 201, 205
Stiles, Ezra, 16
Storer, Bellamy, 96, 97
Story, Joseph, 96
Stowe, Calvin, 83
Strong, Josiah, 119–121, 257
Sunday, Billy, 23, 35
Synagogue Council of America, 229
Systematic Theology (Hodge), 163

Taft, Alphonso, 96, 97, 104
Taft, William H., 40
Taylor, Edward, 17
Thoughts on the Revival (Ed-
    wards), 49
Tillich, Paul, 8, 9, 212–213, 254
*Tinker v. Des Moines Ind. Com-
    munity School District*, 217
Tocqueville, Alexis de, 11, 13, 14,
    51, 192, 252
Torcasso v. Watkins, 211–213
Truman, Harry S., 222
Tweed, William Marcy, 88
Tyack, David B., 153

Ulich, Robert, 244
U.S. Supreme Court
    on education, 45
    separationist principle, 192–218
    churches, the public and, 219–
        252
United States v. Seeger, 211–213
University of Pennsylvania, 249, 251
University of Virginia, 80, 81

Van Dusen, Henry P., 226, 227
Vatican I, 105
Vatican II, 234, 238
Vickers, Thomas, 93, 95, 96, 100,
    104, 105
Vietnam War, 217
Votaw, Clyde W., 165

Wallace, George, 224
Ware, Henry, 71
Washington, George, 222
Weigle, Luther A., 189–190
Wenner, George U., 171
Wertenbaker, T. J., 50
White, Byron R., 201
Whitefield, George, 22–23
Whitehead, Alfred North, 9
Whitman, Marcus, 23
Whitney, Dr. John R., 264
Whyte, William, 141
Wigglesworth, Michael, 17
William and Mary College, 79, 80

Williams, Roger, 22
Wilson, Woodrow, 40, 41, 42
Winthrop, John, 21, 41, 42
Wirt, William, 174
Wise, Rabbi Isaac Mayer, 31, 93
Witherspoon, John, 50, 52
Woolman, John, 35, 52

Yale University, 51

Zionism, 25, 147
Zorach v. Clauson, 181, 193, 194, 198, 199, 206, 216–217, 230, 239